The Economist

POCKET
WORLD IN
FIGURES

2018 Edition

Published by
Profile Books Ltd
3 Holford Yard
Bevin Way
London WC1X 9HD

Published under exclusive licence from
The Economist by Profile Books, 2017

Material researched by

Andrea Burgess, Lisa Davies, Graham Douglas, Mark Doyle,
Ian Emery, Conrad Heine, Carol Howard, David McKelvey,
Georgina McKelvey, Guy Scriven, Christopher Wilson

Typeset in Econ Sans Condensed by MacGuru Ltd

Printed and bound in Italy by L.E.G.O. Spa

A CIP catalogue record for this book is available
from the British Library

ISBN 978 1 78125 744 9

Contents

7   Introduction
8   Notes

11   Part I   World rankings

Geography and demographics

12   **Countries: *natural facts***
Countries: the largest   Largest exclusive economic zones
Mountains: the highest   Rivers: the longest
Deserts: the largest non-polar   Lakes: the largest

14   **Population: *size and growth***
Largest populations, 2015   Largest populations, 2030
Fastest-growing populations   Slowest-growing populations

16   **Population: *matters of breeding and sex***
Total births   Teenage births   Highest and lowest fertility rates
Highest and lowest contraception rates

18   **Population: *age***
Median age biggest change over 50 years
Oldest and youngest populations

19   **City living**
Biggest cities   Fastest- and slowest-growing cities
Biggest urban populations   Highest and lowest urban growth
Highest and lowest rural growth   City liveability index
Tallest buildings

22   **Migrants, refugees and asylum seekers**
Biggest migrant populations   Biggest destination country for migrants
Refugees by country of origin
Countries with largest refugee populations
Origin of asylum applications to industrialised countries
Countries where asylum applications were lodged

Economics

24   **The world economy**
Biggest economies   Biggest economies by purchasing power
Regional GDP   Regional purchasing power
Regional population   Regional international trade

26   **Living standards**
Highest and lowest GDP per person
Highest and lowest purchasing power

28   **The quality of life**
Highest and lowest human development index
Inequality-adjusted human development index
Highest and lowest Gini coefficient

30   **Economic growth**
Highest economic growth   Lowest economic growth
Highest services growth   Lowest services growth

32 **Trading places**
Biggest exporters   Most and least trade-dependent
Biggest traders of goods   Biggest earners from services and income

34 **Balance of payments:** *current account*
Largest surpluses   Largest deficits
Largest surpluses as % of GDP   Largest deficits as % of GDP
Official reserves   Official gold reserves   Workers' remittances

37 **Exchange rates**
The Economist's Big Mac index

38 **Inflation**
Highest and lowest consumer-price inflation
Commodity prices: change   House prices: change

40 **Debt**
Highest foreign debt   Highest foreign debt burden
Highest debt and debt service ratios   Household debt

42 **Aid**
Largest recipients   Largest donors   Biggest changes to aid

44 **Industry and services**
Largest industrial output
Highest and lowest growth in industrial output
Largest manufacturing output   Largest services output

46 **Agriculture and fisheries**
Largest agricultural output   Most and least economically dependent
Fisheries and aquaculture production
Biggest producers: cereals, meat, fruit, vegetables, roots and tubers

48 **Commodities**
Leading producers and consumers of: wheat, rice, sugar, coarse grains,
tea, coffee, cocoa, orange juice, copper, lead, zinc, tin, nickel, aluminium,
precious metals, rubber, cotton, major oil seeds and vegetable oils, oil,
natural gas, coal   Top proved oil reserves

54 **Energy**
Largest producers   Largest consumers
Most and least energy-efficient
Highest and lowest net energy importers
Largest consumption per person   Sources of electricity

56 **Labour markets**
Highest and lowest labour-force participation
Most male and female workforces   Highest rate of unemployment
Highest rate of youth unemployment   Minimum wage
Average hours worked   Poverty pay

Business

59 **Business costs and foreign direct investment**
Office rents   Foreign direct investment

60 **Business creativity and research**
Entrepreneurial activity   Brain drains
R&D expenditure   Innovation index

62 Businesses and banks
Largest non-financial companies   Largest banks
Largest sovereign-wealth funds

64 Stockmarkets
Largest market capitalisation
Largest gains and losses in global stockmarkets
Largest value traded   Number of listed companies

Politics and society

66 Public finance
Government debt   Government spending   Tax revenue

67 Democracy
Most and least democratic   Most and fewest parliamentary seats
Women in parliament

68 Education
Highest and lowest primary enrolment
Highest secondary enrolment   Highest tertiary enrolment
Least literate   Highest and lowest education spending

70 Marriage and divorce
Highest marriage rates   Lowest marriage rates
Highest divorce rates   Lowest divorce rates
Youngest and oldest mean age of women at first marriage

72 Households, living costs and giving
Biggest number of households   Average household size
Highest and lowest cost of living   World Giving Index

74 Transport: *roads and cars*
Longest road networks   Densest road networks
Most crowded road networks   Most road deaths
Fastest-growing car ownership   Slowest-growing car ownership
Car production   Cars sold

78 Transport: *planes and trains*
Most air travel   Busiest airports   Longest railway networks
Most rail passengers   Most rail freight

80 Transport: *shipping*
Largest merchant fleets by country of domicile and country of
registration

81 Crime and punishment
Murders   Robberies   Prisoners

82 War and terrorism
Defence spending   Armed forces   Arms traders
Terrorist attacks

84 Space and peace
Space missions   Orbital launches   Global Peace Index

85 Environment
Biggest emitters of carbon dioxide
Largest amount of carbon dioxide emitted per person
Most polluted capital cities   Lowest access to improved sanitation
Lowest access to electricity   Largest forests   Most forested

Biggest decrease and increase in forestation   Most dams
Largest reservoirs   Slums   Environmental Performance Index
Worst natural catastrophes

Health and welfare

90 Life expectancy
Highest life expectancy   Highest male life expectancy
Highest female life expectancy   Lowest life expectancy
Lowest male life expectancy   Lowest female life expectancy

92 Death rates and infant mortality
Highest death rates   Highest infant mortality
Lowest death rates   Lowest infant mortality

94 Death and disease
Diabetes   Cardiovascular disease
Chronic respiratory diseases   Tuberculosis
Measles and DPT immunisation   HIV/AIDS prevalence and deaths

96 Health
Highest health spending   Lowest health spending
Highest and lowest population per doctor   Obesity
Highest and lowest food deficits

Culture and entertainment

98 Telephones and the internet
Mobile telephones   Landline telephones   Internet users
Broadband

100 Arts and entertainment
Music sales   Book publishing
Cinema attendances   Oscar nominations by ethnicity

102 The press
Daily newspapers   Press freedom

103 Nobel prize winners
Peace   Medicine   Literature   Economics   Physics   Chemistry
Total wins by country of birth

104 Sports champions and cheats
World Cup winners and finalists: men's and women's football, cricket,
Davis Cup winners   Summer Olympics, athletes sent per gold medal
Anti-doping rule violations

106 Vices
Beer drinkers   Smokers   Gambling losses

107 Tourism
Most tourist arrivals   Biggest tourist spenders
Largest tourist receipts

109 Part II Country profiles

242 WORLD RANKINGS QUIZ
248 Glossary
250 List of countries
254 Sources

Introduction

This 2018 edition of *The Economist Pocket World in Figures* presents and analyses data about the world in two sections:

The **world rankings** consider and rank the performance of 185 countries against a range of indicators in six sections: geography and demographics, economics, business, politics and society, health and welfare, and culture and entertainment. The countries included are those which had (in 2015) a population of at least 1m or a GDP of at least $3bn; they are listed on pages 250–53. New rankings this year include topics as diverse as the average number of births, biggest destination countries for migrants, largest merchant fleets by flags of convenience, terrorist attacks, dams, reservoirs and countries with most urban population living in slums. Some of the rankings data are shown as charts and graphs.

The **country profiles** look in detail at 64 major countries, listed on page 109, plus profiles of the euro area and the world.

Test your *Pocket World in Figures* knowledge with our **World Rankings Quiz** on pages 242–7. Answers can be found in the corresponding world rankings section.

Notes

The extent and quality of the statistics available vary from country to country. Every care has been taken to specify the broad definitions on which the data are based and to indicate cases where data quality or technical difficulties are such that interpretation of the figures is likely to be seriously affected. Nevertheless, figures from individual countries may differ from standard international statistical definitions. The term "country" can also refer to territories or economic entities.

Definitions of the statistics shown are given on the relevant page or in the glossary on pages 248–9. Figures may not add exactly to totals, or percentages to 100, because of rounding or, in the case of GDP, statistical adjustment. Sums of money have generally been converted to US dollars at the official exchange rate ruling at the time to which the figures refer.

Some country definitions
Macedonia is officially known as the Former Yugoslav Republic of Macedonia. Data for Cyprus normally refer to Greek Cyprus only. Data for China do not include Hong Kong or Macau. For countries such as Morocco they exclude disputed areas. Congo-Kinshasa refers to the Democratic Republic of Congo, formerly known as Zaire. Congo-Brazzaville refers to the other Congo. Euro area data normally refer to the 19 members that had adopted the euro as at December 31 2016: Austria, Belgium, Cyprus, Estonia, Finland, France, Germany, Greece, Ireland, Italy, Latvia, Lithuania, Luxembourg, Malta, Netherlands, Portugal, Slovakia, Slovenia and Spain. Euro area (18) excludes Lithuania, which adopted the euro on January 1 2015. Euro area (15) refers to the 15 countries in the euro area that are members of the OECD. Data referring to the European Union include the UK, which in June 2016 voted in a referendum to leave the EU. Negotiations over the country's departure will take some time. For more information about the EU, euro area and OECD see the glossary on pages 248–9.

Statistical basis
The all-important factor in a book of this kind is to be able to make reliable comparisons between countries. Although this is never quite possible for the reasons stated above, the best route, which this book takes, is

to compare data for the same year or period and to use actual, not estimated, figures wherever possible. In some cases, only OECD members are considered. Where a country's data are excessively out of date, they are excluded. The research for this edition was carried out in 2017 using the latest available sources that present data on an internationally comparable basis.

Data in the country profiles, unless otherwise indicated, refer to the year ending December 31 2015. Life expectancy, crude birth, death and fertility rates are based on 2015–20 estimated averages; energy data are for 2014 and religion data for 2010; marriage and divorce, employment, health and education, consumer goods and services data refer to the latest year for which figures are available.

Other definitions

Data shown in country profiles may not always be consistent with those shown in the world rankings because the definitions or years covered can differ.

Statistics for principal exports and principal imports are normally based on customs statistics. These are generally compiled on different definitions to the visible exports and imports figures shown in the balance of payments section.

Energy-consumption data are not always reliable, particularly for the major oil-producing countries; consumption per person data may therefore be higher than in reality. Energy exports can exceed production and imports can exceed consumption if transit operations distort trade data or oil is imported for refining and re-exported.

Abbreviations and conventions
(see also glossary on pages 248–9)

bn	billion (one thousand million)	km	kilometre
		m	million
EU	European Union	PPP	purchasing power parity
GDP	gross domestic product	TOE	tonnes of oil equivalent
GNI	gross national income	trn	trillion (one thousand billion)
ha	hectare		
kg	kilogram	...	not available

World rankings

Countries: natural facts

Countries: the largest[a]

'000 sq km

1	Russia	17,098	36	Turkey	785
2	Canada	9,985	37	Chile	756
3	United States	9,832	38	Zambia	753
4	China	9,563	39	Myanmar	677
5	Brazil	8,516	40	Afghanistan	653
6	Australia	7,741	41	South Sudan	644
7	India	3,287	42	Somalia	638
8	Argentina	2,780	43	Central African Rep.	623
9	Kazakhstan	2,725	44	Ukraine	604
10	Algeria	2,382	45	Madagascar	587
11	Congo-Kinshasa	2,345	46	Botswana	582
12	Saudi Arabia	2,150	47	Kenya	580
13	Mexico	1,964	48	France	549
14	Indonesia	1,911	49	Yemen	528
15	Sudan	1,879	50	Thailand	513
16	Libya	1,760	51	Spain	506
17	Iran	1,745	52	Turkmenistan	488
18	Mongolia	1,564	53	Cameroon	475
19	Peru	1,285	54	Papua New Guinea	463
20	Chad	1,284	55	Morocco	447
21	Niger	1,267		Sweden	447
22	Angola	1,247		Uzbekistan	447
23	Mali	1,240	58	Iraq	435
24	South Africa	1,219	59	Paraguay	407
25	Colombia	1,142	60	Zimbabwe	391
26	Ethiopia	1,104	61	Norway	385
27	Bolivia	1,099	62	Japan	378
28	Mauritania	1,031	63	Germany	357
29	Egypt	1,001	64	Congo-Brazzaville	342
30	Tanzania	947	65	Finland	338
31	Nigeria	924	66	Malaysia	331
32	Venezuela	912		Vietnam	331
33	Namibia	824	68	Ivory Coast	322
34	Mozambique	799			
35	Pakistan	796			

Largest exclusive economic zones[b]

Million sq km

		Marine territory	Land area				Marine territory	Land area
1	United States	11.4	9.832	10	Brazil		3.7	8.516
2	France	11.0	0.549		Chile		3.7	0.756
3	Australia	8.5	7.741	12	Mexico		3.2	1.964
4	Russia	7.6	17.098	13	Denmark		2.5	0.043
5	United Kingdom	6.8	0.244	14	Norway		2.4	0.385
6	New Zealand	6.7	0.268		Papua New Guinea		2.4	0.463
7	Indonesia	6.2	1.911	16	India		2.3	3.287
8	Canada	5.6	9.985	17	Portugal		1.7	0.092
9	Japan	4.5	0.378					

a Includes freshwater.   b Area extending 200 nautical miles (370km) from the coast.

Mountains: the highest[a]

		Location	Height (m)
1	Everest	China–Nepal	8,848
2	K2 (Godwin Austen)	China–Pakistan	8,611
3	Kangchenjunga	India–Nepal	8,586
4	Lhotse	China–Nepal	8,516
5	Makalu	China–Nepal	8,463
6	Cho Oyu	China–Nepal	8,201
7	Dhaulagiri	Nepal	8,167
8	Manaslu	Nepal	8,163
9	Nanga Parbat	Pakistan	8,126
10	Annapurna I	Nepal	8,091

Rivers: the longest

		Location	Length (km)
1	Nile	Africa	6,695
2	Amazon	South America	6,516
3	Yangtze (Chang Jiang)	Asia	6,380
4	Mississippi–Missouri system	North America	5,959
5	Ob'-Irtysh	Asia	5,568
6	Yenisey–Angara–Selanga	Asia	5,550
7	Yellow (Huang He)	Asia	5,464
8	Congo	Africa	4,667

Deserts: the largest non-polar

		Location	Area ('000 sq km)
1	Sahara	Northern Africa	8,600
2	Arabian	South-western Asia	2,300
3	Gobi	Mongolia/China	1,300
4	Patagonian	Argentina	673
5	Syrian	Middle East	520
6	Great Basin	South-western United States	490
7	Great Victoria	Western and Southern Australia	419
8	Great Sandy	Western Australia	395

Lakes: the largest

		Location	Area ('000 sq km)
1	Caspian Sea	Central Asia	371
2	Superior	Canada/United States	82
3	Victoria	East Africa	69
4	Huron	Canada/United States	60
5	Michigan	United States	58
6	Tanganyika	East Africa	33
7	Baikal	Russia	31
	Great Bear	Canada	31

a Includes separate peaks which are part of the same massif.
Notes: Estimates of the lengths of rivers vary widely depending on, eg, the path to take through a delta. The definition of a desert is normally a mean annual precipitation value equal to 250ml or less.

Population: size and growth

Largest populations
m, 2015

1	China	1,376.0	37	Iraq	36.4
2	India	1,311.1	38	Canada	35.9
3	United States	321.8	39	Morocco	34.4
4	Indonesia	257.6	40	Afghanistan	32.5
5	Brazil	207.8	41	Saudi Arabia	31.5
6	Pakistan	188.9	42	Peru	31.4
7	Nigeria	182.2	43	Venezuela	31.1
8	Bangladesh	161.0	44	Malaysia	30.3
9	Russia	143.5	45	Uzbekistan	29.9
10	Mexico	127.0	46	Nepal	28.5
11	Japan	126.6	47	Mozambique	28.0
12	Philippines	100.7	48	Ghana	27.4
13	Ethiopia	99.4	49	Yemen	26.8
14	Vietnam	93.4	50	North Korea	25.2
15	Egypt	91.5	51	Angola	25.0
16	Germany	80.7	52	Madagascar	24.2
17	Iran	79.1	53	Australia	24.0
18	Turkey	78.7	54	Taiwan	23.4
19	Congo-Kinshasa	77.3	55	Cameroon	23.3
20	Thailand	68.0	56	Ivory Coast	22.7
21	United Kingdom	64.7	57	Sri Lanka	20.7
22	France	64.4	58	Niger	19.9
23	Italy	59.8	59	Romania	19.5
24	South Africa	54.5	60	Syria	18.5
25	Myanmar	53.9	61	Burkina Faso	18.1
26	Tanzania	53.5	62	Chile	17.9
27	South Korea	50.3	63	Kazakhstan	17.6
28	Colombia	48.2		Mali	17.6
29	Kenya	46.1	65	Malawi	17.2
	Spain	46.1	66	Netherlands	16.9
31	Ukraine	44.8	67	Guatemala	16.3
32	Argentina	43.4	68	Zambia	16.2
33	Sudan	40.2	69	Ecuador	16.1
34	Algeria	39.7	70	Cambodia	15.6
35	Uganda	39.0		Zimbabwe	15.6
36	Poland	38.6	72	Senegal	15.1

Largest populations
m, 2030

1	India	1,527.7	11	Ethiopia	138.3
2	China	1,415.5	12	Philippines	123.6
3	United States	355.8	13	Congo-Kinshasa	120.3
4	Indonesia	295.5	14	Japan	120.1
5	Nigeria	262.6	15	Egypt	117.1
6	Pakistan	244.9	16	Vietnam	105.2
7	Brazil	228.7	17	Iran	88.5
8	Bangladesh	186.5	18	Turkey	87.7
9	Mexico	148.1	19	Tanzania	82.9
10	Russia	138.7	20	Germany	79.3

Note: Populations include migrant workers.

Fastest-growing populations
Total % change, 2010–20

1	Oman	63.6	24	Guinea	30.4
2	Niger	49.2	25	Afghanistan	30.3
3	Kuwait	41.1	26	Benin	30.0
4	South Sudan	40.4	27	French Guiana	29.9
5	Qatar	38.8	28	Togo	29.8
6	Burundi	38.7	29	Nigeria	29.7
7	Uganda	38.3	30	Somalia	29.6
8	Chad	38.1	31	Congo-Brazzaville	29.4
9	Angola	37.8		Kenya	29.4
10	Gambia, The	37.4	33	Liberia	28.6
11	Congo-Kinshasa	36.7	34	Cameroon	27.9
12	Tanzania	36.4		Ethiopia	27.9
13	Iraq	36.0	36	Mauritania	27.3
14	Lebanon	35.8		Yemen	27.3
15	Zambia	35.7	38	Ivory Coast	27.0
16	Malawi	35.6	39	Guinea-Bissau	26.6
17	Senegal	35.0	40	Rwanda	26.3
18	Mali	34.9	41	Eritrea	25.6
19	Burkina Faso	33.5	42	Ghana	25.5
20	Equatorial Guinea	33.2		Sudan	25.5
21	Madagascar	31.9	44	Jordan	25.3
22	Mozambique	31.5	45	Zimbabwe	25.0
23	West Bank & Gaza	31.1	46	Namibia	24.5

Slowest-growing populations
Total % change, 2010–20

1	Andorra	-16.7	26	Cuba	0.5
2	Lithuania	-10.5		Slovakia	0.5
3	Latvia	-8.2	28	Czech Republic	0.6
4	Bulgaria	-7.1		Montenegro	0.6
	Romania	-7.1	30	Virgin Islands (US)	0.9
6	Georgia	-6.4	31	Albania	1.1
7	Bermuda	-4.7		Slovenia	1.1
8	Ukraine	-4.3	33	Macedonia	1.3
9	Serbia	-4.2		Syria	1.3
10	Portugal	-4.0	35	Taiwan	2.1
11	Croatia	-3.6	36	Armenia	2.5
12	Hungary	-3.3	37	Malta	2.7
13	Greece	-3.2		Monaco	2.7
14	Estonia	-2.8	39	Thailand	2.8
15	Bosnia & Herz.	-2.0	40	Barbados	2.9
16	Japan	-1.8	41	Austria	3.1
17	Moldova	-1.5	42	El Salvador	3.2
18	Belarus	-1.3	43	Netherlands	3.3
19	Puerto Rico	-0.9	44	Mauritius	3.4
	Spain	-0.9	45	Jamaica	3.6
21	Poland	-0.4		Uruguay	3.6
22	Russia	-0.2	47	Trinidad & Tobago	3.8
23	Germany	-0.1	48	Finland	4.0
24	Martinique	0.0	49	Denmark	4.1
25	Italy	0.3			

Population: matters of breeding and sex

Total births
Average annual number, m, 2015–20

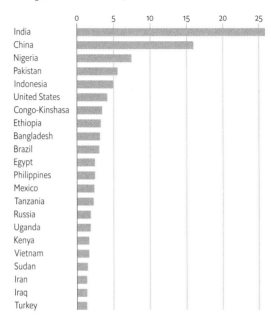

Teenage births
Births per 1,000 women aged 15–19, 2015–20

Highest		Lowest	
1 Niger	196.3	**1** North Korea	0.4
2 Mali	170.3	**2** South Korea	1.4
3 Angola	152.6	**3** Switzerland	2.4
4 Ivory Coast	136.0	**4** Hong Kong	2.9
5 Guinea	135.4	Macau	2.9
6 Malawi	132.1	**6** Slovenia	3.1
7 Mozambique	125.7	**7** Netherlands	3.5
8 Congo-Kinshasa	120.9	**8** Denmark	3.6
9 Chad	114.9	Japan	3.6
10 Tanzania	114.4	**10** Singapore	3.7
11 Sierra Leone	111.0	**11** Iceland	4.0
12 Gambia, The	110.2	**12** Maldives	4.1
13 Congo-Brazzaville	109.9	**13** Cyprus	4.5
14 Madagascar	109.5	**14** Luxembourg	4.9
15 Zimbabwe	106.0	**15** Germany	5.4
16 Nigeria	104.1	**16** Oman	5.5
17 Equatorial Guinea	103.0	**17** Austria	5.6
18 Burkina Faso	101.6	Italy	5.6

Fertility rates
Average number of children per woman, 2015

Highest			Lowest		
1	Niger	6.8	**1**	Macau	1.0
2	Burundi	6.1		Singapore	1.0
	Mali	6.1	**3**	Taiwan	1.1
4	Somalia	6.0	**4**	Hong Kong	1.2
5	Burkina Faso	5.9	**5**	Bosnia & Herz.	1.3
	Uganda	5.9		Poland	1.3
7	Zambia	5.7		Romania	1.3
8	Malawi	5.6		Slovenia	1.3
9	Angola	5.4		South Korea	1.3
10	Afghanistan	5.3	**10**	Andorra	1.4
	South Sudan	5.3		Czech Republic	1.4
12	Ethiopia	5.2		Germany	1.4
	Mozambique	5.2		Greece	1.4
	Nigeria	5.2		Hungary	1.4
15	Benin	5.0		Italy	1.4
	Timor-Leste	5.0		Japan	1.4
17	Guinea	4.9		Serbia	1.4
	Tanzania	4.9		Slovakia	1.4
19	Cameroon	4.8			
	Sierra Leone	4.8			
21	Congo-Brazzaville	4.7			
	Congo-Kinshasa	4.7			
	Liberia	4.7			
24	Chad	4.6			
	Equatorial Guinea	4.6			
26	Gabon	4.5			
	Rwanda	4.5			
	Togo	4.5			

Women[a] who use modern methods of contraception
2015 or latest, %

Highest			Lowest		
1	China	82.5	**1**	South Sudan	2.6
2	United Kingdom	80.0	**2**	Chad	2.9
3	Thailand	76.5	**3**	Guinea	4.6
4	Costa Rica	75.7	**4**	Somalia	5.8
5	Nicaragua	75.4	**5**	Congo-Kinshasa	8.5
6	Brazil	75.2	**6**	Gambia, The	9.8
7	Hong Kong	75.1		Niger	9.8
8	Uruguay	73.8	**8**	Montenegro	10.2
9	Cuba	72.3	**9**	Benin	10.4
10	Finland	72.2	**10**	Equatorial Guinea	10.6
	France	72.2	**11**	Nigeria	10.8
	Switzerland	72.2	**12**	Mali	11.4
13	Colombia	71.7	**13**	Mauritania	12.5
14	Norway	71.5	**14**	Angola	12.6
15	Canada	71.1		Central African Rep.	12.6

a Married women aged 15–49; excludes traditional methods of contraception, such as the rhythm method.

Population: age

Median age[a]

Biggest increase over 50 years
● 1965 ● 2015

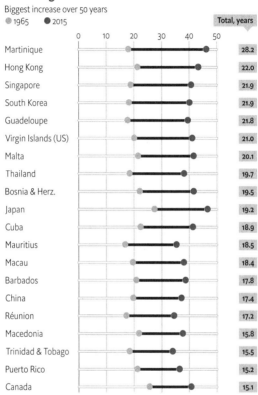

Total, years

Martinique	28.2
Hong Kong	22.0
Singapore	21.9
South Korea	21.9
Guadeloupe	21.8
Virgin Islands (US)	21.0
Malta	20.1
Thailand	19.7
Bosnia & Herz.	19.5
Japan	19.2
Cuba	18.9
Mauritius	18.5
Macau	18.4
Barbados	17.8
China	17.4
Réunion	17.2
Macedonia	15.8
Trinidad & Tobago	15.5
Puerto Rico	15.2
Canada	15.1

Most old people
% of population aged 70 or over, 2015

1	Monaco	22.9
2	Japan	18.9
3	Italy	16.3
4	Germany	16.1
5	Greece	15.4
6	Portugal	15.0
7	Latvia	14.5
8	Lithuania	14.3
9	Estonia	13.8
10	Austria	13.7
	Spain	13.7
12	Sweden	13.4

Most young people
% of population aged 0–24, 2015

1	Uganda	68.4
2	Niger	68.3
3	Chad	68.0
4	Angola	67.1
5	Mali	66.7
6	Somalia	66.6
7	Zambia	66.0
8	Gambia, The	65.8
	Malawi	65.8
10	Burkina Faso	65.5
	Congo-Kinshasa	65.5
12	Mozambique	65.3

a Age at which there is an equal number of people above and below.

City living

Biggest cities[a]
Population, m, 2016

1	Tokyo, Japan	38.1
2	Delhi, India	26.5
3	Shanghai, China	24.5
4	Mumbai, India	21.4
5	São Paulo, Brazil	21.3
6	Beijing, China	21.2
	Mexico City, Mexico	21.2
8	Osaka, Japan	20.3
9	Cairo, Egypt	19.1
10	New York, US	18.6
11	Dhaka, Bangladesh	18.2
12	Karachi, Pakistan	17.1
13	Buenos Aires, Argentina	15.3
14	Kolkata, India	15.0
15	Istanbul, Turkey	14.4
16	Chongqing, China	13.7
	Lagos, Nigeria	13.7
18	Guangzhou, China	13.1
	Manila, Philippines	13.1
20	Rio de Janeiro, Brazil	13.0
21	Los Angeles, US	12.3
	Moscow, Russia	12.3
23	Kinshasa, Congo-Kinshasa	12.1
24	Tianjin, China	11.6
25	Paris, France	10.9

26	Shenzhen, China	10.8
27	Bangalore, India	10.5
	Jakarta, Indonesia	10.5
29	London, UK	10.4
30	Chennai, India	10.2
31	Lima, Peru	10.1
32	Bogotá, Colombia	10.0
33	Seoul, South Korea	9.8
34	Johannesburg, South Africa	9.6
35	Bangkok, Thailand	9.4
	Nagoya, Japan	9.4
37	Hyderabad, India	9.2
38	Lahore, Pakistan	9.0
39	Chicago, US	8.8
40	Tehran, Iran	8.5
41	Wuhan, China	8.0
42	Chengdu, China	7.8
43	Nanjing, China	7.6
	Ahmadabad, India	7.6
45	Ho Chi Minh City, Vietnam	7.5
	Dongguan, China	7.5
47	Hong Kong	7.4
48	Foshan, China	7.1
49	Kuala Lumpur, Malaysia	7.0
50	Baghdad, Iraq	6.8

City growth[b]
Total % change, 2010–20

Fastest

1	Samut Prakan, Thailand	134.0
2	Batam, Indonesia	103.9
3	Mogadishu, Somalia	95.1
4	Ouagadougou, Burkina Faso	93.1
6	Xiamen, China	90.8
7	Yinchuan, China	80.8
8	Denpasar, Indonesia	80.4
9	Abuja, Nigeria	77.0
10	Can Tho, Vietnam	74.6
11	Dar es Salaam, Tanzania	73.8
12	Zhongshan, China	73.7
13	Kannur, India	73.3
14	Suqian, China	72.5
15	Suzhou, China	72.0
16	Malappuram, India	71.7
17	Hama, Syria	70.9
18	Bamako, Mali	69.2
19	Huambo, Angola	68.2

Slowest

1	Dnipropetrovsk, Ukraine	-9.3
2	Sendai, Japan	-7.8
3	Nizhniy Novgorod, Russia	-7.7
4	Saratov, Russia	-6.9
5	Donetsk, Ukraine	-6.5
6	Zaporizhia, Ukraine	-5.8
7	Khulna, Bangladesh	-5.4
8	Pusan, South Korea	-4.7
9	Yerevan, Armenia	-3.9
10	Detroit, US	-3.3
11	Perm, Russia	-3.0
12	Thessaloniki, Greece	-2.9
13	Buffalo, US	-2.8
14	Havana, Cuba	-2.6
15	Changwon, South Korea	-2.0
	Kitakyushu, Japan	-2.0
17	Kharkiv, Ukraine	-1.9
18	Sapporo, Japan	-1.6
19	Daegu, South Korea	-1.5

a Urban agglomerations. Data may change from year to year based on reassessments of agglomeration boundaries.
b Cities with a population of at least 750,000 in 2010.

Urban populations

% 2020

Highest			Lowest		
1	Bermuda	100.0	1	Trinidad & Tobago	8.1
	Hong Kong	100.0	2	Papua New Guinea	13.3
	Macau	100.0	3	Burundi	13.6
	Monaco	100.0	4	Liechtenstein	14.4
	Singapore	100.0	5	Malawi	17.3
6	Qatar	99.5	6	Uganda	17.9
7	Guadeloupe	98.5	7	Sri Lanka	18.8
8	Kuwait	98.4	8	South Sudan	20.1
9	Belgium	98.0	9	Niger	20.3
10	Uruguay	96.0	10	Nepal	20.6
11	Malta	95.9	11	Swaziland	21.5
	Virgin Islands (US)	95.9	12	Ethiopia	21.8
13	Réunion	95.6	13	Cambodia	22.0
14	Japan	95.3	14	Chad	23.4

Urban growth

Total % change, 2010–20

Highest			Lowest		
1	Rwanda	82.4	1	Trinidad & Tobago	-9.9
2	Burkina Faso	74.8	2	Latvia	-5.9
3	Burundi	74.6	3	Moldova	-5.3
4	Uganda	71.0	4	Lithuania	-4.2
5	Oman	70.8	5	Estonia	-4.0
6	Niger	70.2	6	Bulgaria	-3.5
7	Tanzania	67.8	7	Ukraine	-3.3
8	Mali	65.3	8	Serbia	-3.1
9	Eritrea	63.5	9	Slovakia	-2.0
10	Angola	61.4	10	Russia	-1.4
11	Ethiopia	61.1	11	Puerto Rico	-1.2
12	Madagascar	58.1	12	Armenia	-1.1
13	Laos	57.3	13	Georgia	-0.9

Rural growth

Total % change, 2010–20

Highest			Lowest		
1	Andorra	55.6	1	Japan	-50.8
2	Niger	42.5	2	Qatar	-50.0
3	South Sudan	35.6	3	Netherlands	-42.7
4	Uganda	33.0	4	Virgin Islands (US)	-33.3
5	Zimbabwe	32.9	5	Dominican Rep.	-26.3
6	Chad	31.8	6	Uruguay	-25.5
7	Burundi	31.7	7	Costa Rica	-22.2
8	Oman	31.5	8	Malta	-21.7
9	Malawi	29.7	9	Réunion	-19.6
10	Zambia	27.9	10	Belarus	-19.3
11	Eritrea	27.1		Thailand	-19.3
12	Equatorial Guinea	27.0	12	China	-19.1
13	Iraq	26.6	13	Bulgaria	-18.3
14	Senegal	24.5	14	Albania	-18.1

City liveability[a]

100 = ideal, 0 = intolerable, 2016

Best

1	Melbourne, Australia	97.5
2	Vienna, Austria	97.4
3	Vancouver, Canada	97.3
4	Toronto, Canada	97.2
5	Adelaide, Australia	96.6
	Calgary, Canada	96.6
7	Perth, Australia	95.9
8	Auckland, New Zealand	95.7
9	Helsinki, Finland	95.6
10	Hamburg, Germany	95.0
11	Sydney, Australia	94.9
12	Montreal, Canada	94.8
13	Tokyo, Japan	94.7
14	Osaka, Japan	94.5
15	Zurich, Switzerland	94.3

Worst

1	Damascus, Syria	30.2
2	Tripoli, Libya	35.9
3	Lagos, Nigeria	36.0
4	Dhaka, Bangladesh	38.7
5	Port Moresby, Papua New Guinea	38.9
6	Algiers, Algeria	40.9
	Karachi, Pakistan	40.9
8	Harare, Zimbabwe	42.6
9	Douala, Cameroon	44.0
10	Kiev, Ukraine	47.8
11	Dakar, Senegal	48.3
12	Abidjan, Ivory Coast	49.7
13	Tehran, Iran	50.8

▌ Tallest buildings[b]

Height, metres

a EIU liveability index, based on a range of factors including stability, health care, culture, education, infrastructure.   b Completed.

Migrants, refugees and asylum seekers

Migrants[a] by country of origin

m, 2015

1	India	15.6		South Korea	2.3
2	Mexico	12.3	28	France	2.1
3	Russia	10.6	29	Somalia	2.0
4	China	9.5		Uzbekistan	2.0
5	Bangladesh	7.2	31	Sudan	1.9
6	Pakistan	5.9	32	Algeria	1.8
7	Ukraine	5.8		Malaysia	1.8
8	Philippines	5.3		Puerto Rico	1.8
9	Syria	5.0	35	Bosnia & Herz.	1.7
10	United Kingdom	4.9	36	Nepal	1.6
11	Afghanistan	4.8		Sri Lanka	1.6
12	Poland	4.4	38	Belarus	1.5
13	Kazakhstan	4.1		Brazil	1.5
14	Germany	4.0		Burkina Faso	1.5
15	Indonesia	3.9		Iraq	1.5
16	West Bank & Gaza	3.6	42	Congo-Kinshasa	1.4
17	Romania	3.4		Cuba	1.4
18	Egypt	3.3		El Salvador	1.4
19	Turkey	3.1		Peru	1.4
20	United States	3.0	46	Canada	1.3
21	Italy	2.9		Dominican Republic	1.3
	Myanmar	2.9		Laos	1.3
23	Morocco	2.8		Spain	1.3
24	Colombia	2.6	50	Bulgaria	1.2
	Vietnam	2.6		Cambodia	1.2
26	Portugal	2.3		Haiti	1.2

Biggest destination country for migrant groups

'000, 2015

1	Mexico	12,050.0	United States
2	India	3,499.3	United Arab Emirates
3	Russia	3,276.8	Ukraine
4	Ukraine	3,270.0	Russia
5	Bangladesh	3,171.0	India
6	Kazakhstan	2,560.3	Russia
7	Afghanistan	2,348.4	Iran
8	China	2,307.8	Hong Kong
9	West Bank & Gaza	2,142.8	Jordan
10	Myanmar	1,978.3	Thailand
11	Poland	1,930.1	Germany
12	Philippines	1,896.0	United States
13	Puerto Rico	1,744.4	United States
14	Turkey	1,656.0	Germany
15	Syria	1,568.5	Turkey
16	Algeria	1,430.7	France
17	Vietnam	1,302.9	United States
18	Burkina Faso	1,294.3	Ivory Coast
19	Indonesia	1,294.0	Saudi Arabia
20	United Kingdom	1,289.4	Australia

a Living outside their country of birth.

Refugees[a] by country of origin

'000, 2015

1	Syria	4,872.6	11	Ukraine	321.3
2	Afghanistan	2,666.3	12	Vietnam	313.2
3	Somalia	1,123.1	13	Pakistan	297.8
4	South Sudan	778.7	14	Burundi	292.8
5	Sudan	628.8	15	Rwanda	286.4
6	Congo-Kinshasa	541.5	16	Iraq	264.1
7	Central African Rep.	471.1	17	China	212.9
8	Myanmar	451.8	18	Nigeria	168.0
9	Eritrea	411.3	19	Mali	154.2
10	Colombia	340.2	20	Sri Lanka	121.4

Countries with largest refugee[a] populations

'000, 2015

1	Turkey	2,541.4	11	Cameroon	343.0
2	Pakistan	1,561.2	12	Germany	316.1
3	Lebanon	1,070.9	13	Russia	314.5
4	Iran	979.4	14	Sudan	309.6
5	Ethiopia	736.1	15	China	301.1
6	Jordan	664.1	16	Iraq	277.7
7	Kenya	553.9	17	United States	273.2
8	Uganda	477.2	18	France	273.1
9	Congo-Kinshasa	383.1	19	Yemen	267.2
10	Chad	369.5	20	South Sudan	263.0

Applications for asylum by country of origin

'000, 2015

1	Syria	782.3	11	Nigeria	55.8
2	Afghanistan	486.7	12	Somalia	44.2
3	Iraq	300.6	13	Bangladesh	42.8
4	Ukraine	177.7	14	Ethiopia	36.9
5	Serbia[b]	133.6	15	Zimbabwe	36.3
6	Pakistan	92.8	16	China	30.7
7	Albania	74.2	17	Russia	28.7
8	Congo-Kinshasa	66.3	18	Sudan	27.9
9	Eritrea	62.9	19	Myanmar	24.9
10	Iran	60.5	20	El Salvador	22.9

Countries where asylum applications were lodged

'000, 2015

1	Serbia[b]	578.1	11	Italy	83.2
2	Germany	476.6	12	United Kingdom	53.3
3	Hungary	351.6	13	Belgium	49.3
4	Sweden	173.8	14	Netherlands	45.1
5	Russia	152.5	15	Switzerland	39.5
6	United States	136.0	16	Norway	36.7
7	Turkey	134.8	17	Uganda	35.9
8	South Africa	120.5	18	Finland	29.5
9	France	118.5	19	Egypt	23.1
10	Austria	89.9	20	Denmark	22.7

a According to UNHCR. Includes people in "refugee-like situations".
b Includes Kosovo.

The world economy

Biggest economies
GDP, $bn, 2015

1	United States	18,037	23	Sweden	496
2	China	11,226	24	Nigeria	494
3	Japan	4,382	25	Poland	477
4	Germany	3,365	26	Belgium	455
5	United Kingdom	2,863	27	Thailand	399
6	France[a]	2,420	28	Norway	387
7	India	2,088	29	Austria	377
8	Italy	1,826	30	Iran	374
9	Brazil	1,801	31	United Arab Emirates	370
10	Canada	1,553	32	Egypt	332
11	South Korea	1,383	33	South Africa	315
12	Russia	1,366	34	Hong Kong	309
13	Australia	1,230	35	Denmark	301
14	Spain	1,194	36	Israel	299
15	Mexico	1,151	37	Singapore	297
16	Indonesia	861	38	Malaysia	296
17	Turkey	859	39	Colombia	292
18	Netherlands	751		Philippines	292
19	Switzerland	671	41	Ireland	283
20	Saudi Arabia	652	42	Pakistan	271
21	Argentina	632	43	Venezuela	260
22	Taiwan	525	44	Chile	243

Biggest economies by purchasing power
GDP PPP, $bn, 2015

1	China	19,696	24	Poland	1,012
2	United States	18,037	25	Pakistan	932
3	India	8,003	26	Argentina	883
4	Japan	5,119	27	Netherlands	840
5	Germany	3,860	28	Malaysia	817
6	Russia	3,760	29	Philippines	744
7	Brazil	3,216	30	South Africa	728
8	Indonesia	2,850	31	Colombia	667
9	United Kingdom	2,701	32	United Arab Emirates	643
10	France[a]	2,666	33	Algeria	580
11	Mexico	2,234		Bangladesh	580
12	Italy	2,186		Iraq	580
13	Turkey	1,908	36	Vietnam	553
14	South Korea	1,856	37	Venezuela	514
15	Saudi Arabia	1,704	38	Belgium	497
16	Canada	1,637	39	Switzerland	483
17	Spain	1,613	40	Singapore	477
18	Iran	1,347	41	Sweden	476
19	Australia	1,144	42	Kazakhstan	441
20	Thailand	1,114	43	Chile	426
21	Taiwan	1,102	44	Hong Kong	416
22	Nigeria	1,094		Romania	416
23	Egypt	1,072	46	Austria	406

Note: For a list of 185 countries with their GDPs, see pages 250–53. "Advanced economies" refers to 39 countries as defined by the IMF.
a Includes overseas territories.   b IMF coverage.

Regional GDP

$bn, 2016		*% annual growth 2011–17*	
World	75,278	World	3.4
Advanced economies	46,076	Advanced economies	1.7
G7	35,447	G7	1.6
Euro area (19)	11,879	Euro area (19)	0.9
Other Asia	16,107	Other Asia	6.7
Latin America & Caribbean	5,003	Latin America & Caribbean	1.2
Other Europe & CIS	3,571	Other Europe & CIS	2.3
Middle East, N. Africa, Afghanistan & Pakistan	3,110	Middle East, N. Africa, Afghanistan & Pakistan	3.3
Sub-Saharan Africa	1,412	Sub-Saharan Africa	3.7

Regional purchasing power

GDP, % of total, 2016		*$ per person, 2016*	
World	100	World	16,439
Advanced economies	41.9	Advanced economies	47,383
G7	31.0	G7	48,978
Euro area (19)	11.8	Euro area (19)	41,672
Other Asia	31.6	Other Asia	10,675
Latin America & Caribbean	7.9	Latin America & Caribbean	15,358
Other Europe & CIS	8.0	Other Europe & CIS	20,875
Middle East, N. Africa, Afghanistan & Pakistan	7.6	Middle East, N. Africa, Afghanistan & Pakistan	13,702
Sub-Saharan Africa	3.0	Sub-Saharan Africa	3,837

Regional population

% of total (7.3bn), 2016		*No. of countries[b], 2016*	
World	100.0	World	190
Advanced economies	16.7	Advanced economies	23
G7	10.4	G7	7
Euro area (19)	4.6	Euro area (19)	19
Other Asia	48.7	Other Asia	30
Latin America & Caribbean	8.4	Latin America & Caribbean	32
Other Europe & CIS	6.3	Other Europe & CIS	24
Middle East, N. Africa, Afghanistan & Pakistan	9.0	Middle East, N. Africa, Afghanistan & Pakistan	22
Sub-Saharan Africa	13.0	Sub-Saharan Africa	45

Regional international trade

Exports of goods & services *% of total, 2016*		*Current-account balances* *$bn, 2016*	
World	100.0	World	286
Advanced economies	64.4	Advanced economies	375
G7	34.7	G7	-138
Euro area (19)	26.3	Euro area (19)	400
Other Asia	17.9	Other Asia	217
Latin America & Caribbean	5.0	Latin America & Caribbean	-107
Other Europe & CIS	5.9	Other Europe & CIS	-37
Middle East, N. Africa, Afghanistan & Pakistan	5.2	Middle East, N. Africa, Afghanistan & Pakistan	-105
Sub-Saharan Africa	1.5	Sub-Saharan Africa	-56

Living standards

Highest GDP per person
$, 2015

1	Liechtenstein	159,030	**31**	Japan	34,616
2	Monaco	156,462	**32**	Brunei	32,328
3	Bermuda	97,553	**33**	Italy	30,532
4	Luxembourg	94,718	**34**	Martinique	30,000
5	Switzerland	80,802	**35**	New Caledonia	29,790
6	Macau	76,963	**36**	Kuwait	29,251
7	Qatar	74,837	**37**	Guam	28,670
8	Norway	74,342	**38**	Puerto Rico	27,812
9	Ireland	60,303	**39**	South Korea	27,490
10	Channel Islands[a]	51,166	**40**	Spain	25,891
11	United States	56,049	**41**	Malta	25,733
12	Iceland	55,947	**42**	Réunion	24,444
13	Singapore	53,006	**43**	Guadeloupe	24,000
14	Denmark	52,861	**44**	Taiwan	22,446
15	Australia	51,238	**45**	Bahrain	22,228
16	Sweden	50,581	**46**	Bahamas	22,135
17	Netherlands	44,420	**47**	Saudi Arabia	20,691
18	United Kingdom	44,255	**48**	Slovenia	20,380
19	Austria	43,855	**49**	Portugal	19,342
20	Canada	43,254	**50**	Greece	17,723
21	Hong Kong	42,384	**51**	Czech Republic	17,634
22	Finland	42,269	**52**	Estonia	17,286
23	Germany	41,701	**53**	Equatorial Guinea	17,274
24	Belgium	40,295	**54**	French Polynesia	17,118
25	United Arab Emirates	40,250	**55**	Trinidad & Tobago	16,828
26	Andorra	40,166	**56**	French Guiana	16,667
27	New Zealand	38,501	**57**	Cyprus	16,308
28	Virgin Islands (US)[b]	37,650	**58**	Slovakia	16,169
29	France[c]	37,580	**59**	Uruguay	15,620
30	Israel	36,965	**60**	Oman	15,518

Lowest GDP per person
$, 2015

1	Burundi	268	**17**	North Korea	646
2	Central African Rep.	325	**18**	Ethiopia	651
3	Niger	361	**19**	Sierra Leone	699
4	Malawi	373	**20**	Rwanda	714
5	Madagascar	403	**21**	Mali	745
6	Gambia, The	446	**22**	Nepal	748
7	Liberia	453	**23**	Benin	761
8	Congo-Kinshasa	498	**24**	Chad	782
9	Mozambique	529	**25**	Haiti	810
10	Guinea	535	**26**	Tanzania	853
11	Somalia	549	**27**	Eritrea	880
12	Togo	571	**28**	Senegal	905
13	Guinea-Bissau	578	**29**	Zimbabwe	908
14	Afghanistan	606	**30**	Tajikistan	924
15	Burkina Faso	614	**31**	South Sudan	1,007
16	Uganda	644	**32**	Myanmar	1,105

a 2010   b 2004   c Includes overseas territories.

Highest purchasing power

GDP per person in PPP (US = 100), 2015

1	Monaco	302.9	35	Japan	72.1
2	Qatar	256.6	36	Oman	70.2
3	Macau	191.2	37	Virgin Islands (US)	67.7
4	Luxembourg	169.2	38	New Zealand	66.6
5	Singapore	151.9	39	South Korea	65.8
6	Brunei	147.9	40	Italy	65.2
7	Liechtenstein	142.7	41	Puerto Rico	63.5
8	Kuwait	133.8	42	Israel	62.8
9	United Arab Emirates	124.6	43	Spain	62.4
10	Norway	122.2	44	Trinidad & Tobago	57.7
11	Ireland	115.7	45	Czech Republic	57.4
12	Switzerland	103.9	46	Martinique	56.3
13	Channel Islands	102.6	47	Slovenia	54.2
14	Hong Kong	101.7	48	Slovakia	53.7
15	Bermuda	101.4	49	New Caledonia	52.1
16	United States	100.0	50	Estonia	51.3
17	Saudi Arabia	96.5	51	Lithuania	51.1
18	Iceland	90.5	52	Portugal	50.4
19	Netherlands	88.7	53	Malaysia	48.1
20	Sweden	86.6	54	Hungary	47.1
21	Germany	85.3	55	Poland	46.8
22	Australia	85.0	56	Russia	46.7
23	Austria	84.2	57	Greece	46.3
24	Taiwan	84.0	58	Guadeloupe	45.6
25	Denmark	83.7	59	Kazakhstan	44.7
26	Bahrain	81.8	60	Latvia	43.7
27	Canada	81.4	61	Guam	43.6
28	Andorra	80.6		Réunion	43.6
29	Belgium	78.4	63	Turkey	43.2
30	Equatorial Guinea	77.6	64	Chile	42.5
31	United Kingdom	74.5		French Polynesia	42.5
32	France	73.9	66	Cyprus	42.3
33	Finland	73.1	67	Panama	40.0
34	Malta	72.5	68	Cuba	39.9

Lowest purchasing power

GDP per person in PPP (US = 100), 2015

1	Somalia	0.73	15	Ethiopia	2.91
2	Central African Rep.	1.10	16	Eritrea	2.94
3	Burundi	1.25	17	Gambia, The	2.95
4	Congo-Kinshasa	1.45	18	Burkina Faso	3.03
5	Liberia	1.49	19	Haiti	3.14
6	Niger	1.70	20	Zimbabwe	3.21
7	Malawi	2.12	21	Rwanda	3.27
8	Guinea	2.13	22	Afghanistan	3.40
	Mozambique	2.13	23	South Sudan	3.41
10	Madagascar	2.62	24	Mali	3.62
11	Togo	2.67	25	Benin	3.66
12	Guinea-Bissau	2.68	26	Uganda	3.67
13	Sierra Leone	2.78	27	Chad	3.89
14	North Korea	2.83	28	Senegal	4.34

The quality of life

Human development index[a]
Highest, 2015

1	Norway	94.9	32	Andorra	85.8
2	Australia	93.9	33	Cyprus	85.6
	Switzerland	93.9		Malta	85.6
4	Germany	92.6		Qatar	85.6
5	Denmark	92.5	36	Poland	85.5
	Singapore	92.5	37	Lithuania	84.8
7	Netherlands	92.4	38	Chile	84.7
8	Ireland	92.3		Saudi Arabia	84.7
9	Iceland	92.1	40	Slovakia	84.5
10	Canada	92.0	41	Portugal	84.3
	United States	92.0	42	United Arab Emirates	84.0
12	Hong Kong	91.7	43	Hungary	83.6
13	New Zealand	91.5	44	Latvia	83.0
14	Sweden	91.3	45	Argentina	82.7
15	Liechtenstein	91.2		Croatia	82.7
16	United Kingdom	90.9	47	Bahrain	82.4
17	Japan	90.3	48	Montenegro	80.7
18	South Korea	90.1	49	Russia	80.4
19	Israel	89.9	50	Romania	80.2
20	Luxembourg	89.8	51	Kuwait	80.0
21	France	89.7	52	Belarus	79.6
22	Belgium	89.6		Oman	79.6
23	Finland	89.5	54	Barbados	79.5
24	Austria	89.3		Uruguay	79.5
25	Slovenia	89.0	56	Bulgaria	79.4
26	Italy	88.7		Kazakhstan	79.4
27	Spain	88.4	58	Bahamas	79.2
28	Czech Republic	87.8	59	Malaysia	78.9
29	Greece	86.6	60	Panama	78.8
30	Brunei	86.5	61	Mauritius	78.1
	Estonia	86.5	62	Trinidad & Tobago	78.0

Human development index[a]
Lowest, 2015

1	Central African Rep.	35.2	12	Liberia	42.7
2	Niger	35.3	13	Congo-Kinshasa	43.5
3	Chad	39.6	14	Mali	44.2
4	Burkina Faso	40.2	15	Ethiopia	44.8
5	Burundi	40.4	16	Gambia, The	45.2
6	Guinea	41.4	17	Ivory Coast	47.4
7	Mozambique	41.8	18	Malawi	47.6
	South Sudan	41.8	19	Afghanistan	47.9
9	Eritrea	42.0	20	Yemen	48.2
	Sierra Leone	42.0	21	Benin	48.5
11	Guinea-Bissau	42.4	22	Togo	48.7

a GDP or GDP per person is often taken as a measure of how developed a country is, but its usefulness is limited as it refers only to economic welfare. The UN Development Programme combines statistics on average and expected years of schooling and life expectancy with income levels (now GNI per person, valued in PPP US$). The HDI is shown here scaled from 0 to 100; countries scoring over 80 are considered to have very high human development, 70–79 high, 55–69 medium and those under 55 low.

Inequality-adjusted human development index[a]

Highest, 2015

1	Norway	89.8	21	Japan	79.1
2	Iceland	86.8		Spain	79.1
3	Australia	86.1	23	Estonia	78.8
	Netherlands	86.1	24	Malta	78.6
5	Germany	85.9	25	Italy	78.4
	Switzerland	85.9	26	Israel	77.8
7	Denmark	85.8	27	Poland	77.4
8	Sweden	85.1	28	Hungary	77.1
9	Ireland	85.0	29	Cyprus	76.2
10	Finland	84.3	30	Lithuania	75.9
11	Canada	83.9	31	Greece	75.8
12	Slovenia	83.8	32	Portugal	75.5
13	United Kingdom	83.6	33	South Korea	75.3
14	Czech Republic	83.0	34	Croatia	75.2
15	Luxembourg	82.7	35	Belarus	74.5
16	Belgium	82.1	36	Latvia	74.2
17	Austria	81.5	37	Montenegro	73.6
18	France	81.3	38	Russia	72.5
19	United States	79.6	39	Kazakhstan	71.4
20	Slovakia	79.3		Romania	71.4

Gini coefficient[b]

Highest, 2010–15

1	South Africa	63.4
2	Namibia	61.0
3	Haiti	60.8
4	Botswana	60.5
5	Central African Rep.	56.2
6	Zambia	55.6
7	Lesotho	54.2
8	Colombia	53.5
9	Paraguay	51.7
10	Brazil	51.5
	Swaziland	51.5
12	Guinea-Bissau	50.7
	Panama	50.7
14	Honduras	50.6
15	Chile	50.5
16	Rwanda	50.4
17	Congo-Brazzaville	48.9
18	Guatemala	48.7
19	Costa Rica	48.5
	Kenya	48.5

Lowest, 2010–15

1	Ukraine	24.1
2	Slovenia	25.6
3	Norway	25.9
4	Czech Republic	26.1
	Slovakia	26.1
6	Kazakhstan	26.3
7	Kyrgyzstan	26.8
	Moldova	26.8
9	Iceland	26.9
10	Finland	27.1
11	Belarus	27.2
12	Sweden	27.3
13	Romania	27.5
14	Belgium	27.6
15	Netherlands	28.0
16	Albania	29.0
17	Denmark	29.1
	Serbia	29.1
19	Germany	30.1
20	Austria	30.5

a Where there is inequality in the distribution of health, education and income, the IHDI of an average person in society is less than the ordinary HDI.
b The lower its value, the more equally household income is distributed.

Economic growth

Economic growth
Average annual % increase in real GDP, 2005–15

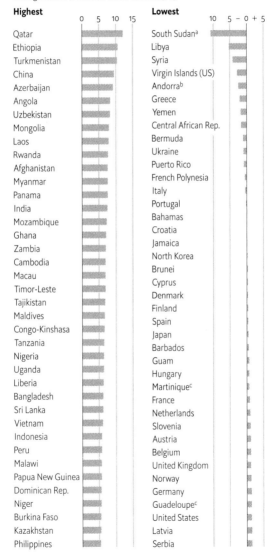

Highest		Lowest	
Qatar		South Sudan[a]	
Ethiopia		Libya	
Turkmenistan		Syria	
China		Virgin Islands (US)	
Azerbaijan		Andorra[b]	
Angola		Greece	
Uzbekistan		Yemen	
Mongolia		Central African Rep.	
Laos		Bermuda	
Rwanda		Ukraine	
Afghanistan		Puerto Rico	
Myanmar		French Polynesia	
Panama		Italy	
India		Portugal	
Mozambique		Bahamas	
Ghana		Croatia	
Zambia		Jamaica	
Cambodia		North Korea	
Macau		Brunei	
Timor-Leste		Cyprus	
Tajikistan		Denmark	
Maldives		Finland	
Congo-Kinshasa		Spain	
Tanzania		Japan	
Nigeria		Barbados	
Uganda		Guam	
Liberia		Hungary	
Bangladesh		Martinique[c]	
Sri Lanka		France	
Vietnam		Netherlands	
Indonesia		Slovenia	
Peru		Austria	
Malawi		Belgium	
Papua New Guinea		United Kingdom	
Dominican Rep.		Norway	
Niger		Germany	
Burkina Faso		Guadeloupe[c]	
Kazakhstan		United States	
Philippines		Latvia	
		Serbia	

a 2011–15   b 2005–13   c 2005–14

Highest economic growth
Average annual % increase in real GDP, 1995–2005

1	Equatorial Guinea	45.3	11	Armenia	8.6
2	Iraq[a]	16.5		Chad	8.6
3	Sudan	15.5		Sierra Leone	8.6
4	Myanmar[b]	11.8	14	Cambodia	8.3
5	Mozambique	10.2	15	Angola	8.2
6	Turkmenistan	9.9	16	Bosnia & Herz.[c]	8.0
7	Qatar	9.7		West Bank & Gaza	8.0
8	Azerbaijan	9.5	18	Trinidad & Tobago	7.9
9	China	9.2	19	Maldives	7.8
10	Rwanda	8.7	20	Ireland	7.6

Lowest economic growth
Average annual % change in real GDP, 1995–2005

1	Zimbabwe[a]	-6.5		Japan	1.0
2	Congo-Kinshasa	-0.8	12	Germany	1.2
3	Central African Rep.	0.4		Paraguay	1.2
4	Togo	0.5		Uruguay	1.2
5	Channel Islands[a]	0.6	15	Burundi	1.4
	Gabon	0.6	16	Italy	1.5
7	Jamaica	0.7		Papua New Guinea	1.5
8	North Korea	0.8	18	Guyana	1.6
9	Guinea-Bissau	1.0		Venezuela	1.6
	Haiti	1.0	20	Brunei	1.7

Highest services growth
Average annual % increase in real terms, 2007–15

1	Mali	13.3	10	Angola[d]	8.7
2	Ethiopia	12.8	11	Zambia	8.6
3	Myanmar	10.1	12	Mongolia	8.5
	Qatar	10.1		Mozambique	8.5
5	Afghanistan	10.0		Tajikistan	8.5
6	Zimbabwe	9.7	15	Nigeria	8.3
7	India	9.4	16	Congo-Kinshasa	8.1
8	China	9.0	17	Uzbekistan	8.0
9	Rwanda	8.8	18	Timor-Leste[a]	7.9

Lowest services growth
Average annual % change in real terms, 2007–15

1	Greece	-2.9		Portugal	0.1
2	Ukraine	-2.1	11	Central African Rep.	0.2
3	Estonia	-0.6		Denmark	0.2
4	Bahamas	-0.5		Latvia	0.2
5	Italy	-0.4	14	Serbia	0.5
6	Croatia	-0.3	15	Iceland[e]	0.7
7	Jamaica	0.0		Slovenia	0.7
	Japan[d]	0.0	17	Cyprus	0.8
9	Finland	0.1		Germany	0.8

a 1998–2005   b 1997–2005   c 1996–2005   d 2007–14   e 2007–13
Note: Rankings of highest and lowest industrial growth 2007–15 can be found on page 44.

Trading places

Biggest exporters
% of total world exports (goods, services and income), 2015

1	Euro area (19)	16.28	22	Luxembourg	1.40
2	United States	12.72	23	Thailand	1.17
3	China	11.10	24	Australia	1.15
4	Germany	7.46		Hong Kong	1.15
5	Japan	4.29	26	Sweden	1.14
6	United Kingdom	4.16	27	Poland	1.04
7	France	3.89	28	Saudi Arabia	1.02
8	Netherlands	3.62	29	Brazil	0.99
9	South Korea	2.78	30	Austria	0.97
10	Italy	2.53	31	Malaysia	0.93
11	Switzerland	2.39	32	Turkey	0.85
12	Canada	2.35	33	Denmark	0.82
13	Spain	1.90	34	Norway	0.78
14	India	1.85	35	Vietnam	0.73
15	Russia	1.80	36	Indonesia	0.72
16	Ireland	1.76	37	Czech Republic	0.67
17	Belgium	1.75	38	Hungary	0.51
18	Mexico	1.72	39	South Africa	0.44
19	United Arab Emirates	1.58	40	Finland	0.43
20	Taiwan	1.55	41	Israel	0.42
21	Singapore	1.54		Qatar	0.42

Trade dependency
Trade[a] as % of GDP, 2015

Most			Least		
1	Slovakia	83.2	1	Sudan	6.0
2	Vietnam	82.7	2	Bermuda	8.1
3	Hungary	71.2	3	Argentina	9.0
4	United Arab Emirates	70.8	4	Brazil	10.1
5	Czech Republic	68.5	5	Hong Kong	10.2
6	Lesotho	65.7		Nigeria	10.2
7	Lithuania	62.7	7	Yemen	10.4
8	Libya[b]	60.6	8	Egypt	10.5
9	Slovenia	60.3		United States	10.5
10	Puerto Rico	58.7	10	Timor-Leste	10.8
11	Netherlands	57.5	11	Pakistan	11.4
12	Belgium	55.8	12	Burundi	12.5
13	Estonia	55.1	13	Cuba[b]	13.2
14	Ireland	54.8	14	Venezuela	14.2
15	Malaysia	54.6	15	Central African Rep.[c]	14.3
16	Cambodia[c]	54.0	16	Iran	14.9
17	Bulgaria	52.6	17	Uganda	15.0
18	Bahrain[c]	51.0	18	Japan	15.1
19	Thailand	50.8	19	Colombia	15.4
20	Belarus	49.9	20	French Polynesia	15.8
21	Singapore	49.5			

Notes: The figures are drawn wherever possible from balance of payment statistics, so have differing definitions from statistics taken from customs or similar sources. For Hong Kong and Singapore, only domestic exports and retained imports are used. Euro area data exclude intra-euro area trade.

a Average of imports plus exports of goods.   b 2013   c 2014

Biggest traders of goods[a]

% of world, 2016

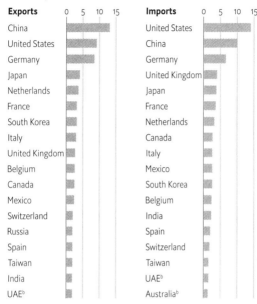

Exports		Imports	
China		United States	
United States		China	
Germany		Germany	
Japan		United Kingdom	
Netherlands		Japan	
France		France	
South Korea		Netherlands	
Italy		Canada	
United Kingdom		Italy	
Belgium		Mexico	
Canada		South Korea	
Mexico		Belgium	
Switzerland		India	
Russia		Spain	
Spain		Switzerland	
Taiwan		Taiwan	
India		UAE[b]	
UAE[b]		Australia[b]	

Biggest earners from services and income

% of world exports of services and income, 2015

1	Euro area (19)	18.26	**19**	South Korea	1.43
2	United States	18.03		Sweden	1.43
3	United Kingdom	6.53	**21**	Denmark	1.09
4	China	6.05	**22**	Austria	1.06
5	Germany	5.65	**23**	Russia	1.05
6	France	4.94	**24**	Australia	1.03
7	Japan	4.76	**25**	Taiwan	1.02
8	Netherlands	4.61	**26**	Norway	0.98
9	Luxembourg	3.74	**27**	United Arab Emirates	0.92
10	Hong Kong	3.16	**28**	Thailand	0.78
	Switzerland	3.15	**29**	Poland	0.68
12	Ireland	2.49	**30**	Turkey	0.60
13	Singapore	2.39	**31**	Malaysia	0.56
14	Spain	2.07	**32**	Brazil	0.54
15	India	2.01	**33**	Israel	0.53
16	Belgium	1.93	**34**	Finland	0.49
17	Italy	1.85	**35**	Saudi Arabia	0.47
18	Canada	1.78	**36**	Greece	0.46

a Individual countries only.   b Estimate.

Balance of payments: current account

Largest surpluses
$m, 2015

1	Euro area (19)	358,322	26	Philippines	7,266
2	China	330,602	27	Austria	7,020
3	Germany	279,969	28	Puerto Rico	6,331
4	Japan	135,608	29	Papua New Guinea	5,326
5	South Korea	105,940	30	Iraq	4,121
6	Switzerland	77,378	31	Hungary	3,946
7	Taiwan	76,165	32	Luxembourg	2,962
8	Russia	69,000	33	Bangladesh	2,687
9	Netherlands	65,129	34	Croatia	2,492
10	Singapore	53,757	35	Nepal	2,447
11	Norway	33,746	36	Slovenia	2,216
12	Thailand	32,149	37	Brunei	2,071
13	Italy	29,348	38	Belgium	1,936
14	Ireland	28,967	39	Cuba[a]	1,850
15	Denmark	27,582	40	Czech Republic	1,683
16	Sweden	23,250	41	Bahrain[b]	1,124
17	United Arab Emirates	17,253	42	Botswana	1,120
18	Spain	16,208	43	Trinidad & Tobago	957
19	Qatar	13,751	44	Vietnam	906
20	Israel	13,642	45	Bermuda	886
21	Macau	11,557	46	Iceland	854
22	Hong Kong	10,264	47	Malta	539
23	Iran	9,016	48	Estonia	493
24	Malaysia	8,960	49	French Polynesia	348
25	Kuwait	8,584	50	Swaziland	281

Largest deficits
$m, 2015

1	United States	-462,961	22	Sudan	-5,933
2	United Kingdom	-122,571	23	Mozambique	-5,833
3	Brazil	-58,882	24	New Zealand	-5,501
4	Australia	-58,280	25	Kazakhstan	-5,464
5	Saudi Arabia	-56,724	26	Afghanistan	-5,121
6	Canada	-53,083	27	France	-4,861
7	Mexico	-33,347	28	Chile	-4,761
8	Turkey	-32,118	29	Kenya	-4,038
9	Algeria	-27,229	30	Myanmar	-3,921
10	India	-22,457	31	Tunisia	-3,850
11	Venezuela	-20,360	32	Panama	-3,377
12	Colombia	-18,922	33	Jordan	-3,332
13	Indonesia	-17,586	34	Tanzania	-3,312
14	Argentina	-16,806	35	Yemen	-3,026
15	Egypt	-16,787	36	Poland	-2,932
16	Nigeria	-15,763	37	Ghana	-2,809
17	South Africa	-13,644	38	Costa Rica	-2,493
18	Oman	-10,807	39	Uganda	-2,353
19	Angola	-10,273	40	Laos	-2,264
20	Peru	-9,210	41	Ecuador	-2,201
21	Lebanon	-8,146	42	Morocco	-2,161

Note: Euro area data exclude intra-euro area trade.
a 2013   b 2014

Largest surpluses as % of GDP

$m, 2015

1	Papua New Guinea	25.1		Iceland	5.1
2	Macau	25.0		Luxembourg	5.1
3	Singapore	18.1	28	Russia	5.0
4	Brunei	16.0	29	Sweden	4.7
5	Bermuda	14.9		United Arab Emirates	4.7
6	Taiwan	14.5	31	Israel	4.6
7	Nepal	11.5	32	Trinidad & Tobago	3.7
	Switzerland	11.5	33	Bahrain[a]	3.4
9	Ireland	10.2	34	Hong Kong	3.3
10	Denmark	9.2		Hungary	3.3
11	Netherlands	8.7	36	Euro area (19)	3.1
	Norway	8.7		Japan	3.1
13	Qatar	8.4	38	China	3.0
14	Germany	8.3		Malaysia	3.0
15	Thailand	8.1	40	Philippines	2.5
16	Botswana	7.8	41	Cuba[b]	2.4
17	South Korea	7.7		Iran	2.4
	Timor-Leste	7.7	43	Iraq	2.3
19	Kuwait	7.2	44	Estonia	2.2
20	Swaziland	7.0	45	Guinea-Bissau	2.1
21	Puerto Rico	6.2	46	Austria	1.9
22	French Polynesia	5.7	47	Italy	1.6
23	Malta	5.5	48	Spain	1.4
24	Slovenia	5.2	49	Bangladesh	1.3
25	Croatia	5.1	50	Czech Republic	0.9

Largest deficits as % of GDP

$m, 2015

1	Liberia	-41.9	22	Togo	-11.3
2	Mozambique	-39.4	23	Malawi	-11.0
3	Afghanistan	-26.5	24	Gambia, The	-10.8
4	Sierra Leone[a]	-26.3	25	Albania	-10.7
5	Niger	-20.8		Zimbabwe	-10.7
6	Mauritania	-19.2	27	Angola	-10.0
7	Laos	-18.3	28	Cambodia[a]	-9.9
8	Guinea[a]	-17.9	29	Uganda	-9.3
9	Oman	-16.9	30	Benin	-9.0
10	Algeria	-16.5	31	Jordan	-8.9
	Lebanon	-16.5		Tunisia	-8.9
12	Bahamas	-15.9	33	Saudi Arabia	-8.7
13	Suriname	-15.6	34	Lesotho	-8.6
14	Kyrgyzstan	-14.9	35	Burkina Faso	-8.4
15	Namibia	-14.8	36	Haiti	-8.3
16	Rwanda	-13.6	37	Nicaragua	-8.2
17	West Bank & Gaza	-13.5	38	Mongolia	-8.1
18	Montenegro	-13.2	39	Yemen	-8.0
19	Burundi	-13.1	40	Venezuela	-7.8
20	Georgia	-12.7	41	Ghana	-7.5
21	Chad	-12.4	42	Tanzania	-7.3

a 2014   b 2013

Official reserves[a]

$m, end-2016

1	China	3,097,955	16	Thailand	171,797
2	Japan	1,216,642	17	France	146,258
3	Euro area (19)	743,548	18	Italy	135,527
4	Switzerland	679,077	19	United Kingdom	134,982
5	Saudi Arabia	547,313	20	Algeria	120,816
6	Taiwan	449,879	21	Indonesia	116,382
7	United States	407,250	22	Poland	114,345
8	Hong Kong	386,241	23	Turkey	106,006
9	Russia	377,312	24	Israel	98,447
10	South Korea	370,171	25	Malaysia	94,487
11	Brazil	364,995	26	Czech Republic	85,727
12	India	361,784	27	United Arab Emirates	85,392
13	Singapore	251,079	28	Canada	82,718
14	Germany	184,574	29	Philippines	80,698
15	Mexico	177,993	30	Libya[b]	74,112

Official gold reserves

Market prices, $m, end-2016

1	Euro area (19)	399,111	14	Turkey	13,952
2	United States	300,959	15	Saudi Arabia	11,948
3	Germany	124,992	16	United Kingdom	11,481
4	Italy	90,724	17	Lebanon	10,614
5	France	90,133	18	Spain	10,419
6	China	68,179	19	Austria	10,360
7	Russia	59,767	20	Kazakhstan	9,549
8	Switzerland	38,482	21	Belgium	8,414
9	Japan	28,315	22	Philippines	7,265
10	Netherlands	22,662	23	Algeria	6,425
11	India	20,639	24	Thailand	5,639
12	Taiwan	15,675	25	Singapore	4,714
13	Portugal	14,153	26	Sweden	4,652

Workers' remittances

Inflows, $m, 2015

1	India	68,910	16	Lebanon	7,481
2	China	63,938	17	United States	7,069
3	Philippines	28,483	18	Sri Lanka	6,980
4	Mexico	26,233	19	Morocco	6,904
5	France	23,352	20	Russia	6,870
6	Nigeria	21,060	21	Poland	6,783
7	Pakistan	19,306	22	Nepal	6,730
8	Egypt	18,325	23	Guatemala	6,573
9	Bangladesh	15,388	24	South Korea	6,454
10	Germany	15,362	25	Thailand	5,895
11	Vietnam	13,000	26	Ukraine	5,845
12	Spain	10,281	27	Jordan	5,348
13	Belgium	9,790	28	Dominican Rep.	5,196
14	Indonesia	9,659	29	United Kingdom	5,003
15	Italy	9,517	30	Colombia	4,680

a Foreign exchange, SDRs, IMF position and gold at market prices.   b End-September.

Exchange rates

The Economist's Big Mac index

Local currency under(-)/over(+) valuation against $^a, %
January 2017

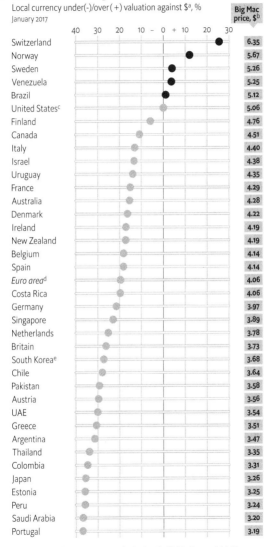

	Big Mac price, $^b
Switzerland	6.35
Norway	5.67
Sweden	5.26
Venezuela	5.25
Brazil	5.12
United States^c	5.06
Finland	4.76
Canada	4.51
Italy	4.40
Israel	4.38
Uruguay	4.35
France	4.29
Australia	4.28
Denmark	4.22
Ireland	4.19
New Zealand	4.19
Belgium	4.14
Spain	4.14
Euro area^d	4.06
Costa Rica	4.06
Germany	3.97
Singapore	3.89
Netherlands	3.78
Britain	3.73
South Korea^e	3.68
Chile	3.64
Pakistan	3.58
Austria	3.56
UAE	3.54
Greece	3.51
Argentina	3.47
Thailand	3.35
Colombia	3.31
Japan	3.26
Estonia	3.25
Peru	3.24
Saudi Arabia	3.20
Portugal	3.19

a Based on purchasing-power parity: local price of a Big Mac burger divided by United States price.   b At market exchange rates.   c Average of four cities.
d Weighted average of prices in euro area.   e Average of five cities.

Inflation

Consumer-price inflation

Highest, 2016, %

1	South Sudan[a]	379.8
2	Venezuela	254.9
3	Suriname	55.5
4	Angola[a]	32.4
5	Libya[a]	27.1
6	Congo-Kinshasa[a]	22.4
7	Malawi[a]	21.7
8	Mozambique	19.2
9	Zambia	17.9
10	Sudan[a]	17.8
11	Ghana[a]	17.5
12	Nigeria	15.7
13	Kazakhstan	14.6
14	Ukraine	13.9
15	Haiti	13.4
16	Azerbaijan[a]	12.4
17	Belarus[a]	11.8
18	Sierra Leone	11.3
19	Argentina	10.6
20	Egypt	10.2
21	Nepal	9.9
22	Uruguay	9.6

Lowest, 2016, %

1	Mali	-1.8
2	Romania	-1.6
	Zimbabwe	-1.6
4	Armenia[a]	-1.4
5	Bulgaria	-1.3
	Timor-Leste	-1.3
7	Cyprus	-1.2
8	Bosnia & Herz.	-1.1
	Chad[a]	-1.1
	Croatia[a]	-1.1
11	Benin	-0.8
	Jordan	-0.8
	Lebanon	-0.8
14	Brunei	-0.7
15	Poland	-0.6
16	Israel	-0.5
	Singapore	-0.5
	Slovakia[a]	-0.5
19	Montenegro	-0.4
	Switzerland	-0.4

Highest average annual consumer-price inflation, 2011–16, %

1	Venezuela[a]	85.1
2	South Sudan[a]	61
3	Sudan[a]	28.3
4	Malawi[a]	23.4
5	Belarus	23.1
6	Iran	19.9
7	Yemen[a]	14.1
8	Ghana[a]	13.7
	Ukraine	13.7
10	Angola[a]	13.4
11	Suriname	13.0
12	Ethiopia	11.2
13	Nigeria	10.7
14	Guinea[a]	10.6
15	Argentina	10.5
16	Sierra Leone	10.4
17	Uzbekistan[a]	9.8
	Zambia	9.8
19	Egypt	9.4
20	Libya[a]	9.3
21	Nepal	8.9
22	Uruguay	8.8
23	Mongolia	8.5

Lowest average annual consumer-price inflation, 2011–16, %

1	Greece	-0.5
	Switzerland	-0.5
3	Bulgaria	-0.3
4	Bosnia & Herz.[a]	-0.2
5	Brunei	-0.2
6	Cyprus	0.1
7	Zimbabwe	0.2
8	Senegal	0.4
9	Ireland	0.5
	Israel	0.5
	Puerto Rico	0.5
12	Poland	0.6
	Spain	0.6
14	El Salvador	0.7
	Japan	0.7
	Latvia	0.7
	Sweden	0.7
18	Croatia[a]	0.8
	France	0.8
	Niger	0.8
	Portugal	0.8
	Slovakia[a]	0.8
	Slovenia[a]	0.8

a Estimate.

Commodity prices

End 2016, % change on a year earlier			2011–16, % change		
1	Rubber	44.1	1	Zinc	40.1
2	Coconut oil	43.3	2	Timber	19.0
3	Tea	29.2	3	Coconut oil	17.0
4	Wool (Aus)	28.0	4	Wool (Aus)	14.0
5	Sugar	22.0	5	Tin	9.5
6	Zinc	20.9	6	Lead	5.0
7	Lead	15.0	7	Hides	4.0
	Palm oil	15.0	8	Cocoa	0.8
9	Cotton	12.8	9	Soya meal	0.1
10	Tin	11.9	10	Beef (Aus)	-1.8
11	Soya oil	5.2	11	Beef (US)	-2.4
12	Lamb	0.0	12	Tea	-6.5
13	Oil[a]	-3.4	13	Lamb	-10.5
14	Soyabeans	-4.7	14	Aluminium	-12.6
15	Aluminium	-5.2	15	Cotton	-14.9
16	Gold	-6.0	16	Soyabeans	-17.6
17	Timber	-9.0	17	Sugar	-21.0
18	Rice	-10.1	18	Palm oil	-22.2
19	Coffee	-10.8	19	Rubber	-22.9
20	Copper	-13.4	20	Copper	-27.8
21	Corn	-14.9	21	Gold	-29.5
22	Soya meal	-16.6		Wool (NZ)	-29.5
23	Wool (NZ)	-20.7	23	Coffee	-31.2
24	Beef (Aus)	-24.0	24	Soya oil	-33.3
25	Beef (US)	-24.8	25	Rice	-36.1
26	Cocoa	-25.2	26	Wheat	-39.0

The Economist's house prices

Q3 2016[b], % change on a year earlier			Q3 2010–Q3 2016[b], % change		
1	China	14.3	1	India	136.3
2	Turkey	14.0	2	Turkey	117.1
3	New Zealand	12.6	3	Brazil	89.8
4	Hungary	11.6	4	Hong Kong	87.2
5	Canada	11.4	5	Colombia	78.2
6	Colombia	10.8	6	Estonia	62.9
	Latvia	10.8	7	New Zealand	60.2
8	Iceland	10.2	8	Iceland	54.2
9	Israel	8.2	9	Israel	51.0
10	India	8.1	10	Sweden	47.5
11	Norway	7.9	11	Indonesia	42.3
12	Portugal	7.6	12	Chile	41.4
	Slovakia	7.6		Norway	41.4
14	Estonia	7.4	14	South Africa	40.0
	United Kingdom	7.4	15	Germany	39.1
16	Sweden	7.1		Latvia	39.1
17	Ireland	7.0	17	Canada	38.6
18	Czech Republic	6.9	18	Austria	38.4
19	Mexica	6.7	19	China	36.9
20	Germany	6.2	20	Mexico	35.6

a West Texas Intermediate. b Or latest.

Debt

Highest foreign debt[a]

$bn, 2015

1	China	1,418.3	26	Colombia	111.0
2	Brazil	543.4	27	Romania	96.0
3	Hong Kong	491.9	28	Israel	89.1
4	India	479.6	29	Panama	87.7
5	Russia	467.7	30	Vietnam	77.8
6	Singapore	465.5	31	Philippines	77.7
7	Mexico	426.3	32	Peru	65.9
8	Turkey	397.7	33	Pakistan	65.5
9	South Korea	376.6	34	Iraq	60.0
10	Poland	331.4	35	Croatia	49.4
11	Indonesia	308.5		Sudan	49.4
12	United Arab Emirates	203.3	37	Egypt	46.6
13	Malaysia	191.0	38	Sri Lanka	43.9
14	Saudi Arabia	171.5	39	Morocco	43.0
15	Argentina	159.7	40	Bangladesh	38.6
16	Taiwan	159.0	41	Belarus	37.9
17	Chile	156.2	42	Bulgaria	37.5
18	Kazakhstan	154.3	43	Kuwait	35.4
19	Qatar	143.4	44	Lebanon	35.1
20	South Africa	137.9	45	Serbia	30.8
21	Thailand	129.7	46	Nigeria	29.0
22	Hungary	127.4	47	Cuba	28.9
23	Czech Republic	126.3	48	Angola	28.0
24	Venezuela	123.7	49	Bahrain	27.7
25	Ukraine	122.8	50	Tunisia	27.4

Highest foreign debt burden[a]

Total foreign debt as % of GDP, 2015

1	Mongolia	183.5	21	Estonia	81.5
2	Panama	171.5	22	Mauritania	79.1
3	Hong Kong	159.0	23	Bosnia & Herz.	77.1
4	Singapore	156.8	24	Bulgaria	74.7
5	Ukraine	135.5	25	Lebanon	72.9
6	Mauritius	125.3	26	Albania	72.5
7	Kyrgyzstan	112.1	27	Poland	69.5
8	Hungary	104.8	28	Belarus	69.4
9	Papua New Guinea	102.7	29	Macedonia	69.1
10	Croatia	101.5	30	Jordan	68.6
11	Jamaica	100.1	31	Czech Republic	68.2
12	Georgia	95.3	32	Mozambique	67.9
13	Bahrain	88.9	33	Chile	64.9
14	Moldova	88.7	34	Malaysia	64.4
15	Laos	87.4	35	Tunisia	63.6
16	Qatar	87.1	36	Zimbabwe	60.6
17	Kazakhstan	86.0	37	El Salvador	58.7
18	Armenia	84.8	38	Paraguay	57.0
19	Serbia	82.9		Tajikistan	57.0
20	Nicaragua	82.6			

a Foreign debt is debt owed to non-residents and repayable in foreign currency; the figures shown include liabilities of government, public and private sectors. Longer-established developed countries have been excluded.

Highest foreign debt[a]

As % of exports of goods and services, 2015

1	Sudan	888.8		15	Uruguay	211.1
2	Mongolia	394.5		16	Jamaica	206.4
3	Venezuela	310.8		17	Papua New Guinea	205.4
4	Laos	309.4		18	Colombia	203.4
5	Central African Rep.	304.4		19	Mauritania	201.3
6	Panama	290.6		20	Chile	201.1
7	Kazakhstan	280.0		21	Sierra Leone	197.9
8	Ethiopia	262.9		22	Turkey	195.0
9	Brazil	227.7		23	Albania	191.2
10	Mozambique	226.3		24	Sri Lanka	182.8
11	Burundi	218.2		25	Kyrgyzstan	182.3
12	Argentina	217.2		26	Croatia	179.8
13	Niger	212.7		27	Georgia	175.2
14	Ukraine	211.3		28	Nicaragua	174.8

Highest debt service ratio[b]

Average, %, 2015

1	Syria	68.4		15	Mauritius	28.3
2	Kazakhstan	63.4		16	Armenia	28.1
3	Venezuela	60.3		17	Turkey	26.9
4	Jamaica	58.8		18	Hungary	25.9
5	Ukraine	56.9		19	Colombia	25.6
6	Brazil	37.6		20	Georgia	24.5
7	Croatia	35.5		21	Argentina	24.4
8	Chile	33.1		22	Dominican Rep.	23.3
9	Cuba	32.6		23	Russia	23.0
10	Mongolia	32.1		24	Bosnia & Herz.	22.9
11	Bulgaria	30.3		25	Serbia	22.5
	Indonesia	30.3		26	Ecuador	21.9
13	Romania	30.1		27	Albania	21.0
14	Sudan	28.4		28	Macedonia	20.5

Household debt[c]

As % of net disposable income, 2015

1	Denmark	292.0		13	Japan[d]	129.5
2	Netherlands	277.1		14	Spain	121.9
3	Norway	221.8		15	Greece	118.5
4	Australia	211.8		16	Belgium	114.3
5	Switzerland	211.2		17	United States	111.6
6	Sweden	179.1		18	France	108.3
7	Ireland	177.9		19	Austria	93.5
8	Canada	175.1		20	Germany	92.9
9	South Korea	169.9		21	Italy	89.2
10	United Kingdom	149.5		22	Estonia	81.9
11	Portugal	136.4		23	Czech Republic	68.7
12	Finland	129.7		24	Slovakia	68.0

b Debt service is the sum of interest and principal repayments (amortisation) due on outstanding foreign debt. The debt service ratio is debt service as a percentage of exports of goods, non-factor services, primary income and workers' remittances.
c OECD countries.   d 2012

Aid

Largest recipients of bilateral and multilateral aid

$bn, 2015

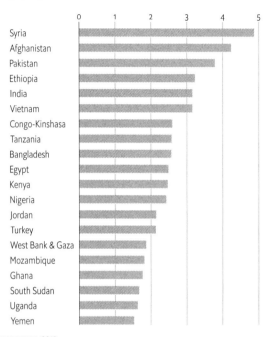

Syria	
Afghanistan	
Pakistan	
Ethiopia	
India	
Vietnam	
Congo-Kinshasa	
Tanzania	
Bangladesh	
Egypt	
Kenya	
Nigeria	
Jordan	
Turkey	
West Bank & Gaza	
Mozambique	
Ghana	
South Sudan	
Uganda	
Yemen	

$ per person, 2015

1	West Bank & Gaza	423.6	21	Bosnia & Herz.	93.2
2	Jordan	283.1		Rwanda	93.2
3	Syria	263.9	23	Moldova	87.9
4	Kosovo	243.7	24	Mongolia	79.6
5	Liberia	243.0	25	Mauritania	78.2
6	Timor-Leste	170.5	26	Papua New Guinea	77.4
7	Lebanon	166.7	27	Nicaragua	74.7
8	Montenegro	160.6	28	Bolivia	73.4
9	Sierra Leone	146.7	29	Swaziland	72.0
10	South Sudan	135.7	30	Laos	69.3
11	Afghanistan	130.3	31	Mali	68.2
12	Kyrgyzstan	129.1	32	Honduras	66.5
13	Georgia	121.7	33	Maldives	65.6
14	Somalia	116.2	34	Mozambique	64.9
15	Albania	115.7	35	Ghana	64.5
16	Armenia	115.2	36	Malawi	61.0
17	Fiji	114.9	37	Mauritius	60.6
18	Macedonia	103.1	38	Senegal	58.1
19	Central African Rep.	99.4	39	Namibia	57.9
20	Haiti	97.3	40	Gabon	57.2

Largest bilateral and multilateral donors[a]

$m, 2015

			As % of GDP					As % of GDP
1	United States	30,986	0.17		**16**	Denmark	2,566	0.85
2	United Kingdom	18,545	0.70		**17**	South Korea	1,915	0.14
3	Germany	17,940	0.52		**18**	Belgium	1,905	0.42
4	Japan	9,203	0.21		**19**	Spain	1,397	0.12
5	France	9,039	0.37		**20**	Austria	1,324	0.35
6	Sweden	7,089	1.40		**21**	Finland	1,288	0.55
7	Saudi Arabia	6,758	1.05		**22**	Russia	1,161	0.09
8	Netherlands	5,726	0.75		**23**	Ireland	718	0.32
9	United Arab Emirates	4,381	1.18		**24**	New Zealand	442	0.27
10	Norway	4,278	1.05		**25**	Poland	441	0.10
11	Canada	4,277	0.28		**26**	Luxembourg	363	0.95
12	Italy	4,004	0.22		**27**	Portugal	308	0.16
13	Turkey	3,919	0.50		**28**	Kuwait	304	0.26
14	Switzerland	3,562	0.52		**29**	Taiwan	255	0.05
15	Australia	3,494	0.29		**30**	Greece	239	0.12

Biggest changes to aid

2015 compared with 2011, $m

Increases			Decreases		
1	Syria	4,546.4	**1**	Congo-Kinshasa	-2,927.2
2	Egypt	2,063.4	**2**	Afghanistan	-2,627.9
3	South Sudan	1,239.0	**3**	Turkey	-1,143.5
4	Jordan	1,175.9	**4**	Serbia	-1,066.6
5	Bangladesh	1,078.7	**5**	Sudan	-842.5
6	Yemen	1,054.4	**6**	Ivory Coast	-782.9
7	Myanmar	788.6	**7**	Mexico	-664.3
8	Philippines	699.0	**8**	Haiti	-649.1
9	Ukraine	679.7	**9**	West Bank & Gaza	-561.6
10	Nigeria	663.9	**10**	Libya	-483.5
11	Sierra Leone	522.5	**11**	Vietnam	-461.8
12	Lebanon	499.7	**12**	Tunisia	-450.7
13	Cuba	465.7	**13**	Indonesia	-444.7
14	Guinea	336.3	**14**	Iraq	-429.7
15	Liberia	332.2	**15**	Togo	-342.8
16	Colombia	329.8	**16**	Bosnia & Herz.	-270.7
17	Nepal	329.1	**17**	Peru	-266.0
18	Pakistan	292.4	**18**	Ethiopia	-258.6
19	China	271.1	**19**	Mozambique	-250.4
20	Malawi	251.9	**20**	Benin	-242.4
21	Kyrgyzstan	245.7	**21**	Nicaragua	-237.4
22	Uzbekistan	243.7	**22**	Zambia	-236.3
23	Madagascar	229.9	**23**	Azerbaijan	-217.8
24	Niger	221.2	**24**	Burundi	-205.2
25	Central African Rep.	218.2	**25**	El Salvador	-189.6
26	Thailand	192.8	**26**	Sri Lanka	-186.1
27	Angola	187.2	**27**	Rwanda	-181.1
28	Brazil	177.6	**28**	Senegal	-175.4

a China also provides aid, but does not disclose amounts.

Industry and services

Largest industrial output

$bn, 2015

1	China	4,529	23	Iran[a]	159
2	United States[a]	3,471	24	Poland	144
3	Japan[a]	1,224	25	Thailand	141
4	Germany	923	26	Argentina	138
5	India	563	27	Netherlands	135
6	Canada[b]	498	28	Egypt	122
7	United Kingdom	495	29	Norway	119
8	South Korea	476	30	Sweden	115
9	France	422	31	Ireland	109
10	Russia	389	32	Malaysia	108
11	Italy	385	33	Nicarugua	98
12	Mexico	349		Puerto Rico[b]	98
13	Brazil	346	35	Qatar.	96
14	Indonesia	345	36	Austria	95
15	Australia	319	37	Colombia	91
16	Saudi Arabia	297	38	Belgium	90
17	Spain	256		Philippines	90
18	Taiwan	185	40	South Africa	83
19	United Arab Emirates	177	41	Iraq	76
20	Turkey	168	42	Singapore	73
21	Switzerland	166	43	Chile	72
	Venezuela[b]	166			

Highest growth in industrial output

Average annual % increase in real terms, 2007–15

1	Timor-Leste[c]	24.1		China	9.2
2	Liberia	16.9	12	Niger	9.1
3	Ethiopia	15.9	13	Rwanda	9.0
4	Myanmar	15.1	14	Kosovo	8.5
5	Laos	13.3	15	Bangladesh	8.4
6	Panama	12.1	16	Tanzania	8.2
7	Uzbekistan	11.5	17	Cambodia	7.8
8	Ghana	10.3		Iraq	7.8
9	Qatar	9.3		Mongolia	7.8
10	Chad	9.2	20	Macedonia	7.5

Lowest growth in industrial output

Average annual % change in real terms, 2006–14

1	Cyprus	-7.8		Jamaica	-2.2
2	Bermuda[d]	-7.5	13	Botswana	-1.7
3	Greece	-7.2	14	Luxembourg	-1.6
4	Ukraine	-6.3	15	Slovenia	-1.5
5	Finland	-3.2		Trinidad & Tobago	-1.5
6	Croatia	-3.1	17	Armenia	-1.3
	Spain	-3.1		Central African Rep.	-1.3
8	Italy	-2.6	19	Iran[c]	-1.1
9	Latvia	-2.5	20	France	-1.0
10	Portugal	-2.4		Netherlands	-1.0
11	Brunei	-2.2		Puerto Rico[e]	-1.0

a 2014   b 2013   c 2007–14   d 2007–12   e 2007–13

Largest manufacturing output
$bn, 2015

1	China[a]	2,857	**21**	Argentina	85
2	United States	2,068		Australia	85
3	Japan[b]	851	**23**	Poland	83
4	Germany	690	**24**	Netherlands	79
5	South Korea	370		Saudi Arabia	79
6	India	315	**26**	Sweden	75
7	Italy	258	**27**	Malaysia	68
8	United Kingdom	249	**28**	Austria	63
9	France	243	**29**	Philippines	59
10	Mexico	196	**30**	Belgium	58
11	Canada[a]	183	**31**	Egypt	56
12	Brazil	182	**32**	Singapore	55
13	Indonesia	180	**33**	Iran[b]	49
14	Russia	169	**34**	Puerto Rico[a]	48
15	Taiwan	158	**35**	Nigeria	46
16	Spain	154	**36**	Czech Republic	45
17	Switzerland	117	**37**	Venezuela[a]	43
18	Turkey	112	**38**	Romania[b]	42
19	Thailand	106	**39**	Denmark	38a
20	Ireland	97			

Largest services output
$bn, 2015

1	United States[b]	13,084	**27**	Poland	268
2	China	5,558	**28**	Austria	236
3	Japan[b]	3,528	**29**	Norway	219
4	Germany	2,085	**30**	Iran[b]	218
5	United Kingdom	2,039		Thailand	218
6	France	1,703	**32**	Singapore	202
7	Italy	1,214	**33**	Denmark	198
8	Canada[a]	1,196	**34**	South Africa	193
9	Brazil	1,126	**35**	United Arab Emirates	191
10	India	1,007	**36**	Egypt	176
11	Australia	899	**37**	Philippines	172
12	Spain	799	**38**	Malaysia	163
13	Russia	748	**39**	Colombia	158
	South Korea	748	**40**	Venezuela[a]	155
15	Mexico	677	**41**	Ireland	151
16	Netherlands	527	**42**	Pakistan	142
17	Switzerland	479	**43**	Finland	142
18	Turkey	412	**44**	Chile	139
19	Indonesia	400	**45**	Greece	138
20	Saudi Arabia	335	**46**	Portugal	131
21	Taiwan	328	**47**	New Zealand[c]	115
22	Argentina	323	**48**	Kazakhstan	109
23	Sweden	318	**49**	Bangladesh	105
24	Belgium	314	**50**	Peru	102
25	Nigeria	283	**51**	Czech Republic	99
26	Hong Kong	274	**52**	Iraq	96

a 2013   b 2014   c 2012

Agriculture and fisheries

Largest agricultural output
$bn, 2015

1	China	977	16	Thailand	36
2	India	332	17	Vietnam	33
3	United States[a]	224	18	Canada	32
4	Indonesia	117	19	Australia	31
5	Nigeria	100		Sudan	31
6	Brazil	77	21	Argentina	30
7	Pakistan	65		Philippines	30
8	Russia	55	23	Bangladesh	29
9	Turkey	54		South Korea	29
10	Japan[a]	53	25	Spain	28
11	Iran[a]	39	26	Malaysia	25
12	France	38	27	Ethiopia	23
	Mexico	38	28	Algeria	19
14	Egypt	37		Germany	19
	Italy	37		Kenya	19

Most economically dependent on agriculture
% of GDP from agriculture, 2015

1	Sierra Leone	61.3	15	Kenya	32.9
2	Chad	52.4	16	Tanzania	31.1
3	Guinea-Bissau[b]	43.7	17	Malawi	29.5
4	Burundi	43.0	18	Cambodia	28.2
5	Central African Rep.	42.4	19	Laos	27.4
6	Ethiopia	41.0	20	Myanmar	26.7
	Mali	41.0	21	Uganda	25.8
8	Togo	40.7	22	Madagascar	25.6
9	Niger	39.9	23	Benin	25.3
10	Sudan	39.3	24	Mozambique	25.2
11	Liberia	35.0	25	Pakistan	25.1
12	Rwanda	34.6	26	Tajikistan	25.0
13	Burkina Faso	34.2	27	Cameroon	22.8
14	Nepal	33.0	28	Ivory Coast	22.7

Least economically dependent on agriculture
% of GDP from agriculture, 2015

1	Macau	0.0		United Kingdom	0.7
	Singapore	0.0	14	Bermuda[c]	0.8
3	Hong Kong	0.1		Puerto Rico[b]	0.8
4	Luxembourg	0.2	16	Ireland	1.0
	Qatar	0.2	17	Brunei	1.1
6	Bahrain	0.3		Japan[a]	1.1
7	Trinidad & Tobago	0.5	19	Denmark	1.2
8	Andorra[b]	0.6	20	Austria	1.3
	Germany	0.6		Sweden	1.3
	Kuwait	0.6		United States[a]	1.3
11	Belgium	0.7	23	Malta	1.4
	Switzerland	0.7	24	Oman	1.6

a 2014 b 2013 c 2012

Fisheries and aquaculture production
Fish, crustaceans and molluscs, million tonnes, 2015

1	China	64.1	16	Malaysia	1.7
2	Indonesia	10.7	17	Mexico	1.6
3	India[a]	10.1	18	Egypt[a]	1.5
4	Vietnam	6.2	19	Morocco	1.4
5	United States	5.5	20	Brazil[a]	1.3
6	Peru	4.9		Iceland	1.3
7	Russia	4.6		Spain	1.3
8	Japan	4.1		Taiwan	1.3
9	Bangladesh	3.7	24	Ecuador	1.1
	Norway	3.7	25	Canada	1.0
11	Myanmar[a]	2.9		Iran	1.0
	Philippines	2.9		Nigeria	1.0
13	Chile	2.8	28	Denmark	0.9
14	Thailand	2.5		United Kingdom	0.9
15	South Korea[a]	2.1	30	Argentina	0.8

Biggest producers
'000 tonnes, 2014

Cereals

1	China	557,407	6	Indonesia	89,855
2	United States	442,849	7	France	73,331
3	India	295,360	8	Ukraine	63,378
4	Russia	103,136	9	Bangladesh	55,759
5	Brazil	101,402	10	Germany	52,010

Meat

1	China	84,798	6	India	6,601
2	United States	42,565	7	Mexico	6,224
3	Brazil	26,053	8	Spain	5,742
4	Russia	9,070	9	France	5,489
5	Germany	8,356	10	Argentina	5,193

Fruit

1	China	158,424	6	Spain	17,764
2	India	88,475	7	Indonesia	17,365
3	Brazil	37,410	8	Philippines	16,233
4	United States	25,952	9	Italy	15,645
5	Mexico	17,851	10	Turkey	14,291

Vegetables

1	China	596,110	6	Egypt	19,352
2	India	126,579	7	Vietnam	17,951
3	United States	36,599	8	Russia	16,894
4	Turkey	28,186	9	Mexico	14,286
5	Iran	21,456	10	Spain	14,173

Roots and tubers

1	China	173,355	5	Thailand	30,484
2	Nigeria	108,069	6	Brazil	27,716
3	India	55,622	7	Indonesia	27,599
4	Russia	31,501	8	Ghana	25,079

a Estimate.

Commodities

Wheat

Top 10 producers, 2015–16
'000 tonnes

1	EU28	159,600
2	China	130,200
3	India	86,500
4	Russia	61,000
5	United States	56,100
6	Canada	27,600
7	Ukraine	27,300
8	Pakistan	25,500
9	Australia	24,200
10	Turkey	22,600

Top 10 consumers, 2015–16
'000 tonnes

1	EU28	128,890
2	China	116,900
3	India	88,710
4	Russia	37,140
5	United States	32,060
6	Pakistan	24,330
7	Egypt	20,430
8	Turkey	20,370
9	Iran	18,180
10	Ukraine	11,800

Rice[a]

Top 10 producers, 2015–16
'000 tonnes

1	China	145,770
2	India	104,408
3	Indonesia	36,200
4	Bangladesh	34,500
5	Vietnam	27,584
6	Thailand	15,800
7	Myanmar	12,160
8	Philippines	11,000
9	Japan	7,670
10	Brazil	7,210

Top 10 consumers, 2015–16
'000 tonnes

1	China	144,000
2	India	93,568
3	Indonesia	37,800
4	Bangladesh	35,100
5	Vietnam	22,600
6	Philippines	13,000
7	Myanmar	10,750
8	Thailand	9,100
9	Japan	8,600
10	Brazil	7,850

Sugar[b]

Top 10 producers, 2015
'000 tonnes

1	Brazil	34,240
2	India	28,870
3	EU28	15,300
4	Thailand	11,000
5	China	10,260
6	United States	7,700
7	Pakistan	6,130
8	Mexico	5,880
9	Russia	5,100
10	Australia	4,820

Top 10 consumers, 2015
'000 tonnes

1	India	26,000
2	EU28	17,880
3	China	15,450
4	Brazil	11,010
5	United States	10,830
6	Indonesia	6,050
7	Russia	5,500
8	Pakistan	4,860
9	Mexico	4,370
10	Egypt	3,270

Coarse grains[c]

Top 5 producers, 2015–16
'000 tonnes

1	United States	367,399
2	China	233,325
3	EU28	152,157
4	Brazil	68,729
5	Argentina	48,334

Top 5 consumers, 2015–16
'000 tonnes

1	United States	313,248
2	China	240,059
3	EU28	149,378
4	Brazil	60,063
5	Mexico	45,718

a Milled. b Raw. c Includes: maize (corn), barley, sorghum, oats, rye, millet, triticale and other. d Tonnes at 65 degrees brix.

Tea

Top 10 producers, 2014
'000 tonnes

1	China	2,096
2	India	1,207
3	Kenya	445
4	Sri Lanka	338
5	Vietnam	228
6	Turkey	227
7	Indonesia	154
8	Iran	119
9	Myanmar	99
10	Argentina	85

Top 10 consumers, 2015
'000 tonnes

1	China	1,978
2	India	999
3	Turkey	306
4	Russia	165
5	Pakistan	152
6	United States	127
7	United Kingdom	115
8	Japan	110
9	Egypt	90
10	Bangladesh	78

Coffee

Top 10 producers, 2016
'000 tonnes

1	Brazil	3,300
2	Vietnam	1,530
3	Colombia	870
4	Indonesia	600
5	Ethiopia	396
6	Honduras	356
7	India	320
8	Peru	228
	Uganda	228
10	Guatemala	210

Top 10 consumers, 2015–16
'000 tonnes

1	EU28	2,573
2	United States	1,520
3	Brazil	1,230
4	Japan	467
5	Indonesia	270
6	Russia	258
7	Ethiopia	222
8	Canada	212
9	Vietnam	138
10	India	135

Cocoa

Top 10 producers, 2015–16
'000 tonnes

1	Ivory Coast	1,581
2	Ghana	778
3	Indonesia	320
4	Ecuador	232
5	Cameroon	211
6	Nigeria	200
7	Brazil	140
8	Peru	95
9	Dominican Rep.	72
10	Colombia	53

Top 10 consumers, 2015–16
'000 tonnes

1	Netherlands	535
2	Ivory Coast	492
3	Germany	430
4	United States	398
5	Indonesia	382
6	Brazil	335
7	Ghana	202
8	Malaysia	194
9	France	138
10	Spain	112

Orange juice[d]

Top 5 producers, 2015–16
'000 tonnes

1	Brazil	848
2	United States	383
3	Mexico	165
4	EU28	100
5	South Africa	45

Top 5 consumers, 2015–16
'000 tonnes

1	EU28	825
2	United States	634
3	Canada	94
4	China	83
5	Japan	78

Copper

Top 10 producers[a], 2015		*Top 10 consumers[b], 2015*	
'000 tonnes		*'000 tonnes*	
1 Chile	5,764	**1** China	11,353
2 Peru	1,705	**2** EU28	3,338
3 China	1,667	**3** United States	1,796
4 United States	1,410	**4** Germany	1,219
5 Congo-Kinshasa	1039	**5** Japan	997
6 Australia	964	**6** South Korea	705
7 EU28	861	**7** Italy	613
8 Zambia	758	**8** India	491
9 Russia	740	**9** Taiwan	471
10 Canada	697	**10** Turkey	455

Lead

Top 10 producers[a], 2014		*Top 10 consumers[b], 2015*	
'000 tonnes		*'000 tonnes*	
1 China	2,335	**1** China	3,804
2 Australia	653	**2** EU28	1,617
3 United States	371	**3** United States	1,590
4 Peru	316	**4** South Korea	602
5 Mexico	254	**5** India	539
6 EU28	208	**6** Germany	357
7 Russia	196	**7** Japan	269
8 India	139	**8** Brazil	240
9 Sweden	79	**9** Spain	238
10 Turkey	76	**10** Mexico	235

Zinc

Top 10 producers[a], 2015		*Top 10 consumers[c], 2015*	
'000 tonnes		*'000 tonnes*	
1 China	4,750	**1** China	6,483
2 Australia	1,583	**2** EU28	2,114
3 Peru	1,422	**3** United States	931
4 India	826	**4** India	612
5 United States	808	**5** South Korea	590
6 EU28	699	**6** Germany	479
7 Mexico	677		Japan	479
8 Bolivia	442	**8** Belgium	450
9 Kazakhstan	384	**9** Italy	258
10 Canada	277	**10** Turkey	230

Tin

Top 5 producers[a], 2015		*Top 5 consumers[b], 2015*	
'000 tonnes		*'000 tonnes*	
1 China	146.6	**1** China	175.8
2 Indonesia	68.4	**2** EU28	51.5
3 Myanmar	28.6	**3** United States	31.4
4 Brazil	25.5	**4** Japan	26.8
5 Bolivia	20.1	**5** Germany	17.9

Nickel

Top 10 producers[a], 2015
'000 tonnes

1	Philippines	464.5
2	Russia	261.0
3	Canada	234.9
4	Australia	225.2
5	New Caledonia	186.1
6	Indonesia	128.6
7	China	100.8
8	Brazil	89.3
9	South Africa	56.7
10	Guatemala	56.5

Top 10 consumers[b], 2015
'000 tonnes

1	China	836.1
2	EU28	301.6
3	United States	152.0
4	Japan	150.6
5	South Korea	83.4
6	Italy	60.5
7	Germany	60.2
8	Taiwan	60.0
9	India	37.1
10	Belgium	35.0

Aluminium

Top 10 producers[d], 2015
'000 tonnes

1	China	31,410
2	Russia	3,529
3	Canada	2,880
4	United Arab Emirates	2,464
5	EU28	2,217
6	India	1,886
7	Australia	1,646
8	United States	1,587
9	Norway	1,241
10	Bahrain	961

Top 10 consumers[e], 2015
'000 tonnes

1	China	31,068
2	EU28	6,679
3	United States	5,325
4	Germany	2,163
5	Japan	1,779
6	India	1,476
7	South Korea	1,366
8	Turkey	952
9	United Arab Emirates	835
10	Brazil	801

Precious metals

Gold [a]
Top 10 producers, 2015
tonnes

1	China	450.1
2	Australia	277.8
3	Russia	255.8
4	United States	212.3
5	Canada	160.8
6	Peru	145.0
7	South Africa	144.5
8	Mexico	124.6
9	Uzbekistan	103.0
10	Indonesia	92.2

Silver [a]
Top 10 producers, 2015
tonnes

1	Mexico	5,592
2	Peru	4,102
3	China	3,393
4	EU28	2,024
5	Russia	1,571
6	Chile	1,504
7	Australia	1,430
8	Bolivia	1,306
9	Kazakhstan	1,305
10	Poland	1,230

Platinum
Top 3 producers, 2015
tonnes

1	South Africa	142.1
2	Russia	20.8
3	Zimbabwe	12.5

Palladium
Top 3 producers, 2015
tonnes

1	South Africa	76.1
2	Russia	69
3	United States/Canada	24.6

a Mine production.   b Refined consumption.   c Slab consumption.
d Primary refined production.   e Primary refined consumption.

Rubber (natural and synthetic)

Top 10 producers, 2015		*Top 10 consumers, 2015*	
'000 tonnes		*'000 tonnes*	
1 Thailand	4,724	**1** China	8,897
2 China	3,645	**2** EU28	3,629
3 Indonesia	3,145	**3** United States	2,905
4 United States	2,392	**4** Japan	1,587
5 EU28	2,381	**5** India	1,536
6 Japan	1,668	**6** Thailand	1,072
7 South Korea	1,502	**7** Brazil	929
8 Russia	1,390	**8** Malaysia	898
9 Vietnam	1,017	**9** Russia	520
10 India	767	**10** Indonesia	509

Cotton

Top 10 producers, 2015–16		*Top 10 consumers, 2015–16*	
'000 tonnes		*'000 tonnes*	
1 India	5,746	**1** China	7,442
2 China	4,753	**2** India	5,296
3 United States	2,806	**3** Pakistan	2,256
4 Pakistan	1,537	**4** Turkey	1,500
5 Brazil	1,289	**5** Bangladesh	1,324
6 Uzbekistan	832	**6** Vietnam	1,007
7 Turkey	640	**7** United States	751
8 Australia	626	**8** Brazil	733
9 Turkmenistan	315	**9** Indonesia	654
10 Burkina Faso	244	**10** Mexico	418

Major oil seeds[a]

Top 5 producers, 2015–16		*Top 5 consumers, 2015–16*	
'000 tonnes		*'000 tonnes*	
1 United States	115,879	**1** China	141,677
2 Brazil	98,974	**2** United States	63,104
3 Argentina	60,777	**3** EU28	51,515
4 China	54,454	**4** Brazil	45,568
5 India	29,043	**5** India	28,659

Major vegetable oils[b]

Top 5 producers, 2015–16		*Top 5 consumers, 2015–16*	
'000 tonnes		*'000 tonnes*	
1 Indonesia	32,000	**1** China	29,859
2 China	22,329	**2** EU28	23,185
3 Malaysia	17,801	**3** India	18,345
4 EU28	16,096	**4** United States	13,028
5 United States	10,883	**5** Indonesia	9,463

a Soyabeans, rapeseed (canola), cottonseed, sunflowerseed and groundnuts
(peanuts).   b Palm, soyabean, rapeseed and sunflowerseed oil.
c Includes crude oil, shale oil, oil sands and natural gas liquids.   d Opec member.
e Opec membership suspended 30 November 2016.

Oil[c]

Top 10 producers, 2016
'000 barrels per day

1	United States	12,354
2	Saudi Arabia[e]	12,349
3	Russia	11,227
4	Iran[d]	4,600
5	Iraq[d]	4,465
6	Canada	4,460
7	United Arab Emirates[d]	4,073
8	China	3,999
9	Kuwait[d]	3,151
10	Brazil	2,605

Top 10 consumers, 2016
'000 barrels per day

1	United States	19,631
2	China	12,381
3	India	4,489
4	Japan	4,037
5	Saudi Arabia[d]	3,906
6	Russia	3,203
7	Brazil	3,018
8	South Korea	2,763
9	Germany	2,394
10	Canada	2,343

Natural gas

Top 10 producers, 2016
Billion cubic metres

1	United States	749.2
2	Russia	579.4
3	Iran[d]	202.4
4	Qatar[d]	181.2
5	Canada	152.0
6	China	138.4
7	Norway	116.6
8	Saudi Arabia[d]	109.4
9	Algeria[d]	91.3
10	Australia	91.2

Top 10 consumers, 2016
Billion cubic metres

1	United States	778.6
2	Russia	390.9
3	China	210.3
4	Iran[e]	200.8
5	Japan	111.2
6	Saudi Arabia[d]	109.4
7	Canada	99.9
8	Mexico	89.5
9	Germany	80.5
10	United Arab Emirates[d]	76.6

Coal

Top 10 producers, 2016
Million tonnes oil equivalent

1	China	1,685.7
2	United States	364.8
3	Australia	299.3
4	India	288.5
5	Indonesia[e]	255.7
6	Russia	192.8
7	South Africa	142.4
8	Colombia	62.5
9	Poland	52.3
10	Kazakhstan	44.1

Top 10 consumers, 2016
Million tonnes oil equivalent

1	China	1,887.6
2	India	411.9
3	United States	358.4
4	Japan	119.9
5	Russia	87.3
6	South Africa	85.1
7	South Korea	81.6
8	Germany	75.3
9	Indonesia[e]	62.7
10	Poland	48.8

Oil reserves[c]

Top proved reserves, end 2016
% of world total

1	Venezuela[d]	17.6
2	Saudi Arabia[d]	15.6
3	Canada	10
4	Iran[d]	9.3
5	Iraq[d]	9.0

6	Russia	6.4
7	Kuwait[d]	5.9
8	United Arab Emirates[d]	5.7
9	Libya[d]	2.8
	United States	2.8

Energy

Largest producers
Million tonnes of oil equivalent, 2014

1	China	3,073	16	Italy	160
2	United States	2,451	17	Australia	142
3	Russia	772		South Africa	142
4	India	623	19	Spain	137
5	Japan	477	20	Turkey	131
6	Canada	364	21	Thailand	129
7	Germany	322	22	Taiwan	115
8	Brazil	321	23	United Arab Emirates	107
9	South Korea	281	24	Ukraine	106
10	Iran	265	25	Poland	98
11	Saudi Arabia	255	26	Netherlands	96
12	France	254	27	Argentina	94
13	United Kingdom	201	28	Egypt	90
14	Mexico	188	29	Malaysia	87
15	Indonesia	185	30	Venezuela	83

Largest consumers
Million tonnes of oil equivalent, 2013

1	China	3,073	16	Italy	160
2	United States	2,451	17	Australia	142
3	Russia	772		South Africa	142
4	India	623	19	Spain	137
5	Japan	477	20	Turkey	131
6	Canada	364	21	Thailand	129
7	Germany	322	22	Taiwan	115
8	Brazil	321	23	United Arab Emirates	107
9	South Korea	281	24	Ukraine	106
10	Iran	265	25	Poland	98
11	Saudi Arabia	255	26	Netherlands	96
12	France	254	27	Argentina	94
13	United Kingdom	201	28	Egypt	90
14	Mexico	188	29	Malaysia	87
15	Indonesia	185	30	Venezuela	83

Energy efficiency[a]
GDP per unit of energy use, 2014

Most efficient			Least efficient		
1	South Sudan	32.8	1	Congo-Kinshasa	1.9
2	Hong Kong	26.8	2	Trinidad & Tobago	2.2
3	Sri Lanka	20.6	3	Iceland	2.3
4	Cuba	19.6	4	Mozambique	2.5
5	Switzerland	18.5	5	Ethiopia	2.9
6	Panama	18.4		Togo	2.9
7	Colombia	17.9		Turkmenistan	2.9
8	Ireland	17.7	8	Ukraine	3.4
9	Dominican Rep.	17.2	9	Bahrain	4.1
	Malta	17.2	10	Haiti	4.2
11	Mauritius	16.4	11	South Africa	4.6

a 2011 PPP $ per kg of oil equivalent.

Net energy importers

% of commercial energy use, 2014

Highest			Lowest	
1 Hong Kong	99.0		**1** South Sudan	-1,058
2 Lebanon	98.0		**2** Norway	-583
Malta	98.0		**3** Angola	-541
Singapore	98.0		**4** Congo-Brazzaville	-497
5 Jordan	97.0		**5** Qatar	-399
6 Luxembourg	96.0		**6** Kuwait	-391
7 Cyprus	94.0		**7** Brunei	-357
Japan	94.0		**8** Azerbaijan	-310
9 Morocco	91.0		**9** Colombia	-274
10 Moldova	90.0		**10** Iraq	-229
11 Belarus	87.0		**11** Gabon	-213
Dominican Rep.	87.0		**12** Oman	-206

Largest consumption per person

Kg of oil equivalent, 2014

1 Qatar	20,292		**12** Finland	6,213
2 Iceland	17,916		**13** Oman	5,743
3 Trinidad & Tobago	14,447		**14** Norway	5,596
4 Bahrain	10,395		**15** Australia	5,338
5 Kuwait	9,027		**16** South Korea	5,323
6 Brunei	8,515		**17** Singapore	5,122
7 Canada	7,874		**18** Turkmenistan	5,040
8 United Arab Emirates	7,756		**19** Sweden	4,966
9 United States	6,949		**20** Russia	4,943
10 Saudi Arabia	6,913		**21** Belgium	4,699
11 Luxembourg	6,861		**22** Estonia	4,593

Sources of electricity

% of total, 2014

Oil			Gas	
1 South Sudan	99.6		**1** Bahrain	100.0
2 Benin	99.5		Qatar	100.0
Eritrea	99.5		Turkmenistan	100.0
4 Lebanon	98.9		**4** Trinidad & Tobago	99.8
5 Malta	96.7		**5** Brunei	99.0

Hydropower			Nuclear power	
1 Albania	100.0		**1** France	78.6
Paraguay	100.0		**2** Slovakia	57.1
3 Congo-Kinshasa	99.9		**3** Belgium	53.3
4 Nepal	99.8		**4** Hungary	48.6
5 Namibia	99.1		**5** Sweden	47.2

Coal			Renewables excl. hydropower	
1 Kosovo	96.9		**1** Denmark	55.8
2 Botswana	95.8		**2** Nicaragua	45.7
3 South Africa	93.0		**3** El Salvador	45.0
4 Mongolia	92.3		**4** Iceland	33.8
5 Estonia	87.4		**5** Portugal	32.1

Labour markets

Labour-force participation

% of working-age population[a] working or looking for work, 2016 or latest

Highest			Lowest		
1	Madagascar	86.4	1	Jordan	40.1
2	Uganda	85.0	2	Timor-Leste	41.4
3	Rwanda	84.9	3	Syria	41.7
4	Qatar	84.1	4	Moldova	42.3
5	Eritrea	83.9	5	Puerto Rico	42.5
6	Burundi	83.7	6	Iraq	42.6
7	Burkina Faso	83.4	7	Algeria	43.8
8	Ethiopia	83.0	8	Iran	44.7
	Nepal	83.0	9	Bosnia & Herz.	46.0
10	Zimbabwe	82.5	10	Lebanon	47.2
11	Guinea	82.3	11	Mauritania	47.3
12	Equatorial Guinea	82.0	12	Tunisia	47.7
13	Malawi	81.1	13	Sudan	48.2
14	Cambodia	81.0	14	Italy	48.3
15	Togo	80.9	15	Montenegro	48.8
16	North Korea	79.5	16	Gabon	49.2
	United Arab Emirates	79.5	17	Morocco	49.3
18	Mozambique	79.1	18	Egypt	49.6
19	Tanzania	78.5	19	Yemen	49.8
20	Vietnam	78.4	20	Albania	50.3
21	Central African Rep.	78.1		Turkey	50.3
22	Myanmar	77.8	22	Serbia	51.4
23	Laos	77.6	23	Sri Lanka	51.7
24	Botswana	77.5	24	Greece	51.8
25	Ghana	77.1	25	Croatia	52.2
26	Cameroon	76.1		Swaziland	52.2
27	Zambia	75.3			
28	Peru	74.3			

Most male workforce

Highest % men in workforce, 2016

1	United Arab Emirates	87.6
2	Oman	87.2
3	Syria	85.3
4	Saudi Arabia	84.8
5	Qatar	84.7
6	Jordan	82.5
7	Afghanistan	82.4
8	Iraq	82.2
9	Iran	81.9
10	Algeria	80.7
11	Bahrain	80.2
12	West Bank & Gaza	79.6
13	Pakistan	77.8
14	Egypt	76.9
15	India	75.7
16	Lebanon	75.1

Most female workforce

Highest % women in workforce, 2016

1	Mozambique	54.4
	Rwanda	54.4
3	Burundi	51.7
4	Togo	51.2
5	Laos	51.0
6	Nepal	50.8
7	Malawi	50.5
8	Congo-Kinshasa	50.1
9	Ghana	50.0
10	Barbados	49.9
	Lithuania	49.9
12	Myanmar	49.7
13	Latvia	49.6
14	Sierra Leone	49.5
15	Benin	49.4

a Aged 15 and over.

Highest rate of unemployment

% of labour force[e], 2016

1	Kosovo[b]	32.9	**24**	Armenia	16.8
2	Réunion[b]	30.2	**25**	Serbia	16.5
3	Gambia, The	29.7	**26**	Albania	16.3
4	Lesotho	27.4	**27**	Iraq	16.0
5	Macedonia	26.7	**28**	Bahamas	15.3
6	Guadeloupe[b]	26.2	**29**	New Caledonia	14.9
7	South Africa	25.9	**30**	Tunisia	14.8
	West Bank & Gaza[b]	25.9	**31**	Dominican Rep.	14.4
9	Bosnia & Herz.	25.8	**32**	Syria	14.3
10	Namibia	25.6	**33**	Croatia	13.5
11	Swaziland	25.3	**34**	Jamaica	13.3
12	Mozambique	24.4		Sudan	13.3
13	Greece	23.9	**36**	Haiti	13.2
14	French Guiana[b]	23.8		Jordan	13.2
15	Martinique[b]	23.2	**38**	Puerto Rico	12.6
16	Spain	19.4	**39**	Egypt	12.0
17	Libya	19.2	**40**	Cyprus	11.7
18	Gabon	18.5		Mauritania	11.7
19	Botswana	18.4	**42**	Georgia	11.6
20	French Polynesia	17.9	**43**	Brazil	11.5
21	Montenegro	17.5		Italy	11.5
	Oman	17.5	**45**	Barbados	11.4
23	Yemen	17.1		Guyana	11.4

Highest rate of youth unemployment

% of labour force[a] aged 15–24, 2016 estimates

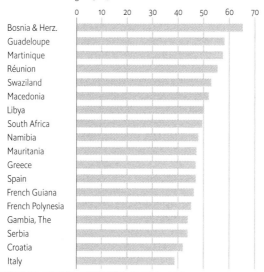

a ILO definition.   b 2015

Minimum wage
As % of the median wage of full-time workers[a], 2015

1	Turkey	70.2	15	South Korea	48.4
2	Chile	66.2	16	Germany	47.8
3	France	62.3	17	Greece	47.4
4	New Zealand	59.8	18	Slovakia	47.3
	Slovenia	59.8	19	Netherlands	45.9
6	Israel	58.1	20	Canada	44.5
7	Portugal	56.9	21	Ireland	44.4
8	Luxembourg	54.8	22	Estonia	41.3
9	Australia	53.5	23	Japan	39.8
10	Hungary	52.5	24	Czech Republic	38.8
11	Latvia	51.8	25	Mexico	37.5
12	Poland	51.3	26	Spain	36.8
13	Belgium	49.2	27	United States	35.8
14	United Kingdom	48.7			

Average hours worked
Per employed person per week, 2015

1	Nepal	53.6	13	Hong Kong	44.0
2	Egypt	53.0	14	South Korea	43.6
3	Myanmar	50.8	15	Vietnam	43.5
4	Qatar	50.0	16	South Africa	43.4
5	Pakistan	47.4	17	Costa Rica	43.0
6	Turkey	46.7	18	Mexico	42.7
7	Macau	46.0	19	Serbia	42.6
8	Malaysia	45.4	20	Colombia	42.2
9	Mongolia	45.0	21	Guatemala	42.0
10	Peru	44.6	22	Dominican Rep.	41.7
11	Singapore	44.2	23	Macedonia	41.5
12	Saudi Arabia	44.1		Montenegro	41.5

Poverty pay
% of workers paid $2 or less per day, 2015

1	Madagascar	94.6	16	Bangladesh	62.8
2	Liberia	93.0	17	Benin	62.6
3	Central African Rep.	90.7		Tanzania	62.6
4	Burundi	88.7	19	Zimbabwe	62.5
5	Afghanistan	87.5	20	Mozambique	61.3
6	Congo-Kinshasa	86.7	21	Togo	60.7
7	Malawi	81.6	22	Sierra Leone	57.8
8	Guinea-Bissau	79.9	23	Laos	56.9
9	Mali	79.0	24	Senegal	56.6
10	Guinea	72.3	25	Burkina Faso	56.2
11	Zambia	71.6	26	India	53.3
12	Eritrea	71.1	27	Uganda	53.1
13	Nigeria	68.9	28	Congo-Brazzaville	51.8
14	Rwanda	68.6	29	Chad	51.2
15	Niger	67.6	30	Lesotho	49.4

a OECD countries.

Business costs and foreign direct investment

Office rents

Rent, taxes and operating expenses, Q1 2016, $ per sq. ft.

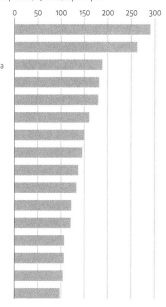

Hong Kong (Central)	
London (West End), UK	
Beijing (Finance Street), China	
Beijing (CBD), China	
Hong Kong (West Kowloon)	
Tokyo (Marunouchi Otemachi), Japan	
New Delhi (Connaught Place, CBD), India	
London (City), UK	
New York (Midtown Manhattan), US	
Shanghai (Pudong), China	
Moscow, Russia	
San Francisco (Downtown), US	
Shanghai (Puxi), China	
Paris, Ile-de-France, France	
Boston (Downtown), US	
San Francisco (Peninsula), US	

Foreign direct investment[a]

Inflows, $m, 2015

1	United States	379,894
2	Hong Kong	174,892
3	China	135,610
4	Ireland	100,542
5	Netherlands	72,649
6	Switzerland	68,838
7	Singapore	65,262
8	Brazil	64,648
9	Canada	48,643
10	India	44,208
11	France	42,883
12	United Kingdom	39,533
13	Germany	31,719
14	Belgium	31,029
15	Mexico	30,285
16	Luxembourg	24,596
17	Australia	22,264

Outflows, $m, 2015

1	United States	299,969
2	Japan	128,654
3	China	127,560
4	Netherlands	113,429
5	Ireland	101,616
6	Germany	94,313
7	Switzerland	70,277
8	Canada	67,182
9	Hong Kong	55,143
10	Luxembourg	39,371
11	Belgium	38,547
12	Singapore	35,485
13	France	35,069
14	Spain	34,586
15	South Korea	27,640
16	Italy	27,607
17	Russia	26,558

Note: CBD is Central Business District.
a Investment in companies in a foreign country.

Business creativity and research

Entrepreneurial activity

Percentage of population aged 18–64 who are either a nascent entrepreneur[a] or owner-manager of a new business, average 2011–16

Highest				Lowest		
1	Zambia	40.7		1	Suriname	3.6
2	Senegal	38.6		2	Bulgaria	4.2
3	Nigeria	36.6			Japan	4.2
4	Uganda	32.2		4	Italy	4.3
5	Ecuador	32.1		5	Morocco	5.0
6	Malawi	31.8		6	Germany	5.1
7	Ghana	31.2			Russia	5.1
8	Cameroon	30.1		8	Denmark	5.2
9	Botswana	28.6			France	5.2
10	Burkina Faso	28.3		10	Malaysia	5.3
11	Bolivia	27.4		11	Belgium	5.5
12	Lebanon	25.7			Spain	5.5
	Namibia	25.7		13	United Arab Emirates	5.9
14	Angola	25.4		14	Slovenia	6.0
15	Chile	24.6		15	Finland	6.1
16	Peru	23.8		16	Norway	6.3
17	Colombia	22.3		17	Macedonia	6.6
18	Thailand	18.4		18	Greece	6.7
19	Brazil	18.1		19	Sweden	7.0
20	Guatemala	18.0		20	Switzerland	7.2
	Philippines	18.0		21	Croatia	7.4
22	Indonesia	17.9		22	Czech Republic	7.5
	Trinidad & Tobago	17.9			South Korea	7.5
24	Argentina	17.0			Tunisia	7.5
25	El Salvador	16.3		25	Algeria	7.6
26	Barbados	16.1				

Brain drains[b]

Highest, 2016				Lowest, 2016		
1	Serbia	1.7		1	Switzerland	6.1
	Venezuela	1.7		2	United Arab Emirates	5.6
3	Bosnia & Herz.	1.9			United States	5.6
	Moldova	1.9		4	Norway	5.5
	Yemen	1.9			Qatar	5.5
6	Romania	2.1			Singapore	5.5
7	Burundi	2.2		7	United Kingdom	5.4
	Croatia	2.2		8	Malaysia	5.3
9	Hungary	2.4		9	Finland	5.2
	Zimbabwe	2.4			Hong Kong	5.2
11	Kyrgyzstan	2.5			Netherlands	5.2
	Mongolia	2.5		12	Luxembourg	5.1
	Ukraine	2.5		13	Sweden	5.0
				14	Chile	4.9
					Iceland	4.9
				16	Canada	4.8
					Germany	4.8

a An individual who has started a new firm which has not paid wages for over three months.
b Scores: 1 = talented people leave for other countries; 7 = they stay and pursue opportunities in the country.

Total expenditure on R&D

$bn, 2015			*% of GDP, 2015*		
1	United States	502.9	**1**	Israel	4.30
2	China	227.6	**2**	South Korea	4.23
3	Japan	144.0	**3**	Japan	3.49
4	Germany	96.7	**4**	Sweden	3.28
5	South Korea	58.3	**5**	Austria	3.10
6	France	53.9	**6**	Taiwan	3.06
7	United Kingdom	48.7	**7**	Denmark	3.02
8	Brazil[b]	39.7	**8**	Switzerland[c]	2.97
9	Australia [b]	32.3	**9**	Finland	2.93
10	Canada[a]	28.8	**10**	Germany	2.88
11	Italy	24.3	**11**	United States	2.80
12	Switzerland[c]	19.7	**12**	Belgium	2.46
13	India[a]	18.3	**13**	France	2.23
14	Sweden	16.2	**14**	Slovenia	2.21
15	Taiwan	16.0	**15**	Iceland	2.20
16	Netherlands	15.1		Singapore[a]	2.20
17	Russia	15.0	**17**	Australia[b]	2.15
18	Spain	14.6	**18**	China	2.09
19	Israel	12.7	**19**	Netherlands	2.01
20	Austria	11.6	**20**	Czech Republic	1.98

Innovation index[d]

2016, 100=maximum score   ● Overall   ● Outputs   ● Inputs

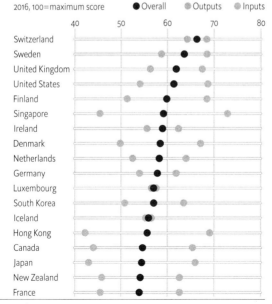

a 2014   b 2013   c 2012
d The innovation index averages countries' capacity for innovation (inputs) and success
in innovation (outputs), based on 79 indicators.

Businesses and banks

Largest non-financial companies

By market capitalisation, $bn, end December 2016

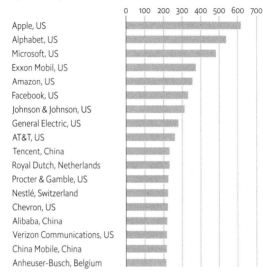

Apple, US
Alphabet, US
Microsoft, US
Exxon Mobil, US
Amazon, US
Facebook, US
Johnson & Johnson, US
General Electric, US
AT&T, US
Tencent, China
Royal Dutch, Netherlands
Procter & Gamble, US
Nestlé, Switzerland
Chevron, US
Alibaba, China
Verizon Communications, US
China Mobile, China
Anheuser-Busch, Belgium

By net profit, $bn, 2016

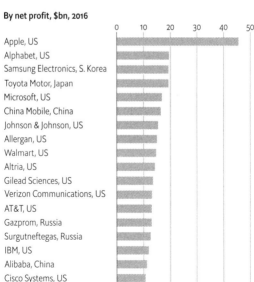

Apple, US
Alphabet, US
Samsung Electronics, S. Korea
Toyota Motor, Japan
Microsoft, US
China Mobile, China
Johnson & Johnson, US
Allergan, US
Walmart, US
Altria, US
Gilead Sciences, US
Verizon Communications, US
AT&T, US
Gazprom, Russia
Surgutneftegas, Russia
IBM, US
Alibaba, China
Cisco Systems, US

Largest banks
By market capitalisation, $bn, end December 2016

1	JPMorgan Chase	United States	308.8
2	Wells Fargo	United States	276.8
3	Industrial & Commercial Bank of China	China	223.4
4	Bank of America	United States	223.3
5	China Construction Bank	China	192.6
6	Citigroup	United States	169.4
7	HSBC	United Kingdom	161.1
8	Agricultural Bank of China	China	144.0
9	Bank of China	China	141.6
10	Commonwealth Bank of Australia	Australia	102.5
11	Royal Bank of Canada	Canada	100.4
12	TD Bank Group	Canada	91.5
13	Mitsubishi UFJ	Japan	87.5
14	BNP Paribas	France	79.6
15	Westpac	Australia	79.0

By assets, $bn, end December 2016

1	Industrial & Commercial Bank of China	China	3,478
2	China Construction Bank	China	3,021
3	Agricultural Bank of China	China	2,820
4	Bank of China	China	2,615
5	Mitsubishi UFJ	Japan	2,590
6	JPMorgan Chase	United States	2,546
7	HSBC	United Kingdom	2,375
8	Bank of America	United States	2,248
9	BNP Paribas	France	2,191
10	Wells Fargo	United States	1,952
11	Citigroup	United States	1,822
12	Japan Post	Japan	1,802
13	Mizuho	Japan	1,752
14	Deutsche Bank	Germany	1,674
15	Crédit Agricole	France	1,608

Largest sovereign-wealth funds
By assets, $bn, April 2017

1	Government Pension Fund, Norway	922
2	Abu Dhabi Investment Authority, UAE	828
3	China Investment Corporation	814
4	Kuwait Investment Authority	592
5	SAMA Foreign Holdings, Saudi Arabia	514
6	Hong Kong Monetary Authority Investment Portfolio	457
7	SAFE Investment Company, China[a]	441
8	Government of Singapore Investment Corporation	350
9	Qatar Investment Authority	335
10	China National Social Security Fund	295

Note: Countries listed refer to the company's domicile.
a   Estimate.

Stockmarkets

Largest market capitalisation

$bn, end 2016

1	NYSE	19,573
2	Nasdaq – US	7,779
3	Japan Exchange Group	5,062
4	Shanghai SE	4,104
5	London SE Group	3,496
6	Euronext	3,493
7	Shenzhen SE	3,217
8	Hong Kong Exchanges	3,193
9	TMX Group	2,042
10	Deutsche Börse	1,732
11	BSE India	1,561
12	National Stock Exchange of India	1,534
13	SIX Swiss Exchange	1,415
14	Australian Securities Exchange[a]	1,317
15	Korea Exchange[b]	1,282
16	Nasdaq OMX Nordic Exchanges[c]	1,260
17	Johannesburg SE	959
18	Taiwan SE	862
19	BM&FBOVESPA	774
20	BME Spanish Exchanges	711
21	Singapore Exchange	649
22	Moscow Exchange	622
23	Saudi SE Tadawul	449
24	Stock Exchange of Thailand	437
25	Indonesia Stock Exchange	434
26	Bursa Malaysia	363
27	Bolsa Mexicana de Valores	334
28	Philippine Stock Exchange	240
29	Oslo Bors	234
30	Tel-Aviv Stock Exchange	215
31	Bolsa de Comercio de Santiago	212
32	Borsa Istanbul	158
33	Qatar Stock Exchange	155
34	Warsaw Stock Exchange	141
35	Abu Dhabi Securities Exchange	121
	Irish Stock Exchange	121
37	Bolsa de Valores de Colombia	103
38	Tehran Stock Exchange	101
	Wiener Borse	101

Stockmarket gains and losses

$ terms, % change December 31st 2015 to December 30th 2016

Largest gains

1	Russia (RTS)	82.1
2	Brazil (BVSP)	68.9
3	Pakistan (KSE)	46.2
4	Hungary (BUX)	32.9
5	Colombia (IGBC)	25.0
6	Canada (S&P TSX)	21.7
7	Norway (OSEAX)	21.2
8	Chile (IGPA)	20.9
9	Thailand (SET)	20.4
10	Argentina (MERV)	18.5
11	Indonesia (JSX)	18.0
12	US (DJIA)	13.4
13	South Africa (FTSE JSE)	13.2
14	Taiwan (TWI)	13.1
15	US (S&P 500)	9.5
16	US (NAScomp)	7.5
17	Netherlands (AEX)	6.2
18	Australia (ASX)	6.1
	Austria (ATX)	6.1
20	Poland (WIG)	5.4

Largest losses

1	Venezuela (IBC)	-95.6
2	China (SSEB)	-25.1
3	Egypt (Case 30)	-23.9
4	China (SSEA)	-18.0
5	Denmark (OMXCB)	-14.2
6	Italy (FTSE MIB)	-12.8
7	Mexico IPC	-11.0
8	Turkey (BIST)	-9.6
9	Switzerland (SMI)	-8.2
10	Malaysia (KLSE)	-7.2
11	Czech Republic (PX)	-6.4
12	Belgium (Bel 20)	-5.4
13	Spain (Madrid SE)	-5.1
14	UK (FTSE 100)	-4.1
15	Europe (FTSEurofirst 300)	-3.5
16	Sweden (OMXS30)	-2.7
17	Euro area (EURO STOXX 50)	-2.2
18	Singapore (STI)	-1.9
19	Israel (TA 125)	-1.8
20	Euro area (FTSE Euro 100)	-1.3

a Includes investment funds. b Includes Kosdaq. c Copenhagen, Helsinki, Iceland, Stockholm, Tallinn, Riga and Vilnius stock exchanges.

Value traded[a]

$bn, 2016

1	Nasdaq – US	31,944	**17**	BME Spanish Exchanges	714
2	NYSE	19,737	**18**	National Stock	
3	BATS Global Markets			Exchange of India	691
	– US	13,683	**19**	BM&FBOVESPA	535
4	Shenzhen SE	11,673	**20**	Taiwan SE	522
5	Shanghai SE	7,535	**21**	Johannesburg SE	404
6	Japan Exchange		**22**	Stock Exchange of	
	Group Inc.	6,354		Thailand	340
7	BATS Chi-x Europe	3,215	**23**	Borsa Istanbul	331
8	London SE Group	3,121	**24**	Saudi SE – Tadawul	309
9	Euronext	1,802	**25**	Singapore Exchange	197
10	Korea Exchange[b]	1,688	**26**	Taipei Exchange	157
11	Hong Kong Exchanges	1,350	**27**	Moscow Exchange	139
12	Deutsche Börse	1,324		Indonesia SE	139
13	TMX Group	1,176	**29**	Mexican Exchange	123
14	Australian Securities		**30**	Oslo Bors	119
	Exchange[c]	911	**31**	Bursa Malaysia	116
15	SIX Swiss Exchange	870	**32**	BSE India	110
16	Nasdaq OMX Nordic		**33**	Tel-Aviv SE	59
	Exchange[d]	779	**34**	Warsaw SE	53

Number of listed companies[e]

End 2016

1	BSE India Limited	5,821	**18**	Warsaw Stock Exchange	893
2	Japan Exchange Group		**19**	Singapore Exchange	757
	Inc.	3,541	**20**	Taipei Exchange	732
3	BME Spanish Exchanges	3,506	**21**	Stock Exchange of	
4	TMX Group	3,419		Thailand	656
5	Nasdaq – US	2,897	**22**	Deutsche Börse	592
6	LSE Group	2,588	**23**	Indonesia Stock Exchange	537
7	NYSE	2,307	**24**	Tel-Aviv Stock Exchange	451
8	Australian Securities		**25**	Borsa Istanbul	381
	Exchange[c]	2,095	**26**	Hanoi Stock Exchange	376
9	Korea Exchange[b]	2,059		Johannesburg Stock	
10	Hong Kong Exchanges	1,973		Exchange	376
11	Shenzhen Stock		**28**	BM&F BOVESPA	349
	Exchange	1,870	**29**	Tehran Stock Exchange	325
12	National Stock Exchange		**30**	Hochiminh Stock	
	of India	1,840		Exchange	320
13	Shanghai Stock		**31**	Bolsa de Comercio de	
	Exchange	1,182		Santiago	298
14	Euronext	1,051	**32**	Colombo Stock Exchange	295
15	Nasdaq Nordic		**33**	Dhaka Stock Exchange	294
	Exchanges[d]	938	**34**	Philippine Stock Exchange	265
16	Taiwan Stock Exchange	911	**35**	Bolsa de Valores de Lima	264
17	Bursa Malaysia	903		SIX Swiss Exchange	264

Note: Figures are not entirely comparable due to different reporting rules and calculations.
a Includes electronic and negotiated deals. b Includes Kosdaq. c Includes investment funds. d Copenhagen, Helsinki, Iceland, Stockholm, Tallinn, Riga and Vilnius stock exchanges. e Domestic and foreign.

Public finance

Government debt
As % of GDP, 2016

1	Japan	233.7	16	Finland	78.0
2	Greece	185.7	17	Netherlands	76.1
3	Italy	159.3	18	Germany	74.7
4	Portugal	151.0	19	Poland	67.5
5	Belgium	127.0	20	Iceland	64.4
6	France	122.7	21	Israel	62.7
7	Spain	118.4	22	Slovakia	59.2
8	United States	115.6	23	Denmark	53.7
9	United Kingdom	112.5	24	Sweden	52.9
10	Euro area (15)	109.1	25	Czech Republic	52.3
11	Austria	106.0	26	Latvia	46.2
12	Canada	100.4	27	Australia	45.4
13	Slovenia	99.4	28	South Korea	44.2
14	Hungary	97.5	29	Switzerland	43.1
15	Ireland	91.0	30	Norway	41.7

Government spending
As % of GDP, 2016

1	Finland	57.5	16	Slovakia	43.6
2	France	56.5	17	Spain	42.8
3	Denmark	55.4	18	Luxembourg	42.4
4	Belgium	53.2	19	Poland	41.7
5	Greece	52.3	20	Iceland	41.4
6	Austria	51.1	21	United Kingdom	41.3
7	Norway	51.0	22	Canada	41.1
8	Sweden	50.3	23	Japan	41.0
9	Hungary	49.9		New Zealand	41.0
10	Italy	49.5	25	Czech Republic	40.4
11	Euro area (15)	48.1	26	Estonia	40.0
12	Portugal	46.2	27	Israel	39.3
13	Slovenia	45.5	28	United States	38.0
14	Netherlands	44.7	29	Latvia	37.1
15	Germany	44.3	30	Australia	36.4

Tax revenue
As % of GDP, 2015

1	Denmark	46.6	14	Greece	36.8
2	France	45.5	15	Slovenia	36.6
3	Belgium	44.8	16	Portugal	34.5
4	Finland	44.0	17	Spain	33.8
5	Austria	43.5	18	Estonia	33.6
6	Italy	43.3	19	Czech Republic	33.5
	Sweden	43.3	20	New Zealand	32.8
8	Hungary	39.4	21	United Kingdom	32.5
9	Norway	38.1	22	Slovakia	32.3
10	Netherlands	37.8	23	Poland	32.1
11	Iceland	37.1	24	Japan	32.0
12	Luxembourg	37.0	25	Canada	31.9
13	Germany	36.9	26	Israel	31.4

Note: Includes only OECD countries.

Democracy

Democracy index
Most democratic = 100, 2016

Most			Least		
1	Norway	87.1	1	Yemen	22.5
2	Switzerland	86.7	2	Libya	29.5
3	Sweden	86.2	3	Pakistan	34.9
4	Finland	86.0	4	Egypt	35.7
5	Denmark	85.1	5	Ivory Coast	38.1
6	Netherlands	83.3	6	China	38.3
7	New Zealand	81.4	7	Bahrain	38.6
8	Germany	81.3	8	Haiti	39.0
9	Ireland	80.9	9	Nigeria	39.3
10	Australia	80.5	10	Guinea	39.4
11	Belgium	80.3		Togo	39.4
12	Austria	79.9	12	Mali	39.5
	Canada	79.9	13	Venezuela	42.2
14	United Kingdom	79.6	14	Morocco	42.5
15	France	78.2		Mozambique	42.5
16	United States	76.5	16	Lebanon	42.9
17	Slovenia	75.9	17	Kyrgyzstan	43.0
18	Japan	75.5		Russia	43.0
19	Spain	75.3	19	Niger	43.2
20	Portugal	74.8	20	Burkina Faso	45.3

Parliamentary seats
Lower or single house, seats per 100,000 population, April 2017

Most			Fewest		
1	Liechtenstein	62.5	1	India	0.04
2	Monaco	60.0	2	United States	0.14
3	Andorra	28.0	3	Pakistan	0.18
4	Maldives	21.3	4	Nigeria	0.20
5	Iceland	21.0	5	Bangladesh	0.22
6	Malta	16.3		China	0.22
7	Montenegro	13.5		Indonesia	0.22
8	Equatorial Guinea	12.5	8	Brazil	0.25
9	Brunei	11.3	9	Philippines	0.29
10	Suriname	10.2	10	Russia	0.31

Women in parliament
Lower or single house, women as % of total seats, April 2017

1	Rwanda	61.3	12	Mozambique	39.6
2	Bolivia	53.1		Norway	39.6
3	Cuba	48.9	14	Spain	39.1
4	Iceland	47.6	15	Argentina	38.9
5	Nicaragua	45.7	16	Ethiopia	38.8
6	Sweden	43.6	17	Timor-Leste	38.5
7	Senegal	42.7	18	Angola	38.2
8	Mexico	42.6	19	Belgium	38.0
9	South Africa	42.1		Ecuador	38.0
10	Finland	42.0	21	Denmark	37.4
11	Namibia	41.3	22	Germany	37.0

Education

Primary enrolment
Number enrolled as % of relevant age group

Highest			Lowest		
1	Madagascar	149	1	Eritrea	50
2	Malawi	146	2	South Sudan	64
3	Timor-Leste	137	3	Sudan	70
4	Nepal	136	4	Niger	73
5	Rwanda	134	5	Mali	76
6	Benin	129	6	Congo-Brazzaville	77
7	Sierra Leone	128	7	Equatorial Guinea	79
8	Burundi	124	8	Syria	80
9	Suriname	123	9	Senegal	82
10	Togo	122		Tanzania	82
11	Sweden	121	11	Guyana	85
12	Bangladesh	120	12	Burkina Faso	88
13	Cambodia	117	13	Puerto Rico	89
	Cameroon	117		Turkmenistan	89
	Georgia	117			
	Philippines	117			

Highest secondary enrolment
Number enrolled as % of relevant age group

1	Belgium	165	12	Iceland	119
2	Finland	149	13	New Zealand	117
3	Australia	138	14	Liechtenstein	116
4	Sweden	133		Portugal	116
5	Netherlands	132	16	Estonia	115
6	Denmark	130		Latvia	115
	Spain	130	18	Norway	113
8	Thailand	129	19	Kazakhstan	112
9	United Kingdom	128	20	France	111
10	Ireland	127		Slovenia	111
11	Costa Rica	123	22	Canada	110

Highest tertiary enrolment[a]
Number enrolled as % of relevant age group

1	Greece	114	11	Argentina	83
2	South Korea	95		Slovenia	83
3	Australia	90	13	Austria	82
	Spain	90		Denmark	82
5	Chile	89		Ukraine	82
6	Belarus	88	16	Iceland	81
7	Finland	87		New Zealand	81
8	Turkey	86	18	Netherlands	79
	United States	86		Russia	79
10	Puerto Rico	84	20	Ireland	78

Notes: Latest available year 2012–16. The gross enrolment ratios shown are the actual number enrolled as a percentage of the number of children in the official primary age group. They may exceed 100 when, eg, children outside the primary age group are receiving primary education.

a Tertiary education includes all levels of post-secondary education including courses leading to awards not equivalent to a university degree, courses leading to a first university degree and postgraduate courses.

Least literate
% adult population

1	Niger	19.1	**19**	Mozambique	58.8
2	Guinea	30.5	**20**	Nigeria	59.6
3	South Sudan	32.0	**21**	Guinea-Bissau	59.8
4	Mali	33.1	**22**	Haiti	60.7
5	Central African Rep.	36.8	**23**	Bangladesh	61.5
6	Burkina Faso	37.7	**24**	Papua New Guinea	63.4
7	Afghanistan	38.2	**25**	Timor-Leste	64.1
8	Benin	38.4	**26**	Madagascar	64.7
9	Chad	40.0		Nepal	64.7
10	Ivory Coast	43.3	**28**	Malawi	66.0
11	Liberia	47.6	**29**	Togo	66.5
12	Sierra Leone	48.4	**30**	Yemen	70.0
13	Ethiopia	49.0	**31**	Angola	71.2
14	Mauritania	52.1		Rwanda	71.2
15	Gambia, The	55.6	**33**	Morocco	71.7
	Senegal	55.6	**34**	India	72.2
17	Pakistan	56.4	**35**	Eritrea	73.8
18	Sudan	58.6		Uganda	73.8

Education spending

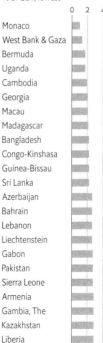

% of GDP, highest

	0 2 4 6 8 10
Denmark	
Zimbabwe	
Malta	
Timor-Leste	
Iceland	
Sweden	
Costa Rica	
Moldova	
Bhutan	
Norway	
Bolivia	
Finland	
Senegal	
Swaziland	
Barbados	
Niger	
Mozambique	
Cyprus	
Puerto Rico	
New Zealand	
Tunisia	
Belize	
Ghana	

% of GDP, lowest

	0 2 4
Monaco	
West Bank & Gaza	
Bermuda	
Uganda	
Cambodia	
Georgia	
Macau	
Madagascar	
Bangladesh	
Congo-Kinshasa	
Guinea-Bissau	
Sri Lanka	
Azerbaijan	
Bahrain	
Lebanon	
Liechtenstein	
Gabon	
Pakistan	
Sierra Leone	
Armenia	
Gambia, The	
Kazakhstan	
Liberia	

Marriage and divorce

Highest marriage rates
Number of marriages per 1,000 population, 2015 or latest available year

1	Tajikistan	11.6	22	Moldova	7.2
2	Lebanon	11.2	23	Georgia	7.0
3	Egypt	11.0	24	Ukraine	6.9
4	Kazakhstan	9.9	25	Jamaica	6.8
5	China	9.6		United States	6.8
	Uzbekistan	9.6	27	Barbados	6.7
	West Bank & Gaza	9.6		Macedonia	6.7
8	Iran	9.3		Malta	6.7
9	Jordan	9.2	30	Israel	6.5
10	Azerbaijan	8.9	31	Cyprus	6.4
	Belarus	8.9	32	Guyana	6.3
12	Kyrgyzstan	8.7		Latvia	6.3
13	Russia	8.5	34	Armenia	6.0
14	Guam	8.3	35	Romania	5.9
15	Albania	8.2		South Korea	5.9
	Bermuda	8.2		Trinidad & Tobago	5.9
17	Hong Kong	7.8	38	Bahamas	5.8
	Turkey	7.8		Macau	5.8
19	Mauritius	7.7		Mongolia	5.8
20	Lithuania	7.6	41	Montenegro	5.7
21	Singapore	7.3			

Lowest marriage rates
Number of marriages per 1,000 population, 2015 or latest available year

1	Qatar	1.8		New Caledonia	3.9
2	Martinique	2.5	24	Kuwait	4.0
3	Argentina	2.8	25	Austria	4.3
4	Guadeloupe	3.0		Czech Republic	4.3
	Luxembourg	3.0	27	Finland	4.5
	Portugal	3.0		New Zealand	4.5
	Uruguay	3.0		United Kingdom	4.5
	Venezuela	3.0	30	Croatia	4.6
9	Italy	3.1		Iceland	4.6
	Peru	3.1		Norway	4.6
11	Slovenia	3.2	33	Estonia	4.7
12	Panama	3.3	34	Bosnia & Herz.	4.8
	Réunion	3.3		Dominican Rep.	4.8
14	Bulgaria	3.4		Germany	4.8
	Spain	3.4		Ireland	4.8
16	Chile	3.5		Mexico	4.8
17	Belgium	3.6	39	Greece	4.9
18	Andorra	3.7		Puerto Rico	4.9
	France	3.7		Slovakia	4.9
20	Suriname	3.8	42	Denmark	5.0
21	Hungary	3.9		Liechtenstein	5.0
	Netherlands	3.9		Poland	5.0

Note: The data are based on latest available figures (no earlier than 2010) and hence will be affected by the population age structure at the time. Marriage rates refer to registered marriages only and, therefore, reflect the customs surrounding registry and efficiency of administration.

Highest divorce rates

Number of divorces per 1,000 population, 2015 or latest available year[a]

1	Russia	4.5	**13**	Sweden		2.7
2	Belarus	3.7	**14**	Luxembourg		2.6
3	Guam	3.6	**15**	Belgium		2.5
4	Denmark	3.4		Czech Republic		2.5
	Puerto Rico	3.4		Finland		2.5
6	Lithuania	3.3	**18**	Estonia		2.4
7	Latvia	3.1		Jordan		2.4
8	Cuba	3.0		Liechtenstein		2.4
	Kazakhstan	3.0	**21**	Cyprus		2.2
	Moldova	3.0		Portugal		2.2
	Ukraine	3.0		Spain		2.2
12	United States	2.8				

Lowest divorce rates

Number of divorces per 1,000 population, 2015 or latest available year[a]

1	Chile	0.1		Panama	1.1
2	Guatemala	0.3		Serbia	1.1
3	Bosnia & Herz.	0.4		Tajikistan	1.1
	Peru	0.4	**19**	Bahamas	1.2
5	Ireland	0.6		New Caledonia	1.2
	Jamaica	0.6		Slovenia	1.2
7	Qatar	0.7	**22**	Albania	1.3
8	Malta	0.8		Azerbaijan	1.3
9	Italy	0.9		Mongolia	1.3
	Mexico	0.9	**25**	Kyrgyzstan	1.4
	Montenegro	0.9		Romania	1.4
	Uzbekistan	0.9		Suriname	1.4
13	Armenia	1.0	**28**	Bulgaria	1.5
14	Macedonia	1.1		Greece	1.5
	Martinique	1.1			

Mean age of women at first marriage

Years, 2012 or latest available year

Youngest[a]			Oldest[b]		
1	Niger	15.7	**1**	Sweden	32.9
2	Bangladesh	16.0	**2**	Denmark	32.1
	Chad	16.0		Iceland	32.1
4	Guinea	16.5	**4**	Ireland	31.2
5	Mali	16.7	**5**	Norway	31.0
6	Sierra Leone	17.1		Spain	31.0
7	Ethiopia	17.4	**7**	Netherlands	30.4
8	Mozambique	17.5	**8**	Finland	30.3
9	India	17.8		Germany	30.3
10	Burkina Faso	17.9	**10**	Italy	30.1
	Malawi	17.9	**11**	France	30.0
	Nepal	17.9	**12**	Luxembourg	29.9
13	Afghanistan	18.0		United Kingdom	29.9
14	Nicaragua	18.1	**14**	Switzerland	29.4

a No earlier than 2010.   b No earlier than 2000.

Households, living costs and giving

Number of households

Biggest, m, 2015

1	China	452.8	21	Ethiopia	21.9
2	India	268.6	22	Turkey	21.2
3	United States	124.5	23	Spain	18.8
4	Indonesia	65.3	24	South Korea	18.7
5	Brazil	62.1	25	Ukraine	17.7
6	Russia	56.5	26	South Africa	15.3
7	Japan	53.0	27	Poland	14.1
8	Germany	41.6	28	Canada	14.0
9	Nigeria	38.3	29	Argentina	13.5
10	Bangladesh	37.1	30	Colombia	13.3
11	Mexico	32.8	31	Congo-Kinshasa	11.5
12	France	29.3	32	Tanzania	11.2
13	Pakistan	28.1	33	Myanmar	11.1
14	Italy	27.3	34	Kenya	10.8
15	United Kingdom	27.2	35	North Korea	9.6
16	Vietnam	27.1	36	Australia	8.8
17	Iran	24.3	37	Uganda	8.2
18	Egypt	23.4	38	Venezuela	7.9
19	Philippines	22.9	39	Peru	7.8
20	Thailand	22.5		Taiwan	7.8

Average household size, people

Biggest, 2015

1	Guinea	8.6
2	Angola	8.5
3	Senegal	8.2
4	Chad	7.9
	Equatorial Guinea	7.9
	Gambia, The	7.9
7	Gabon	7.8
	Guinea-Bissau	7.8
9	Oman	6.9
10	Congo-Kinshasa	6.7
	Mauritania	6.7
	Pakistan	6.7
	Yemen	6.7
14	Maldives	6.5
15	Iraq	6.3
	Papua New Guinea	6.3
	Tajikistan	6.3
	Turkmenistan	6.3
19	Libya	6.1
	Mali	6.1
21	Niger	6.0
22	Kosovo	5.9

Smallest, 2015

1	Germany	1.9
	Sweden	1.9
3	Luxembourg	2.0
4	Finland	2.1
5	France	2.2
	Italy	2.2
	Lithuania	2.2
	Netherlands	2.2
9	Austria	2.3
	Czech Republic	2.3
	Estonia	2.3
12	Bulgaria	2.4
	Denmark	2.4
	Hungary	2.4
	Japan	2.4
	Latvia	2.4
	Slovenia	2.4
	United Kingdom	2.4
19	Portugal	2.5
	Russia	2.5
	Spain	2.5
	Ukraine	2.5

a The cost of living index shown is compiled by the Economist Intelligence Unit for use by companies in determining expatriate compensation: it is a comparison of the cost of maintaining a typical international lifestyle in the country rather than a comparison of the purchasing power of a citizen of the country. The index is based on typical urban prices an international executive and family will face abroad. The prices

Cost of living[a]
December 2016, US = 100

Highest			Lowest		
1	Singapore	120	**1**	Kazakhstan	38
2	Hong Kong	114	**2**	Nigeria	39
3	Japan	110	**3**	Pakistan	44
4	South Korea	108	**4**	Algeria	45
5	France	107	**5**	India	47
	Switzerland	107		Romania	47
7	Denmark	100		Ukraine	47
	United States	100	**8**	Zambia	49
9	Israel	99	**9**	Iran	50
	Norway	99		Syria	50
11	Australia	98		Venezuela	50
12	Finland	92	**12**	Nepal	51
	Iceland	92	**13**	Paraguay	51
	New Zealand	92		South Africa	51
15	Austria	91	**15**	Bulgaria	54
16	United Kingdom	89		Panama	54
17	Ireland	88		Saudi Arabia	54
18	Jordan	85	**18**	Serbia	55
19	Italy	82	**19**	Hungary	56
20	Belgium	81		Senegal	56
	Canada	81		Sri Lanka	56
	New Caledonia	81	**22**	Morocco	57
23	Spain	80	**23**	Oman	58
	Sweden	80		Poland	58
25	China	79			

World Giving Index[b]
Top givers, % of population, 2015

1	Myanmar	70		Turkmenistan	50
2	United States	61	**16**	Iceland	49
3	Australia	60		Malta	49
4	New Zealand	59	**18**	Kuwait	48
5	Sri Lanka	57	**19**	Denmark	47
6	Canada	56		Germany	47
	Indonesia	56	**21**	Finland	46
8	Ireland	54		Malaysia	46
	United Kingdom	54		Switzerland	46
10	United Arab Emirates	53	**24**	Sweden	45
11	Kenya	52	**25**	Mongolia	44
	Netherlands	52		Singapore	44
	Uzbekistan	52		Uganda	44
14	Norway	50			

are for products of international comparable quality found in a supermarket or department store. Prices found in local markets and bazaars are not used unless the available merchandise is of the specified quality and the shopping area itself is safe for executive and family members. New York City prices are used as the base, so United States = 100.

b Three criteria are used to assess giving: in the previous month those surveyed either gave money to charity, gave time to those in need or helped a stranger.

Transport: roads and cars

Longest road networks

Km of road per km² land area, 2015 or latest

1	Monaco	38.5	25	Czech Republic	1.7
2	Macau	13.6		Italy	1.7
3	Malta	9.7		United Kingdom	1.7
4	Bermuda	8.9	28	Austria	1.5
5	Bahrain	5.3		Sri Lanka	1.5
6	Belgium	5.1	30	Cyprus	1.4
7	Singapore	4.9		Estonia	1.4
8	Netherlands	4.1		Ireland	1.4
9	Barbados	3.7		Poland	1.4
10	Japan	3.4	34	Lithuania	1.3
11	Puerto Rico	3.0		Spain	1.3
12	Liechtenstein	2.5	36	Taiwan	1.2
13	Hungary	2.3	37	Latvia	1.1
14	Bangladesh	2.0		Mauritius	1.1
	France	2.0		South Korea	1.1
	Hong Kong	2.0		Sweden	1.1
	Jamaica	2.0	41	Romania	1.0
	Luxembourg	2.0	42	Greece	0.9
19	Guam	1.9		Israel	0.9
	India	1.9		Portugal	0.9
	Slovenia	1.9		Slovakia	0.9
22	Denmark	1.8	46	Costa Rica	0.8
	Germany	1.8		Qatar	0.8
	Switzerland	1.8			

Densest road networks

Km of road per km² land area, 2015 or latest

1	Monaco	38.5		Switzerland	1.8
2	Macau	13.6	25	Czech Republic	1.7
3	Malta	9.7		Italy	1.7
4	Bermuda	8.9		United Kingdom	1.7
5	Bahrain	5.3	28	Austria	1.5
6	Belgium	5.1		Sri Lanka	1.5
7	Singapore	4.9	30	Cyprus	1.4
8	Netherlands	4.1		Estonia	1.4
9	Barbados	3.7		Ireland	1.4
10	Japan	3.4		Poland	1.4
11	Puerto Rico	3	34	Lithuania	1.3
12	Liechtenstein	2.5		Spain	1.3
13	Hungary	2.3	36	Taiwan	1.2
14	Bangladesh	2	37	Latvia	1.1
	France	2		Mauritius	1.1
	Hong Kong	2		South Korea	1.1
	Jamaica	2		Sweden	1.1
	Luxembourg	2	41	Romania	1
19	Guam	1.9	42	Greece	0.9
	India	1.9		Israel	0.9
	Slovenia	1.9		Portugal	0.9
22	Denmark	1.8		Slovakia	0.9
	Germany	1.8			

Most crowded road networks

Number of vehicles per km of road network, 2014 or latest

1	Japan	628.4	26	Liechtenstein	77.3
2	United Arab Emirates	479.0	27	Germany	74.1
3	Monaco	427.3	28	Armenia	73.3
4	Hong Kong	310.6	29	Tunisia	71.5
5	Kuwait	263.7	30	Dominican Rep.	68.1
6	Bahrain	252.3	31	Brunei	67.9
7	Singapore	239.5	32	Barbados	67.5
8	Macau	238.0		Switzerland	67.5
9	South Korea	190.4	34	Portugal	67.1
10	Taiwan	176.2	35	Netherlands	66.5
11	Israel	150.3	36	Croatia	61.5
12	Jordan	148.3	37	Malaysia	58.1
13	Puerto Rico	122.5	38	Argentina	58.0
14	Mauritius	111.8	39	Bermuda	57.9
15	Guam	108.8	40	Morocco	57.6
16	Guatemala	108.0	41	Poland	56.8
17	Malta	101.8	42	Ukraine	56.2
18	Qatar	97.7	43	Chile	55.4
19	Mexico	93.8	44	Greece	55.2
20	Syria	91.9	45	Moldova	53.9
21	United Kingdom	88.1	46	Slovakia	52.4
22	Bulgaria	85.6	47	Kazakhstan	50.0
23	Italy	85.0	48	Ecuador	49.5
24	Thailand	79.8	49	Bahamas	48.2
25	Luxembourg	79.5	50	Finland	48.1

Most road deaths

Fatalities per 100,000 population, 2015

1	Zimbabwe	45.4	24	Dominican Rep.	27.8
2	Venezuela	41.7	25	Benin	27.7
3	Liberia	35.1	26	Saudi Arabia	27.5
4	Malawi	34.2	27	Ethiopia	27.3
5	Congo-Kinshasa	33.5		Uganda	27.3
6	Tanzania	33.4	29	Somalia	26.9
7	Mozambique	33.1	30	Guinea-Bissau	26.8
8	Rwanda	32.9	31	Congo-Brazzaville	26.7
9	Burundi	32.7	32	Ghana	26.1
10	Togo	31.9		Lesotho	26.1
11	Central African Rep.	31.8	34	Libya	25.3
12	Thailand	31.7		Mali	25.3
13	Madagascar	31.4	36	Oman	25.0
14	Burkina Faso	30.7	37	Eritrea	24.9
15	Kenya	30.5		Swaziland	24.9
16	Gambia, The	30.4	39	Zambia	24.7
17	South Sudan	29.3	40	Sudan	24.6
18	Sierra Leone	28.5	41	Angola	24.4
19	Niger	28.4	42	Chad	24.3
20	Cameroon	28.1	43	Mauritania	24.2
	Guinea	28.1	44	Ivory Coast	24.0
22	Iran	28.0		Vietnam	24.0
	Senegal	28.0	46	Algeria	23.7

Fastest-growing car ownership
Change in number of cars per 1,000 population, 1995–2014[a]

1	Bahrain	458.5	26	Canada	101.6
2	Brunei	257.5	27	Norway	100.1
3	Kuwait	208.6	28	Australia	96.9
	Puerto Rico	208.6	29	Iceland	96.7
5	Poland	200.0	30	Bosnia & Herz.	96.0
6	Qatar	175.7	31	Uruguay	95.3
7	New Zealand	173.7	32	Syria	95.0
8	Kazakhstan	166.9	33	South Korea	93.4
9	Libya	152.4	34	Czech Republic	91.4
10	Malta	149.9	35	Mexico	90.8
11	Malaysia	148.2	36	Georgia	81.4
12	Suriname	146.0	37	Chile	78.6
13	Finland	144.6	38	Greece	72.8
14	Lithuania	138.2	39	Romania	71.4
15	Luxembourg	131.7	40	Brazil	71.0
16	Russia	125.0	41	Mauritius	70.8
17	Estonia	122.5	42	Iran	69.8
18	Belarus	120.2	43	Botswana	68.5
19	Slovakia	117.8	44	Jordan	68.3
20	Argentina	117.5	45	China	67.8
21	United Arab Emirates	110.0	46	Bulgaria	66.9
22	Oman	109.0	47	Costa Rica	66.7
23	Kyrgyzstan	108.8	48	Saudi Arabia	66.3
24	Israel	104.9	49	Thailand	66.0
25	Cyprus	102.9	50	Guam	65.5

Slowest-growing car ownership
Change in number of cars per 1,000 population, 1995–2014[a]

1	Latvia	-42.3	22	Madagascar	4.9
2	Germany	-20.4	23	El Salvador	5.1
3	Zambia	-3.6	24	Philippines	5.2
4	Ethiopia	0.2	25	Mali	5.4
5	Sudan	0.3	26	Benin	5.5
6	Burundi	0.6	27	Pakistan	5.6
	Haiti	0.6	28	Mozambique	5.8
8	Bangladesh	0.9	29	Ivory Coast	6.7
9	Bermuda	1.1	30	Tunisia	7.9
10	Malawi	1.5	31	Yemen	8.5
11	Honduras	1.7	32	Jamaica	8.6
12	Liberia	1.8	33	Kenya	9.5
13	Mauritania	2.0	34	Nigeria	9.7
14	Uganda	2.1	35	Sri Lanka	10.2
15	Congo-Kinshasa	2.2	36	Bolivia	10.5
16	Cuba	2.9	37	Senegal	10.8
17	Nicaragua	3.1	38	India	11.3
18	Cameroon	3.2	39	Zimbabwe	13.7
19	Burkina Faso	3.7	40	Vietnam	14.9
20	Tanzania	3.9	41	Ghana	15.9
21	Togo	4.1	42	Egypt	16.2

a Based on 2014 population.

Car production

Number of cars produced, m, 2015

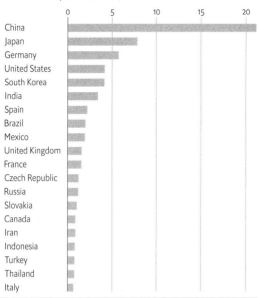

Cars sold

New car registrations, '000, 2015

1	China	21,210	**23**	Poland	355
2	United States	7,517	**24**	Sweden	345
3	Japan	4,216	**25**	Switzerland	324
4	Germany	3,206	**26**	Austria	309
5	India	2,772	**27**	Israel	247
6	United Kingdom	2,634	**28**	Colombia	237
7	Brazil	2,123	**29**	Czech Republic	231
8	France	1,917	**30**	United Arab Emirates	214
9	Italy	1,576	**31**	Chile	212
10	South Korea	1,534		Taiwan	212
11	Russia	1,283	**33**	Denmark	208
12	Spain	1,094	**34**	Pakistan	182
13	Iran	1,055	**35**	Portugal	179
14	Australia	924	**36**	Norway	151
15	Indonesia	756	**37**	Peru	137
16	Turkey	726	**38**	Ireland	125
17	Saudi Arabia	672	**39**	Kuwait	124
18	Malaysia	591	**40**	Oman	121
19	Belgium	501	**41**	Vietnam	117
20	Argentina	481	**42**	Philippines	116
21	Netherlands	449	**43**	Finland	109
22	Thailand	356	**44**	Romania	98

Transport: planes and trains

Most air travel
Passengers carried, m, 2015

1	United States	798.2	16	Thailand	54.3
2	China	436.2	17	Malaysia	50.3
3	United Kingdom	131.4	18	Mexico	45.6
4	Germany	115.5	19	Netherlands	34.9
5	Japan	113.8	20	Singapore	33.3
6	Ireland	113.1	21	Saudi Arabia	32.8
7	Brazil	102.0	22	Philippines	32.2
8	India	98.9	23	Colombia	30.7
9	Turkey	96.6	24	Vietnam	29.9
10	Indonesia	88.7	25	Switzerland	26.8
11	United Arab Emirates	84.7	26	Italy	26.0
12	Canada	80.2	27	Qatar	25.3
13	Australia	69.3	28	Hungary	20.0
14	France	65.0	29	South Africa	17.2
15	Spain	60.8	30	New Zealand	15.3

Busiest airports

Total passengers, m, 2016

1	Atlanta, Hartsfield	104.2
2	Beijing, Capital	94.4
3	Dubai Intl.	83.6
4	Los Angeles, Intl.	80.9
5	Tokyo, Haneda	79.7
6	Chicago, O'Hare	78.3
7	London, Heathrow	75.7
8	Hong Kong, Intl.	70.3
9	Shanghai, Pudong Intl.	66.0
10	Paris, Charles de Gaulle	65.9
11	Dallas, Ft Worth	65.7
12	Amsterdam, Schiphol	63.6
13	Frankfurt, Main	60.8
14	Istanbul, Ataturk	60.2
15	Guangzhou Baiyun, Intl	59.7

Total cargo, m tonnes, 2016

1	Hong Kong, Intl.	4.62
2	Memphis, Intl.	4.32
3	Shanghai, Pudong Intl.	3.44
4	Dubai, Intl.	2.95
5	Seoul, Incheon	2.71
6	Anchorage, Intl.	2.54
7	Louisville, Standiford Field	2.44
8	Tokyo, Narita	2.17
9	Paris, Charles de Gaulle	2.14
10	Frankfurt, Main	2.11
11	Taiwan, Taoyuan Intl.	2.10
12	Miami, Intl.	2.01
	Singapore, Changi	2.01
14	Los Angeles, Intl.	1.99
15	Beijing, Capital	1.93

Average daily aircraft movements, take-offs and landings, 2016

1	Atlanta, Hartsfield	2,461	14	Istanbul, Ataturk	1,275
2	Chicago, O'Hare	2,377	15	Frankfurt, Main	1,268
3	Los Angeles, Intl.	1,910	16	Toronto, Pearson Intl.	1,251
4	Dallas, Ft Worth	1,843	17	Dubai, Intl.	1,244
5	Beijing, Capital	1,661	18	New York, JFK	1,239
6	Denver, Intl.	1,569	19	San Francisco	1,234
7	Charlotte/Douglas, Intl.	1,495	20	Mexico City, Intl.	1,228
8	Las Vegas, McCarran Intl.	1,483	21	Tokyo, Haneda	1,221
9	Shanghai, Pudong Intl.	1,315	22	Phoenix, Skyharbor Intl.	1,207
10	Amsterdam, Schiphol	1,312	23	Guangzhou Baiyun, Intl	1,192
11	London, Heathrow	1,301	24	Newark	1,182
12	Paris, Charles de Gaulle	1,296	25	Miami	1,135
13	Houston, George Bush Intercontinental	1,290			

Longest railway networks
'000 km, 2015 or latest

1	United States	228.2	21	Turkey	10.1
2	Russia	85.3	22	Sweden	9.7
3	China	67.2	23	Czech Republic	9.5
4	India	66.0	24	Pakistan	9.3
5	Canada	52.1	25	Iran	8.6
6	Germany	33.3	26	Hungary	7.9
7	Australia	32.8	27	Finland	5.9
8	France	30.0	28	Belarus	5.5
9	Brazil	29.8		Chile	5.5
10	Mexico	26.7	30	Thailand	5.3
11	Argentina	25.0	31	Egypt	5.2
12	Ukraine	21.0	32	Austria	4.9
13	South Africa	20.5	33	Indonesia	4.7
14	Japan	19.2	34	Sudan	4.3
15	Poland	18.5	35	Norway	4.2
16	Italy	16.7		Uzbekistan	4.2
17	United Kingdom	16.1	37	Bulgaria	4.0
18	Spain	15.7		Switzerland	4.0
19	Kazakhstan	14.8	39	South Korea	3.9
20	Romania	10.8			

Most rail passengers
Km per person per year, 2015 or latest

1	Switzerland	2,311	13	Taiwan	844
2	Japan	1,633	14	Ukraine	839
3	Russia	1,439	15	Belarus	749
4	Austria	1,359	16	Finland	748
5	France	1,315	17	Czech Republic	683
6	Denmark	1,054	18	Italy	657
7	Netherlands	1,051	19	Sweden	642
8	Germany	982	20	Luxembourg	622
9	Kazakhstan	971	21	Norway	594
10	United Kingdom	963	22	Hungary	571
11	Belgium	914		Slovakia	571
12	India	875	24	Spain	557

Most rail freight
Million tonne-km per year, 2015 or latest

1	United States	2,547,253	13	Belarus	40,785
2	Russia	2,304,759	14	France	33,116
3	China	1,980,061	15	Poland	28,720
4	India	681,696	16	Iran	25,014
5	Canada	352,535	17	Uzbekistan	22,686
6	Brazil	267,700	18	Austria	20,804
7	Ukraine	195,054	19	Japan	20,255
8	Kazakhstan	189,759	20	Lithuania	14,036
9	South Africa	134,600	21	Latvia	13,023
10	Mexico	78,770	22	Argentina	12,111
11	Germany	72,913	23	Turkmenistan	11,992
12	Australia	59,649	24	Mongolia	11,463

Transport: shipping

Merchant fleets

Number of vessels, by country of domicile, January 2016

1	China	4,960	11	Turkey	1,540
2	Greece	4,136	12	United Kingdom	1,329
3	Japan	3,969	13	Netherlands	1,229
4	Germany	3,361	14	Denmark	960
5	Singapore	2,553	15	India	947
6	United States	1,995	16	Taiwan	898
7	Norway	1,854	17	Vietnam	896
8	Indonesia	1,712	18	United Arab Emirates	815
9	Russia	1,680	19	Italy	802
10	South Korea	1,634	20	Malaysia	621

Ships' flags

Largest registered fleets, 2016

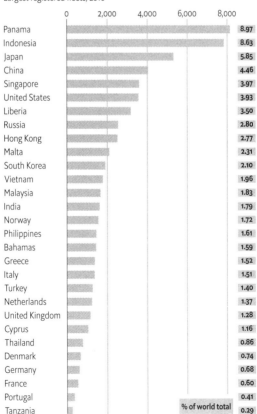

	% of world total
Panama	8.97
Indonesia	8.63
Japan	5.85
China	4.46
Singapore	3.97
United States	3.93
Liberia	3.50
Russia	2.80
Hong Kong	2.77
Malta	2.31
South Korea	2.10
Vietnam	1.96
Malaysia	1.83
India	1.79
Norway	1.72
Philippines	1.61
Bahamas	1.59
Greece	1.52
Italy	1.51
Turkey	1.40
Netherlands	1.37
United Kingdom	1.28
Cyprus	1.16
Thailand	0.86
Denmark	0.74
Germany	0.68
France	0.60
Portugal	0.41
Tanzania	0.29

Crime and punishment

Murders

Homicides per 100,000 pop., 2014 or latest

1	Honduras	74.6
2	El Salvador	64.2
3	Venezuela	62.0
4	Virgin Islands (US)	52.6
5	Lesotho	38.0
6	Jamaica	36.1
7	Belize	34.4
8	South Africa	33.0
9	Guatemala	31.2
10	Bahamas	29.8
11	Colombia	27.9
12	Trinidad & Tobago	25.9
13	Brazil	24.6
14	Guyana	20.4
15	Puerto Rico	18.5
16	Dominican Rep.	17.4
	Panama	17.4
	Swaziland	17.4
19	Namibia	16.9
20	Mexico	15.7

Robberies

Per 100,000 pop., 2014 or latest

1	Belgium	1,529
2	Costa Rica	1,096
3	Argentina	958
4	Chile	599
5	Mexico	589
6	Ecuador	571
7	Uruguay	543
8	Brazil	496
	Nicaragua	496
	Panama	496
11	Paraguay	307
12	Peru	251
13	Honduras	238
14	Maldives	208
15	Guyana	201
16	Colombia	198
17	Trinidad & Tobago	197
18	France	178
19	Spain	153
20	Portugal	150

Prisoners

Total prison pop., 2017 or latest

1	United States	2,145,100
2	China	1,649,804
3	Brazil	650,956
4	Russia	627,702
5	India	419,623
6	Thailand	286,861
7	Mexico	233,469
8	Iran	225,624
9	Indonesia	210,682
10	Turkey	201,177
11	South Africa	161,984
12	Philippines	142,168
13	Vietnam	130,679
14	Colombia	119,269
15	Ethiopia	111,050
16	Egypt	106,000
17	United Kingdom	85,442
18	Peru	82,200
19	Pakistan	80,169
20	Morocco	79,368
21	Argentina	72,693
22	Poland	72,677
23	Myanmar	70,000
24	Bangladesh	69,719
25	France	68,432
26	Nigeria	68,259
27	Germany	62,865

Per 100,000 pop., 2017 or latest

1	United States	666
2	Turkmenistan	583
3	El Salvador	579
4	Virgin Islands (US)	542
5	Cuba	510
6	Guam	438
7	Russia	434
	Rwanda	434
9	Panama	426
10	Thailand	424
11	Bahamas	363
12	Bermuda	354
13	Costa Rica	352
14	Puerto Rico	349
15	Barbados	322
16	Brazil	316
17	Belarus	314
18	Bahrain	301
19	South Africa	291
	Uruguay	291
21	Iran	287
22	Swaziland	282
23	Trinidad & Tobago	272
24	Taiwan	266
25	Israel	265
26	Mongolia	262
27	Peru	259

War and terrorism

Defence spending
As % of GDP, 2016

1	Oman	15.3		Azerbaijan	4.0
2	Afghanistan	14.0	14	Iran	3.9
3	Iraq	11.6		Mali	3.9
4	Saudi Arabia	8.9	16	Brunei	3.8
5	Congo-Brazzaville	6.4	17	Russia[a]	3.7
6	Algeria	6.3	18	Lebanon	3.5
7	Israel	6.1		Singapore	3.5
8	Bahrain	4.8	20	Colombia	3.4
9	Botswana	4.4	21	Myanmar	3.3
	Jordan	4.4		United States	3.3
11	Namibia	4.1	23	Cambodia	3.2
12	Armenia	4.0		Morocco	3.2

Defence spending

	$bn, 2016			Per person, $, 2016	
1	United States	604.5	1	Oman	2,714
2	China	145	2	Israel	2,322
3	Saudi Arabia	56.9	3	Saudi Arabia	2,021
4	United Kingdom	52.5	4	Qatar	1,950
5	India	51.1	5	United States	1,866
6	Japan	47.3	6	Singapore	1,773
7	France	47.2	7	Norway	1,134
8	Russia[a]	46.6	8	Bahrain	1,110
9	Germany	38.3	9	Australia	1,052
10	South Korea	33.8	10	Brunei	920
11	Australia	24.2	11	United Kingdom	815
12	Italy	22.3	12	France	706
13	Iraq	17.9	13	South Korea	663
14	Iran	15.9	14	Denmark	634
	Israel	15.9	15	Finland	597

Armed forces
'000, 2017[b]

		Regulars	Reserves			Regulars	Reserves
1	China	2,183	510	16	Mexico	277	82
2	India	1,395	1,155	17	Saudi Arabia	227	0
3	United States	1,347	865	18	Taiwan	215	1,657
4	Russia[a]	831	2,000	19	Ukraine	204	900
5	Pakistan	654	0	20	France	203	28
6	South Korea	630	4,500	21	Sri Lanka	203	6
7	Iran	523	350	22	Morocco	196	150
8	Vietnam	482	5,000	23	South Sudan	185	0
9	Egypt	439	479	24	Israel	177	465
10	Myanmar	406	0	25	Georgia	177	28
11	Indonesia	396	400	26	Italy	175	18
12	Thailand	361	200	27	Afghanistan	171	0
13	Turkey	355	379	28	United Kingdom	152	81
14	Brazil	335	1,340	29	Greece	143	221
15	Colombia	293	35	30	Congo-Kinshasa	134	0

a National defence budget only. b Estimates.

Arms exporters

$m, 2016

1	United States	9,894
2	Russia	6,432
3	Germany	2,813
4	France	2,226
5	China	2,123
6	United Kingdom	1,393
7	Israel	1,260
8	Italy	802
9	South Korea	534
10	Ukraine	528
11	Spain	483
12	Netherlands	466
13	Turkey	277
14	Sweden	249
15	Switzerland	186
16	Portugal	169
17	Norway	150
18	Czech Republic	129
19	Australia	127
	Canada	127

Arms importers

$m, 2016

1	Saudi Arabia	2,979
2	Algeria	2,882
3	India	2,547
4	Iraq	1,734
5	Egypt	1,483
6	South Korea	1,333
7	United Arab Emirates	1,278
8	Vietnam	1,196
9	Australia	1,060
10	China	993
11	Qatar	901
12	Italy	868
13	Pakistan	759
14	Israel	607
15	United States	512
16	Bangladesh	438
17	Turkey	437
18	Oman	393
19	Turkmenistan	392
20	Mexico	388

Terrorist attacks

Number of incidences, 2015

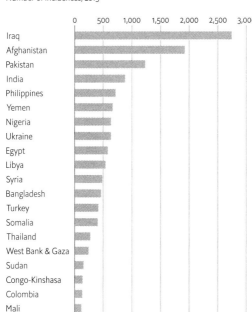

Space and peace

Manned space missions
Firsts and selected events

1957	Man-made satellite
	Dog in space, Laika
1961	Human in space, Yuri Gagarin
1963	Woman in space, Valentina Tereshkova
1964	Space crew, one pilot and two passengers
1965	Spacewalk, Alexei Leonov
	Eight days in space achieved (needed to travel to moon and back)
1968	Live television broadcast from space
1968	Moon orbit
1969	Moon landing
1971	Space station, Salyut
	Drive on Moon
1973	Space laboratory, Skylab
1978	Non-Amercian, non-Soviet, Vladimir Remek (Czechoslovakia)
1982	Space shuttle, *Columbia* (first craft to carry four crew members)
1986	Space shuttle explosion, *Challenger*
	Mir space station activated
1990	Hubble telescope deployed
2001	Dennis Tito, paying space tourist
2003	China manned space flight, Yang Liwei
2004	*SpaceShipOne*, successful private manned suborbital space flight
2010	SpaceX's privately funded spacecraft made an orbital flight
2014	Rosetta probe landed on comet *67P* after 12-year mission

Orbital launches

2016		Commercial	Non-commercial[b]	Total	*2005–16*
1	United States	11	11	22	218
2	China	0	22	22	163
3	Russia	2	15	17	330
4	Europe	8	3	11	92
5	India	0	7	7	37
6	Japan	0	4	4	36
7	Israel	0	1	1	4
	North Korea	0	1	1	4

Global Peace Index[b]

Most peaceful, 2017			*Least peaceful, 2017*		
1	Iceland	1.111	**1**	Syria	3.814
2	New Zealand	1.241	**2**	South Sudan	3.524
3	Portugal	1.258	**3**	Iraq	3.556
4	Austria	1.265	**4**	Afghanistan	3.567
5	Denmark	1.337	**5**	Somalia	3.387
6	Czech Republic	1.360	**6**	Yemen	3.412
7	Slovenia	1.364	**7**	Ukraine	3.184
8	Canada	1.371	**8**	Sudan	3.213
9	Switzerland	1.373	**9**	Libya	3.328
10	Ireland	1.408	**10**	Pakistan	3.058

a Government and non-profit launches.
b Ranks 163 countries using 23 indicators which gauge the level of safety and security in society, the extent of domestic or international conflict and the degree of militarisation.

Environment

Biggest emitters of carbon dioxide
Million tonnes, 2013

1	China	10,249.5	31	United Arab Emirates	169.1
2	United States	5,186.2	32	Iraq	167.8
3	India	2,034.8	33	Pakistan	153.4
4	Russia	1,789.1	34	Vietnam	152.6
5	Japan	1,243.4	35	Algeria	134.2
6	Germany	757.3	36	Uzbekistan	103.2
7	Iran	617.0	37	Czech Republic	98.7
8	South Korea	592.5	38	Philippines	98.2
9	Saudi Arabia	541.4	39	Kuwait	98.0
10	Brazil	503.7	40	Nigeria	95.7
11	Mexico	488.6	41	Belgium	93.6
12	Indonesia	479.4	42	Colombia	89.6
13	Canada	475.7	43	Qatar	85.0
14	South Africa	471.2	44	Chile	83.2
15	United Kingdom	457.5	45	Israel	71.1
16	Australia	377.9	46	Romania	70.7
17	Italy	344.8	47	Greece	69.2
18	France	333.2	48	Bangladesh	69.0
19	Turkey	323.5	49	Turkmenistan	66.9
20	Thailand	303.1	50	Belarus	63.8
21	Poland	302.3	51	Austria	62.4
22	Taiwan	295.0	52	Oman	61.2
23	Ukraine	271.1	53	Norway	59.6
24	Kazakhstan	262.9	54	Morocco	58.6
25	Spain	237.0	55	Peru	57.2
26	Malaysia	236.5	56	Libya	51.0
27	Egypt	213.0	57	Singapore	50.6
28	Argentina	189.8	58	North Korea	50.1
29	Venezuela	185.5	59	Trinidad & Tobago	46.5
30	Netherlands	170.0			

Largest amount of carbon dioxide emitted per person
Tonnes, 2013

1	Qatar	40.5	18	Taiwan	12.6
2	Trinidad & Tobago	34.5	19	Russia	12.5
3	Kuwait	27.3	20	South Korea	11.8
4	Bahrain	23.7	21	Norway	11.7
5	Brunei	18.9	22	Netherlands	10.1
6	Luxembourg	18.7	23	Japan	9.8
	United Arab Emirates	18.7	24	Guam	9.7
8	Saudi Arabia	17.9	25	Czech Republic	9.4
9	United States	16.4		Singapore	9.4
10	Australia	16.3	27	Germany	9.2
11	Oman	15.7	28	South Africa	8.9
12	Kazakhstan	15.4	29	Israel	8.8
13	Estonia	15.1	30	Finland	8.5
14	New Caledonia	14.7	31	Belgium	8.4
15	Mongolia	14.5	32	Bahamas	8.2
16	Canada	13.5	33	Libya	8.1
17	Turkmenistan	12.8			

Most polluted capital cities
Annual mean particulate matter concentration[a], micrograms per cubic metre
2014 or latest

1	Riyadh, Saudi Arabia	368.0	13	Beijing, China	108.0
2	Kabul, Afghanistan	260.0	14	Tunis, Tunisia	90.0
3	Delhi, India	229.1	15	Kathmandu, Nepal	88.3
4	Islamabad, Pakistan	216.9	16	Lima, Peru	87.8
5	Baghdad, Iraq	208.0	17	Muscat, Oman	82.1
6	Cairo, Egypt	179.0	18	San Salvador, El Salvador	77.2
7	Kampala, Uganda	170.4	19	Ankara, Turkey	77.0
8	Doha, Qatar	167.6	20	Tehran, Iran	76.9
9	Ulaanbaatar, Mongolia	165.1	21	Skopje, Macedonia	73.8
10	Dhaka, Bangladesh	158.1	22	Amman, Jordan	68.0
11	Dakar, Senegal	141.3	23	Yaoundé, Cameroon	65.0
12	Abu Dhabi, UAE	132.0	24	Santiago, Chile	64.4

Lowest access to an improved water source
% of population, 2014

1	South Sudan	6.7	15	Benin	19.6
2	Niger	10.8	16	Guinea	20.0
3	Togo	11.6	17	Mozambique	20.4
4	Madagascar	11.9	18	Guinea-Bissau	20.7
5	Chad	12.0	19	Central African Rep.	21.7
6	Sierra Leone	13.1	20	Ivory Coast	22.3
7	Ghana	14.8	21	Sudan	23.6
8	Congo-Brazzaville	14.9	22	Mali	24.2
9	Tanzania	15.0	23	Ethiopia	26.8
10	Eritrea	15.6	24	Haiti	27.4
11	Liberia	16.6	25	Congo-Kinshasa	28.3
12	Papua New Guinea	18.9	26	Nigeria	29.3
13	Uganda	19.0	27	Kenya	30.1
14	Burkina Faso	19.4	28	Lesotho	30.2

Lowest access to electricity
% of population, 2013

1	South Sudan	4.0	17	Papua New Guinea	19.7
2	Burundi	6.5	18	Mozambique	20.2
3	Chad	7.6	19	Zambia	23.6
4	Malawi	9.0	20	Ethiopia	25.2
5	Liberia	9.8	21	Lesotho	25.3
6	Central African Rep.	11.8	22	Mali	26.1
7	Madagascar	12.9	23	Guinea	26.8
8	Sierra Leone	13.5	24	Kenya	28.2
9	Niger	13.8	25	North Korea	31.2
10	Guinea-Bissau	13.9	26	Angola	33.3
	Uganda	13.9	27	Mauritania	36.2
12	Congo-Kinshasa	14.8	28	Zimbabwe	36.5
13	Rwanda	15.2	29	Benin	37.3
14	Tanzania	16.4	30	Haiti	37.5
15	Burkina Faso	16.9	31	Sudan	38.5
16	Somalia	18.1	32	Congo-Brazzaville	42.1

a Particulates less than 10 microns in diameter.

Largest forests

Sq km, 2014

1	Russia	8,149,715
2	Brazil	4,945,220
3	Canada	3,471,156
4	United States	3,098,200
5	China	2,067,791
6	Congo-Kinshasa	1,528,894
7	Australia	1,244,430
8	Indonesia	916,944
9	Peru	741,406
10	India	705,036
11	Mexico	661,316
12	Colombia	585,285
13	Angola	579,808
14	Bolivia	550,530
15	Zambia	488,016
16	Venezuela	468,474
17	Tanzania	464,320
18	Mozambique	381,464
19	Papua New Guinea	335,618
20	Myanmar	295,874
21	Sweden	280,730
22	Argentina	274,088
23	Japan	249,596
24	Gabon	228,000
25	Congo-Brazzaville	223,494
26	Finland	222,180
27	Central African Rep.	221,856
28	Malaysia	221,808
29	Sudan	193,844
30	Cameroon	190,360

Most forested

% of land area, 2014

1	Suriname	98.3
2	Gabon	88.5
3	Guyana	84.0
4	Laos	80.5
5	Papua New Guinea	74.1
6	Finland	73.1
7	Brunei	72.1
8	Guinea-Bissau	70.5
9	Sweden	68.9
10	Japan	68.5
11	Malaysia	67.5
12	Congo-Kinshasa	67.4
13	Zambia	65.6
14	Congo-Brazzaville	65.4
15	South Korea	63.5
16	Panama	62.3
17	Slovenia	62.0
18	Montenegro	61.5
19	Brazil	59.2
20	Peru	57.9
21	Equatorial Guinea	56.3
22	Puerto Rico	55.5
23	Fiji	55.4
24	Cambodia	54.3
25	Latvia	54.0
26	Costa Rica	53.4
27	Venezuela	53.1
28	Colombia	52.8
29	Estonia	52.7
30	Tanzania	52.4

Deforestation

Biggest % change in forested land, 1990–2014

Decrease

1	Togo	-69.7
2	Nigeria	-57.0
3	Uganda	-53.4
4	Mauritania	-45.1
5	Honduras	-42.1
6	Niger	-40.6
7	Pakistan	-40.0
8	North Korea	-37.1
9	Sudan	-36.9
10	Zimbabwe	-35.1
11	Nicaragua	-31.0
12	El Salvador	-28.5
13	Mali	-28.3
14	Timor-Leste	-27.8
15	Cambodia	-26.0
	Paraguay	-26.0
17	Ethiopia	-25.6

Increase

1	Iceland	197.5
2	French Polynesia	181.8
3	Bahrain	168.2
4	Uruguay	128.4
5	Kuwait	81.2
6	Dominican Rep.	76.5
7	Puerto Rico	71.7
8	Egypt	64.5
9	Ireland	60.9
10	Tunisia	60.3
11	Vietnam	56.4
12	Cuba	52.9
13	Rwanda	48.8
14	Spain	33.1
15	Montenegro	32.1
16	Syria	32.0
17	China	31.6

Dams and reservoirs

Most dams[a]

1	China	23,842	16	Germany	371
2	United States	9,261	17	Norway	335
3	India	5,102	18	Albania	307
4	Japan	3,112	19	Zimbabwe	254
5	Brazil	1,411	20	Romania	246
6	Canada	1,170	21	Thailand	218
7	South Africa	1,114	22	Portugal	217
8	Spain	1,063	23	Sweden	190
9	Turkey	972	24	Bulgaria	181
10	Iran	802	25	Austria	171
11	France	712	26	Switzerland	167
12	United Kingdom	596	27	Greece	164
13	Mexico	571	28	Pakistan	163
14	Australia	570	29	Algeria	154
15	Italy	542	30	Morocco	150

Dams

Largest reservoir capacity[a], cubic kms

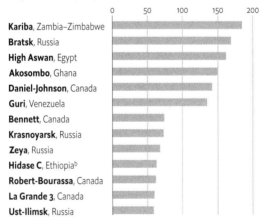

	0	50	100	150	200

Kariba, Zambia–Zimbabwe
Bratsk, Russia
High Aswan, Egypt
Akosombo, Ghana
Daniel-Johnson, Canada
Guri, Venezuela
Bennett, Canada
Krasnoyarsk, Russia
Zeya, Russia
Hidase C, Ethiopia[b]
Robert-Bourassa, Canada
La Grande 3, Canada
Ust-Ilimsk, Russia

Slums

% of urban population living in slums, 2014

1	South Sudan	95.6	8	Madagascar	77.2
2	Central African Rep.	93.3	9	Sierra Leone	75.6
3	Sudan	91.6	10	Congo-Kinshasa	74.8
4	Chad	88.2	11	Haiti	74.4
5	Guinea-Bissau	82.3	12	Ethiopia	73.9
6	Mozambique	80.3	13	Somalia	73.6
7	Mauritania	79.9	14	Niger	70.1

a As of April 2017. b Under construction spring 2017.

Environmental Performance Index

Scores on biodiversity[a], 2016, 0=lowest, 100=highest

Best			Worst		
1	Belgium	100.0	**1**	Somalia	20.9
	Czech Republic	100.0	**2**	Afghanistan	21.3
	Estonia	100.0	**3**	Turkey	22.5
	Germany	100.0	**4**	Haiti	24.4
	Hungary	100.0	**5**	Libya	24.7
	Luxembourg	100.0	**6**	Lesotho	26.2
	Slovakia	100.0	**7**	Barbados	26.5
	Slovenia	100.0	**8**	Syria	31.2
9	Poland	99.8	**9**	Iraq	34.6
10	France	99.5	**10**	Maldives	35.9
11	Croatia	99.0	**11**	Bosnia & Herz.	36.6
	Italy	99.0	**12**	Eritrea	41.1
	United Kingdom	99.0	**13**	Sudan	42.8
14	Lithuania	98.6	**14**	Jordan	42.9
15	Latvia	97.8		Mauritania	42.9
16	Denmark	97.6	**16**	Gambia, The	43.6
17	Zambia	97.1	**17**	Lebanon	43.9
18	Finland	96.9	**18**	Papua New Guinea	46.5
19	Spain	96.7	**19**	Yemen	48.0
20	Portugal	95.8	**20**	Oman	48.7
	Romania	95.8	**21**	Liberia	49.7
22	Namibia	95.7	**22**	Turkmenistan	49.9
	Venezuela	95.7	**23**	Guyana	51.3
24	Greece	94.8	**24**	Swaziland	52.9

Worst natural catastrophes

2015

	Country/region	Type of disaster	Deaths
1	Nepal	Earthquake	8,960
2	India	Heatwave	2,248
3	Pakistan	Heatwave	1,270
4	Europe	Heatwave	1,200
5	Malawi/Mozambique/Zimbabwe	Floods	451
6	China	Ship hit by strong wind	442
7	Afghanistan	Earthquake	399
8	Guatemala	Landslide	350
9	Afghanistan	Avalanches	291
10	India (Chennai)	Flash floods	289
11	India	Monsoon floods	206
12	Pakistan	Monsoon floods	166
13	Myanmar	Monsoon floods	125
14	Egypt	Heatwave	110
15	India (Purnia)	Thunderstorms/hail	100
16	Colombia	Flash floods	93
17	Kenya	Floods	89
18	Philippines/Japan/North Korea	Flooding/landslides	82
19	India (Andhra Pradesh)	Monsoon floods	81
	India (Gujarat)	Monsoon rains	81

a Based on protection of species, land and marine area.

Life expectancy

Highest life expectancy

Years, 2015–20

1	Monaco[a]	89.5	25	Portugal	81.7
2	Hong Kong	84.5	26	Greece	81.6
3	Japan	84.1	27	Finland	81.5
4	Italy	83.8		Germany	81.5
5	Singapore	83.7		Ireland	81.5
6	Switzerland	83.6	30	Belgium	81.4
7	Spain	83.2		Macao	81.4
8	Iceland	83.1	32	Bermuda[a]	81.3
9	Australia	83.0		United Kingdom	81.3
	Israel	83.0	34	Channel Islands	81.2
11	France	82.9		Malta	81.2
12	Andorra[a]	82.8		Virgin Islands (US)	81.2
	South Korea	82.8	37	Slovenia	81.0
	Sweden	82.8	38	Cyprus	80.8
15	Chile	82.7		Réunion	80.8
16	Canada	82.6	40	Denmark	80.7
	Martinique	82.6	41	French Guiana	80.3
18	New Zealand	82.4		Lebanon	80.3
19	Luxembourg	82.3	43	Puerto Rico	80.2
20	Austria	82.1	44	Costa Rica	80.1
	Netherlands	82.1		Taiwan[a]	80.1
	Norway	82.1	46	Cuba	80.0
23	Guadeloupe	82.0		Guam	80.0
24	Liechtenstein[a]	81.9	48	United States	79.6

Highest male life expectancy

Years, 2015–20

1	Monaco[a]	85.6		Japan	80.8
2	Hong Kong	81.7		New Zealand	80.8
	Iceland	81.7	12	Andorra[a]	80.6
4	Switzerland	81.6		Singapore	80.6
5	Israel	81.3	14	Spain	80.5
	Italy	81.3	15	Netherlands	80.3
7	Australia	81.1	16	Luxembourg	80.2
	Sweden	81.1		Norway	80.2
9	Canada	80.8	18	France	80.0

Highest female life expectancy

Years, 2015–20

1	Monaco[a]	93.5		Switzerland	85.5
2	Hong Kong	87.4	11	Chile	85.3
3	Japan	87.3	12	Andorra[a]	85.1
4	Singapore	86.7	13	Australia	85.0
5	Italy	86.0		Guadeloupe	85.0
6	Spain	85.8	15	Israel	84.6
7	South Korea	85.7		Liechtenstein[a]	84.6
8	France	85.6	17	Bermuda[a]	84.5
9	Martinique	85.5		Iceland	84.5

a 2016 estimate.

Lowest life expectancy
Years, 2015–20

1	Swaziland	48.7	26	Ghana	62.0
2	Lesotho	50.4		Liberia	62.0
3	Sierra Leone	52.1	28	Zambia	62.3
4	Chad	52.5	29	Zimbabwe	62.4
5	Ivory Coast	52.8	30	Niger	62.8
6	Central African Rep.	53.3	31	Papua New Guinea	63.2
7	Angola	53.7	32	Kenya	63.3
8	Nigeria	53.8	33	Mauritania	63.6
9	Guinea-Bissau	56.2	34	Congo-Brazzaville	63.9
10	Mozambique	56.2		Haiti	63.9
11	Somalia	56.5	36	Sudan	64.2
12	Cameroon	57.0	37	Yemen	64.5
13	South Sudan	57.1	38	Botswana	64.6
14	South Africa	57.7	39	Eritrea	65.1
15	Burundi	58.1	40	Namibia	65.3
16	Equatorial Guinea	58.6	41	Ethiopia	65.8
17	Mali	59.7		Malawi	65.8
18	Burkina Faso	59.8	43	Gabon	66.0
19	Congo-Kinshasa	59.9		Rwanda	66.0
20	Guinea	60.2	45	Turkmenistan	66.1
21	Benin	60.3	46	Madagascar	66.4
22	Uganda	61.0		Tanzania	66.4
23	Gambia, The	61.1	48	Myanmar	66.5
	Togo	61.1	49	Guyana	66.8
25	Afghanistan	61.5		Pakistan	66.8

Lowest male life expectancy
Years, 2015–20

1	Swaziland	49.5	11	Mozambique	55.0
2	Lesotho	50.3	12	South Africa	55.7
3	Central African Rep.	51.1	13	Cameroon	55.9
4	Chad	51.4	14	Burundi	56.0
5	Sierra Leone	51.5	15	South Sudan	56.1
6	Ivory Coast	52.0	16	Equatorial Guinea	57.3
7	Angola	52.2	17	Congo-Kinshasa	58.4
8	Nigeria	53.3	18	Burkina Faso	58.5
9	Guinea-Bissau	54.4	19	Benin	58.8
10	Somalia	54.9	20	Uganda	58.9

Lowest female life expectancy
Years, 2015–20

1	Swaziland	47.7	10	Guinea-Bissau	58.0
2	Lesotho	50.2	11	South Sudan	58.1
3	Sierra Leone	52.7	12	Cameroon	58.2
4	Chad	53.6		Somalia	58.2
5	Ivory Coast	53.8	14	South Africa	59.3
6	Nigeria	54.1	15	Mali	59.6
7	Angola	55.2	16	Equatorial Guinea	60.0
8	Central African Rep.	55.5	17	Burundi	60.2
9	Mozambique	57.3	18	Guinea	60.7

Death rates and infant mortality

Highest death rates
Number of deaths per 1,000 population, 2015–20

#	Country	Rate		#	Country	Rate
1	Lithuania	16.2			Monacoᵃ	9.6
2	Ukraine	15.7		50	Austria	9.5
3	Bulgaria	15.6		51	North Korea	9.4
4	Latvia	15.4			Uruguay	9.4
5	Swaziland	14.9		53	Mali	9.3
6	Lesotho	14.7			Malta	9.3
7	Belarus	14.6		55	Guinea	9.2
8	Russia	14.3		56	Channel Islands	9.1
9	Romania	13.7			France	9.1
10	Hungary	13.5			Spain	9.1
11	Chad	13.3			United Kingdom	9.1
12	Central African Rep.	13.1		60	Benin	9.0
	Serbia	13.1			Kazakhstan	9.0
14	Croatia	12.8			Martinique	9.0
	Ivory Coast	12.8			Sweden	9.0
	Sierra Leone	12.8		64	Burkina Faso	8.9
17	Angola	12.7		65	Netherlands	8.8
	Estonia	12.7		66	Ghana	8.5
19	South Africa	12.6			Guyana	8.5
20	Nigeria	12.2			Haiti	8.5
21	Moldova	11.7			Uganda	8.5
22	Georgia	11.5		70	Bermudaᵃ	8.4
23	Guinea-Bissau	11.4			Myanmar	8.4
24	Germany	11.3			Thailand	8.4
	Greece	11.3			United States	8.4
	Somalia	11.3		74	Niger	8.3
27	Bosnia & Herz.	11.1		75	Cuba	8.2
28	Barbados	10.9			Gambia, The	8.2
	Japan	10.9			Togo	8.2
	South Sudan	10.9		78	Liberia	8.1
31	Mozambique	10.8			Virgin Islands (US)	8.1
32	Portugal	10.7		80	Mauritius	8.0
33	Cameroon	10.6			Puerto Rico	8.0
	Czech Republic	10.6			Switzerland	8.0
35	Burundi	10.5			Zambia	8.0
36	Poland	10.4		84	Gabon	7.9
37	Equatorial Guinea	10.3			Norway	7.9
	Montenegro	10.3		86	Congo-Brazzaville	7.8
39	Italy	10.2			Turkmenistan	7.8
	Slovakia	10.2			Zimbabwe	7.8
41	Slovenia	10.0		89	Albania	7.7
42	Finland	9.9			Botswana	7.7
43	Trinidad and Tobago	9.8			Mauritania	7.7
44	Belgium	9.7		92	Afghanistan	7.6
	Macedonia	9.7			Azerbaijan	7.6
46	Armenia	9.6			Kenya	7.6
	Congo-Kinshasa	9.6			Papua New Guinea	7.6
	Denmark	9.6			Suriname	7.6

Note: Both death and, in particular, infant mortality rates can be underestimated in certain countries where not all deaths are officially recorded.   a 2016 estimate.

Highest infant mortality
Number of deaths per 1,000 live births, 2015–20

1	Angola	88	**23**	Liberia	52
2	Chad	87		Malawi	52
3	Central African Rep.	84	**25**	Guinea	50
4	Guinea-Bissau	82		Lesotho	50
5	Sierra Leone	81		Niger	50
6	Burundi	71	**28**	Yemen	49
7	Mali	70	**29**	Kenya	48
	Somalia	70		Sudan	48
9	Nigeria	68	**31**	Ghana	47
	South Sudan	68		Zambia	47
11	Congo-Kinshasa	66	**33**	Papua New Guinea	45
12	Cameroon	65	**34**	Congo-Brazzaville	44
13	Afghanistan	64	**35**	Ethiopia	43
14	Benin	63		Gambia, The	43
	Ivory Coast	63		Myanmar	43
	Mauritania	63		Rwanda	43
	Pakistan	63		Turkmenistan	43
18	Equatorial Guinea	62	**40**	Haiti	42
19	Burkina Faso	58		Togo	42
	Swaziland	58	**42**	Uzbekistan	41
21	Mozambique	57	**43**	Zimbabwe	39
22	Uganda	56			

Lowest death rates
No. deaths per 1,000 pop., 2015–20

1	Qatar	1.5
2	United Arab Emirates	1.8
3	Bahrain	2.5
4	Kuwait	2.6
5	Oman	2.7
6	French Guiana	3.0
7	Brunei	3.2
8	Saudi Arabia	3.5
	West Bank & Gaza	3.5
10	Maldives	3.7
11	Jordan	3.8
12	Lebanon	4.5
13	Iran	4.6
14	Nicaragua	4.8
15	Guam	4.9
	Macau	4.9
	Mexico	4.9
18	Costa Rica	5.0
	Honduras	5.0
	Iraq	5.0
21	Algeria	5.1
	Ecuador	5.1
	Panama	5.1
	Singapore	5.1

Lowest infant mortality
No. deaths per 1,000 live births, 2015–20

1	Luxembourg	1
	Singapore	1
3	Czech Republic	2
	Finland	2
	Greece	2
	Hong Kong	2
	Iceland	2
	Ireland	2
	Italy	2
	Japan	2
	Monaco[a]	2
	Norway	2
	South Korea	2
	Sweden	2

Death and disease

Diabetes

Prevalence in pop. aged 20–79, %
2015 age-standardised estimate[a]

1	Mauritius	22.3
2	Kuwait	20.0
	Qatar	20.0
	Saudi Arabia	20.0
5	Bahrain	19.6
6	New Caledonia	19.6
7	French Polynesia	19.4
8	United Arab Emirates	19.3
9	Guam	18.7
10	Malaysia	17.9
11	Egypt	16.7
12	Mexico	15.8
	Réunion	15.8
14	Papua New Guinea	15.3
15	Oman	14.8
16	Fiji	13.8

Cardiovascular disease

No. of deaths per 100,000 pop.,
2012 age standardised estimate[a]

1	Turkmenistan	712.1
2	Kazakhstan	635.5
3	Mongolia	586.7
4	Uzbekistan	577.7
5	Kyrgyzstan	549.4
6	Guyana	544.8
7	Ukraine	536.1
8	Russia	531.0
9	Afghanistan	511.5
10	Tajikistan	510.3
11	Moldova	507.7
12	Armenia	473.9
13	Belarus	464.2
14	Egypt	445.1
15	Azerbaijan	442.2
16	Albania	436.2

Chronic respiratory diseases

Deaths per 100,000 population,
2012 age-standardised estimate[a]

1	India	154.8
2	Nepal	152.3
3	North Korea	133.6
4	Liberia	125.5
5	Myanmar	114.1
6	Bangladesh	106.7
7	Papua New Guinea	106.4
8	Mali	102.5
9	Lesotho	91.9
10	Pakistan	91.4
11	Swaziland	89.5
12	Laos	80.2
13	Central African Rep.	79.5
14	China	77.1
15	Equatorial Guinea	76.3
16	Angola	74.4
17	Afghanistan	65.5
18	Timor-Leste	63.2
19	Namibia	63.1
20	Congo-Kinshasa	61.4
21	Sierra Leone	61.1
22	Philippines	60.7
23	Maldives	60.2

Tuberculosis

Incidence per 100,000 pop., 2015

1	South Africa	834
2	Lesotho	788
3	Swaziland	565
4	North Korea	561
5	Mozambique	551
6	Timor-Leste	498
7	Namibia	489
8	Gabon	465
9	Papua New Guinea	432
10	Mongolia	428
11	Indonesia	395
12	Central African Rep.	391
	Zambia	391
14	Cambodia	380
15	Congo-Brazzaville	379
16	Guinea-Bissau	373
17	Angola	370
18	Myanmar	365
19	Botswana	356
20	Nigeria	322
	Philippines	322
22	Liberia	308
23	Sierra Leone	307
24	Tanzania	306
25	Somalia	274

a Assumes that every country and region has the same age profile (the age profile of the world population has been used).
Note: Statistics are not available for all countries. The number of cases diagnosed and reported depends on the quality of medical practice and administration and can be under-reported in a number of countries.

Measles immunisation

Lowest % of children aged 12–23 months, 2015

1	South Sudan	20
2	Equatorial Guinea	27
3	Somalia	46
4	Central African Rep.	49
5	Guinea	52
6	Haiti	53
	Syria	53
8	Nigeria	54
9	Angola	55
10	Ukraine	56
11	Iraq	57
12	Madagascar	58
13	Papua New Guinea	60
14	Pakistan	61
15	Chad	62
16	Liberia	64
	Montenegro	64
18	Yemen	67

DPT[a] immunisation

Lowest % of children aged 12–23 months, 2015

1	Equatorial Guinea	16
2	Ukraine	23
3	South Sudan	31
4	Syria	41
5	Somalia	42
6	Central African Rep.	47
7	Guinea	51
8	Liberia	52
9	Chad	55
10	Nigeria	56
11	Iraq	58
12	Haiti	60
	Philippines	60
14	Papua New Guinea	62
15	Angola	64
16	Niger	65
17	Mali	68

HIV/AIDS

Prevalence in adults aged 15–49, %, 2015

1	Swaziland	28.8
2	Lesotho	22.7
3	Botswana	22.2
4	South Africa	19.2
5	Zimbabwe	14.7
6	Namibia	13.3
7	Zambia	12.9
8	Mozambique	10.5
9	Malawi	9.1
10	Uganda	7.1
11	Kenya	5.9
12	Equatorial Guinea	4.9
13	Tanzania	4.7
14	Cameroon	4.5
15	Gabon	3.8
16	Central African Rep.	3.7
17	Bahamas	3.2
	Ivory Coast	3.2
19	Rwanda	2.9
20	South Sudan	2.5
21	Togo	2.4
22	Angola	2.2
23	Chad	2.0
24	Gambia, The	1.8
25	Haiti	1.7

AIDS

Deaths per 100,000 population, 2015

1	Lesotho	464
2	South Africa	330
3	Swaziland	295
4	Zimbabwe	186
5	Central African Rep.	159
6	Malawi	157
7	Botswana	141
	Cameroon	141
9	Mozambique	139
10	Equatorial Guinea	130
11	Bahamas	129
12	Namibia	126
13	Zambia	123
14	Ivory Coast	110
15	South Sudan	97
16	Kenya	78
17	Gabon	75
	Haiti	75
19	Uganda	72
20	Togo	70
21	Tanzania	67
22	Chad	61
23	Gambia, The	50
24	Angola	48
25	Ghana	47

a Diphtheria, pertussis and tetanus.

Health

Highest health spending
As % of GDP, 2014

1	United States	17.1
2	Haiti	13.2
3	Sweden	11.9
4	Switzerland	11.7
5	France	11.5
6	Germany	11.3
7	Austria	11.2
8	Cuba	11.1
	Sierra Leone	11.1
10	New Zealand	11.0
11	Netherlands	10.9
12	Denmark	10.8
13	Belgium	10.6
	Lesotho	10.6
15	Canada	10.4
	Serbia	10.4
17	Moldova	10.3
18	Japan	10.2
19	Liberia	10.0
20	Paraguay	9.8
21	Finland	9.7
	Malta	9.7
	Norway	9.7
24	Bosnia & Herz.	9.6
	Malawi	9.6

Lowest health spending
As % of GDP, 2014

1	Timor-Leste	1.5
2	Laos	1.9
3	Turkmenistan	2.1
4	Qatar	2.2
5	Myanmar	2.3
6	Brunei	2.6
	Congo-Kinshasa	2.6
	Pakistan	2.6
9	South Sudan	2.7
10	Bangladesh	2.8
	Indonesia	2.8
12	Kuwait	3.0
	Madagascar	3.0
14	Angola	3.3
	Eritrea	3.3
	Syria	3.3
17	Gabon	3.4
18	Sri Lanka	3.5
19	Bhutan	3.6
	Chad	3.6
	Ghana	3.6
	Oman	3.6
	United Arab Emirates	3.6
24	Nigeria	3.7
25	Equatorial Guinea	3.8
	Mauritania	3.8

Highest pop. per doctor
2014 or latest[a]

1	Liberia	71,429
2	Malawi	52,632
	Niger	52,632
4	Ethiopia	45,455
	Sierra Leone	45,455
6	Tanzania	32,258
7	Somalia	28,571
8	Gambia, The	26,316
9	Mozambique	25,000
10	Guinea-Bissau	22,222
11	Burkina Faso	21,277
12	Togo	18,868
13	Rwanda	17,857
14	Papua New Guinea	17,241
15	Benin	16,949
	Senegal	16,949
17	Mauritania	14,627
18	Timor-Leste	13,699
19	Mali	12,048
	Zimbabwe	12,048

Lowest pop. per doctor
2014 or latest[a]

1	Qatar	129
2	Monaco	140
3	Cuba	149
4	Greece	162
5	Spain	202
6	Belgium	205
7	Austria	207
8	Russia	232
9	Georgia	234
	Norway	234
11	Lithuania	243
12	Portugal	244
13	Switzerland	247
14	Andorra	250
15	Belarus	255
	Sweden	255
17	Germany	257
18	Argentina	259
	Bulgaria	259
20	Italy	266

a 2010–14

Obesity[a]

Adult population 18 years or over, % point increase 1975–2014

● Men　◉ Women

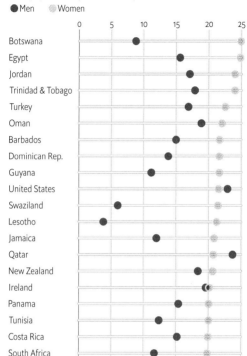

	0	5	10	15	20	25
Botswana						
Egypt						
Jordan						
Trinidad & Tobago						
Turkey						
Oman						
Barbados						
Dominican Rep.						
Guyana						
United States						
Swaziland						
Lesotho						
Jamaica						
Qatar						
New Zealand						
Ireland						
Panama						
Tunisia						
Costa Rica						
South Africa						

Food deficit

Average kilocalories needed[b] per person per day, 2016 or latest

Highest deficit

1	Haiti	546
2	Zambia	405
3	Central African Rep.	380
4	North Korea	343
5	Namibia	325
6	Chad	261
7	Zimbabwe	259
8	Liberia	256
9	Tajikistan	250
10	Tanzania	238
11	Ethiopia	236
12	Rwanda	232

Lowest deficit

1	Turkey	1
2	Argentina	2
3	Tunisia	3
4	South Korea	4
5	Cuba	7
6	Saudi Arabia	9
	Venezuela	9
8	Brazil	10
9	Azerbaijan	12
	Brunei	12
	Egypt	12
12	Jordan	13
	South Africa	13

a Defined as body mass index of 30 or more – see page 248.
b To lift the undernourished from their status.

Telephones and the internet

Mobile telephones
Subscribers per 100 population, 2015

1	Macau	324.4	26	Argentina	146.7
2	Kuwait	231.8	27	Singapore	146.5
3	Hong Kong	228.7	28	Turkmenistan	145.9
4	Maldives	206.7	29	El Salvador	145.3
5	United Arab Emirates	187.3	30	Ukraine	144.0
6	Bahrain	185.3	31	Malaysia	143.9
7	Jordan	179.4	32	Poland	142.7
8	Saudi Arabia	176.6	33	Italy	142.1
9	Panama	174.2	34	Mauritius	140.6
10	Botswana	169.0	35	Mali	139.6
11	South Africa	164.5	36	Lithuania	139.5
12	Montenegro	162.2	37	Gambia, The	137.8
13	Gabon	161.1	38	Suriname	136.8
14	Uruguay	160.2	39	Switzerland	136.5
15	Russia	160.0	40	Finland	135.4
16	Oman	159.9	41	Israel	133.5
17	Qatar	159.1	42	Cambodia	133.0
18	Trinidad & Tobago	157.7	43	Australia	132.8
19	Austria	157.4		Kyrgyzstan	132.8
20	Libya	157.0	45	Indonesia	132.3
21	Kazakhstan	156.9	46	Vietnam	130.6
22	Thailand	152.7	47	Sweden	130.4
23	Costa Rica	150.7	48	Tunisia	129.9
24	Estonia	148.7	49	Ghana	129.7
25	Luxembourg	148.5	50	Chile	129.5

Landline telephones
Per 100 population, 2015

1	Monaco	128.1	16	Andorra	48.0
2	Virgin Islands (US)	71.1	17	Greece	47.3
3	France	59.9	18	Liechtenstein	46.3
4	Taiwan	59.7	19	Portugal	44.1
5	Hong Kong	59.2	20	Canada	43.5
6	South Korea	58.1	21	Israel	43.1
7	Germany	54.9	22	Austria	42.2
8	Barbados	54.6	23	Spain	41.5
9	Malta	53.4	24	Netherlands	41.3
10	United Kingdom	52.0	25	Ireland	40.9
11	Luxembourg	51.0	26	New Zealand	40.2
12	Switzerland	50.3	27	Belgium	40.1
13	Japan	50.2	28	Guam	40.0
14	Iceland	49.9	29	United States	38.4
15	Belarus	49.0	30	Iran	38.3

Internet users

Per 100 population, 2015

1	Bermuda	98.3	26	Australia	84.6
2	Iceland	98.2	27	Austria	83.9
3	Luxembourg	97.3	28	Kuwait	82.1
4	Andorra	96.9		Singapore	82.1
5	Norway	96.8	30	Czech Republic	81.3
6	Liechtenstein	96.6	31	Ireland	80.1
7	Denmark	96.3	32	Puerto Rico	79.5
8	Bahrain	93.5	33	Latvia	79.2
9	Monaco	93.4	34	Spain	78.7
10	Netherlands	93.1	35	Bahamas	78.0
11	Qatar	92.9		Taiwan	78.0
12	Finland	92.7	37	Macau	77.6
13	United Kingdom	92.0		Slovakia	77.6
14	United Arab Emirates	91.2	39	Israel	77.4
15	Japan	91.1	40	Azerbaijan	77.0
16	Sweden	90.6	41	Malta	76.2
17	South Korea	89.6	42	Barbados	76.1
18	Canada	88.5	43	United States	74.5
19	Estonia	88.4	44	Oman	74.2
20	New Zealand	88.2	45	Lebanon	74.0
21	Germany	87.6		New Caledonia	74.0
22	Switzerland	87.5	47	Guam	73.1
23	Belgium	85.1		Slovenia	73.1
24	Hong Kong	84.9	49	Hungary	72.8
25	France	84.7	50	Cyprus	71.7

Broadband

Fixed-broadband subscriptions per 100 population, 2015

1	Monaco	47.9	23	United States	31.0
2	Bermuda	45.7	24	Greece	30.9
3	Switzerland	45.1	25	Japan	30.7
4	Denmark	42.5	26	Estonia	30.0
5	Liechtenstein	41.9	27	Portugal	29.6
6	Netherlands	41.7	28	Macau	29.1
7	France	41.3	29	Austria	28.7
8	South Korea	40.2		Spain	28.7
9	Norway	39.7	31	Australia	28.5
10	United Kingdom	38.6	32	Lithuania	27.8
11	Andorra	37.9	33	Ireland	27.7
12	Malta	37.8	34	Slovenia	27.6
13	Germany	37.2	35	Hungary	27.4
14	Iceland	37.0		Israel	27.4
15	Belgium	36.8	37	Czech Republic	27.3
16	Canada	36.3	38	Barbados	27.2
17	Sweden	36.1	39	Singapore	26.4
18	Luxembourg	35.9	40	Uruguay	26.3
19	Hong Kong	32.1	41	Lebanon	25.4
20	Finland	31.7	42	Latvia	24.8
21	New Zealand	31.6	43	Italy	24.4
22	Belarus	31.4	44	Taiwan	24.3

Arts and entertainment

Music sales

Total including downloads, $bn, 2016

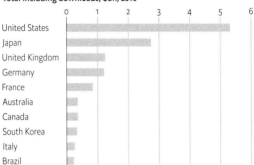

$ per person, 2016

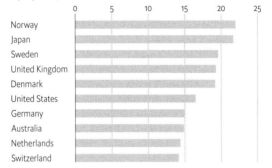

Book publishing
New titles per million population, 2015

1	United Kingdom	2,710	15	United States	1,043
2	Iceland	2,628	16	Georgia[b]	969
3	Denmark	2,326	17	Hungary[a]	920
4	Slovenia[a]	1,831	18	South Korea	909
	Taiwan[a]	1,831	19	Austria[a]	757
6	France	1,643	20	Bosnia & Herz.	731
7	Spain	1,552	21	Russia[a]	699
8	Czech Republic[a]	1,509	22	Sweden	695
9	Netherlands	1,482	23	Argentina	687
	Switzerland	1,482	24	Turkey[a]	670
11	Norway	1,268	25	Finland[b]	640
12	Australia[a]	1,176	26	Japan	603
13	Germany	1,084	27	Poland	547
14	Italy	1,078	28	Belgium	459

a 2013   b 2014

Cinema attendances

Total visits, m, 2015

1	India	2,191.9
2	United States	1,286.8
3	China	1,050.6
4	Mexico	276.0
5	South Korea	219.4
6	France	213.0
7	Russia	171.7
8	Japan	161.1
9	United Kingdom	157.8
10	Brazil	156.0
11	Germany	119.1
12	Italy	112.5
13	Spain	85.9
14	Australia	78.2
15	Malaysia	72.1
16	Turkey	65.4
17	Argentina	49.7
18	Colombia	49.1
19	Philippines	41.9
20	Poland	40.9
21	Peru	40.1
22	Netherlands	31.1
23	Thailand	28.9
24	Hong Kong	28.6
25	Venezuela	27.7
26	Chile	22.4
27	Singapore	22.2
28	South Africa	20.6
29	Belgium	20.4
30	United Arab Emirates	17.6

Visits per person, 2015

1	Iceland	4.3
	South Korea	4.3
3	Singapore	4.0
	United States	4.0
5	Hong Kong	3.9
6	Australia	3.3
	France	3.3
	New Zealand	3.3
9	Bahrain	3.1
	Ireland	3.1
11	United Kingdom	2.4
12	Malaysia	2.3
13	Luxembourg	2.2
	Mexico	2.2
	Norway	2.2
16	Denmark	2.1
	Estonia	2.1
18	Israel	2.0
	United Arab Emirates	2.0
20	Spain	1.9
21	Belgium	1.8
	Italy	1.8
	Netherlands	1.8
24	India	1.7
	Malta	1.7
	Sweden	1.7
	Switzerland	1.7
28	Austria	1.6
29	Germany	1.5
30	Finland	1.4

Oscar nominations by ethnicity

2001–17

Best actor		*Best actress*	
White	68	White	76
Black	11	Black	4
Latino	5	Latino	3
Other	1	Other	2

Supporting actor		*Supporting actress*	
White	71	White	68
Black	7	Black	12
Latino	4	Latino	2
Other	3	Other	3

The press

Daily newspapers
Highest daily circulation, m, 2015

1	India	285.1		16	Egypt	4.7
2	China	142.1		17	Vietnam	4.0
3	Japan	44.2		18	Philippines	3.9
4	United States	42.4		19	Hong Kong	3.8
5	Germany	16.0		20	Italy	3.7
6	United Kingdom	11.3		21	Taiwan	3.5
7	Indonesia	10.9		22	Netherlands	3.4
8	South Korea	10.3		23	Sweden	3.0
9	France	8.9		24	Austria	2.8
10	Brazil	8.4		25	Malaysia	2.7
11	Russia	8.3			Switzerland	2.7
12	Thailand	7.9		27	Saudi Arabia	2.3
13	Mexico	7.0			Ukraine	2.3
14	Canada	5.2		29	Spain	2.1
15	Turkey	5.0				

Press freedom[a]
Scores, 1 = best, 100 = worst, 2015

Most free			Least free		
1	Finland	8.6	1	Eritrea	83.9
2	Netherlands	8.8	2	North Korea	83.8
	Norway	8.8	3	Turkmenistan	83.4
4	Denmark	8.9	4	Syria	81.4
5	New Zealand	10.0	5	China	81.0
6	Costa Rica	11.1	6	Vietnam	74.3
7	Switzerland	11.8	7	Sudan	72.5
8	Sweden	12.3	8	Laos	71.6
9	Ireland	12.4	9	Cuba	70.2
10	Jamaica	12.5	10	Yemen	67.1
11	Austria	13.2	11	Equatorial Guinea	66.5
12	Slovakia	13.3		Iran	66.5
13	Belgium	14.2	13	Somalia	65.4
14	Estonia	14.3	14	Uzbekistan	61.2
15	Luxembourg	14.4	15	Saudi Arabia	59.7
16	Germany	14.8	16	Azerbaijan	57.9
17	Namibia	15.2		Libya	57.9
18	Canada	15.3	18	Bahrain	54.9
	Iceland	15.3	19	Kazakhstan	54.6
20	Uruguay	15.9		Rwanda	54.6
21	Czech Republic	16.7	21	Egypt	54.5
22	Portugal	17.3	22	Iraq	54.4
23	Latvia	17.4	23	Belarus	54.3
24	Australia	17.8	24	Burundi	54.1
25	Ghana	18.0	25	Brunei	53.9
26	Cyprus	18.3	26	Singapore	53.0
27	Liechtenstein	18.4	27	Swaziland	52.4
28	Chile	19.2	28	Congo-Kinshasa	51.0
			29	Turkey	50.8

a Based on data for deaths and violence against journalists, and attacks on organisations, plus 87 questions on media topics.

Nobel prize winners: 1901–2016

Nobel prize winners
By country of residence, 1901–2016

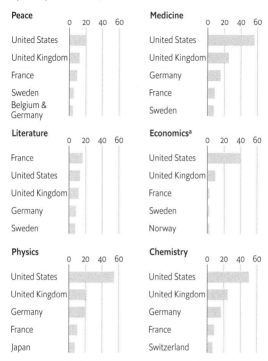

Peace

United States	
United Kingdom	
France	
Sweden	
Belgium & Germany	

Medicine

United States	
United Kingdom	
Germany	
France	
Sweden	

Literature

France	
United States	
United Kingdom	
Germany	
Sweden	

Economics[a]

United States	
United Kingdom	
France	
Sweden	
Norway	

Physics

United States	
United Kingdom	
Germany	
France	
Japan	

Chemistry

United States	
United Kingdom	
Germany	
France	
Switzerland	

Nobel prize winners: 1901–2016
By country of birth

1	United States	259	**14**	China	12
2	United Kingdom	99		Denmark	12
3	Germany	80		Norway	12
4	France	54	**17**	Australia	10
5	Sweden	29	**18**	Belgium	9
6	Poland	26		Hungary	9
	Russia	26		South Africa	9
8	Japan	24	**21**	India	8
9	Italy	19	**22**	Spain	7
10	Canada	18	**23**	Czech Republic	6
	Netherlands	18		Egypt	6
12	Austria	16		Israel	6
	Switzerland	16			

Notes: Prizes by country of residence at time awarded. When prizes have been shared in the same field, one credit given to each country. a Since 1969.

Sports champions and cheats

World Cup winners and finalists

Men's football (since 1930)	Winner	Runner-up
1 Brazil	5	2
2 Germany[a]	4	4
3 Italy	4	2
4 Argentina	2	3
5 Uruguay	2	0
6 France	1	1
7 England	1	0
Spain	1	0
9 Netherlands	0	3
10 Czechoslovakia[b]	0	2
Hungary	0	2
12 Sweden	0	1

Women's football (since 1991)	Winner	Runner-up
1 United States	3	1
2 Germany	2	1
Japan	1	1
Norway	1	1
5 Brazil	0	1
China	0	1
Sweden	0	1

Men's cricket (since 1975)	Winner	Runner-up
1 Australia	5	2
2 India	2	1
West Indies	2	1
4 Sri Lanka	1	2
5 Pakistan	1	1
6 England	0	3
7 New Zealand	0	1

Women's cricket (since 1973)	Winner	Runner-up
1 Australia	6	2
2 England	3	3
3 New Zealand	1	3
4 India	0	1
West Indies	0	1

Davis Cup, tennis (since 1900)[c]	Winner	Runner-up
1 United States	32	29
2 Australia	28	19
3 Great Britain	10	8
4 France	9	8
5 Sweden	7	5
6 Spain	5	4
7 Czech Republic[d]	3	2
Germany[a]	3	2
9 Russia	2	3
10 Italy	1	6

Note: Data as of May 2016.   a Including West Germany.   b Until 1993.
c Excludes finalists who have never won.   d Including Czechoslovakia.

Summer Olympics

Athletes sent per gold medal won, 1896–2016

Soviet Union[a]	
East Germany[b]	
United States	
Ethiopia	
China	
Russia	
Hungary	
Finland	
Jamaica	
Cuba	
Romania	
Kenya	
Australasia	
Germany	
Italy	
Turkey	
Sweden	
Georgia	
Great Britain	
North Korea	
France	
Japan	
Norway	
South Korea	
West Germany[b]	
Australia	
Bulgaria	
Kazakhstan	
Azerbaijan	
Burundi	
Ukraine	
Bahamas	
Iran	

Doping

Anti-doping rule violations, 2015

1	Russia	176	**6**	South Africa	59
2	Italy	129		Turkey	59
3	India	117	**8**	South Korea	51
4	France	84	**9**	United States	50
5	Belgium	67	**10**	Iran	48

a Unified team 1952–92.   b 1968–88

Vices

Beer drinkers

Consumption, litres per person, 2015

1	Czech Republic	142.4
2	Austria	104.7
	Germany	104.7
4	Namibia	102.7
5	Poland	99.0
6	Ireland	97.5
7	Lithuania	97.1
8	Romania	92.1
9	Estonia	91.5
10	Gabon	87.0
11	Spain	82.8
12	Slovenia	81.2
13	Panama	80.1
14	Slovakia	77.9
15	Finland	77.4
16	Latvia	77.3
17	Croatia	76.6
18	United States	75.4

Smokers

Av. ann. consumption of cigarettes per person per day, 2015

1	Moldova	7.1
2	Belarus	6.8
3	Lebanon	6.6
4	Russia	5.4
	Serbia	5.4
6	China	5.2
7	Macedonia	5.0
	Slovenia	5.0
9	Czech Republic	4.8
10	Bulgaria	4.6
11	Georgia	4.5
12	Taiwan	4.2
13	Austria	4.1
	Ukraine	4.1
15	Bosnia & Herz.	4.0
16	Azerbaijan	3.9
	Greece	3.9

Gambling losses[a]

Total, $bn, 2016

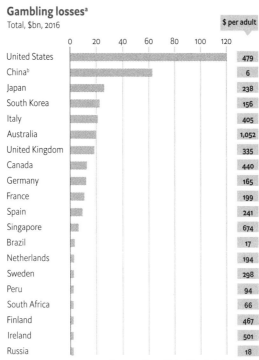

	$ per adult
United States	479
China[b]	6
Japan	238
South Korea	156
Italy	405
Australia	1,052
United Kingdom	335
Canada	440
Germany	165
France	199
Spain	241
Singapore	674
Brazil	17
Netherlands	194
Sweden	298
Peru	94
South Africa	66
Finland	467
Ireland	501
Russia	18

a Data according to H2 Gambling Capital – May 2017.
b Includes Macau and Hong Kong.

Tourism

Most tourist arrivals
Number of arrivals, '000, 2015

1	France	84,452	21	Macau	14,308
2	United States	77,510	22	India	13,284
3	Spain	68,215	23	South Korea	13,232
4	China	56,886	24	Croatia	12,683
5	Italy	50,732	25	Ukraine	12,428
6	Turkey	39,478	26	Singapore	12,051
7	Germany	34,970	27	Bahrain	11,621
8	United Kingdom	34,436	28	Taiwan	10,440
9	Russia	33,729	29	Denmark	10,424
10	Mexico	32,093	30	Indonesia	10,407
11	Thailand	29,923	31	Morocco	10,177
12	Austria	26,719	32	Portugal	9,957
13	Hong Kong	26,686	33	Ireland	9,528
14	Malaysia	25,721	34	Romania	9,331
15	Greece	23,599	35	Switzerland	9,305
16	Japan	19,737	36	Egypt	9,139
17	Saudi Arabia	17,994	37	South Africa	8,904
18	Canada	17,971	38	Czech Republic	8,707
19	Poland	16,722	39	Belgium	8,355
20	Netherlands	15,007	40	Vietnam	7,944

Biggest tourist spenders
$bn, 2015

1	China	292.2	13	Singapore	22.1
2	United States	148.4	14	Saudi Arabia	21.7
3	Germany	88.8	15	Belgium	21.1
4	United Kingdom	79.6		Netherlands	21.1
5	France	46.8	17	Brazil	20.4
6	Russia	38.4	18	Switzerland	18.5
7	Canada	29.5	19	India	17.7
8	Australia	28.3	20	Spain	17.3
9	South Korea	27.6	21	Norway	17.1
10	Italy	24.4	22	Sweden	14.4
11	Japan	23.2	23	Kuwait	13.1
12	Hong Kong	23.1	24	Mexico	12.7

Largest tourist receipts
$bn, 2015

1	United States	246.2	13	Japan	27.3
2	China	114.1	14	India	21.5
3	United Kingdom	60.7	15	Switzerland	19.6
4	Spain	56.4	16	Netherlands	19.3
5	France	54.0	17	South Korea	19.1
6	Thailand	48.5	18	Mexico	18.7
7	Germany	47.4	19	Austria	18.3
8	Hong Kong	42.6	20	Malaysia	17.6
9	Italy	39.4	21	Greece	17.3
10	Turkey	35.4	22	Singapore	16.7
11	Macau	32.0	23	Canada	16.2
12	Australia	31.3	24	United Arab Emirates	16.0

Country profiles

110	Algeria	176	Morocco
112	Argentina	178	Netherlands
114	Australia	180	New Zealand
116	Austria	182	Nigeria
118	Bangladesh	184	Norway
120	Belgium	186	Pakistan
122	Brazil	188	Peru
124	Bulgaria	190	Philippines
126	Cameroon	192	Poland
128	Canada	194	Portugal
130	Chile	196	Romania
132	China	198	Russia
134	Colombia	200	Saudi Arabia
136	Czech Republic	202	Singapore
138	Denmark	204	Slovakia
140	Egypt	206	Slovenia
142	Finland	208	South Africa
144	France	210	South Korea
146	Germany	212	Spain
148	Greece	214	Sweden
150	Hong Kong	216	Switzerland
152	Hungary	218	Taiwan
154	India	220	Thailand
156	Indonesia	222	Turkey
158	Iran	224	Ukraine
160	Ireland	226	United Arab Emirates
162	Israel	228	United Kingdom
164	Italy	230	United States
166	Ivory Coast	232	Venezuela
168	Japan	234	Vietnam
170	Kenya	236	Zimbabwe
172	Malaysia	238	Euro area
174	Mexico	240	World

ALGERIA

| Area, sq km | 2,381,741 | Capital | Algiers |
| Arable as % of total land | 3.1 | Currency | Algerian dinar (AD) |

People

Population, m	39.7	Life expectancy: men	73.4 yrs
Pop. per sq km	16.7	women	78.0 yrs
Average annual growth		Adult literacy	79.6
in pop. 2015–20, %	1.6	Fertility rate (per woman)	2.8
Pop. aged 0–24, %	45.2	Urban population, 2020, %	73.4
Pop. aged 70 and over, %	3.9		per 1,000 pop.
No. of men per 100 women	101.3	Crude birth rate	21.5
Human Development Index	74.5	Crude death rate	5.1

The economy

GDP	$165bn	GDP per head	$4,151
GDP	AD16,592bn	GDP per head in purchasing	
Av. ann. growth in real		power parity (USA=100)	26.1
GDP 2010–15	3.3%	Economic freedom index	46.5

Origins of GDP		**Components of GDP**	
	% of total		% of total
Agriculture	13	Private consumption	41
Industry, of which:	39	Public consumption	21
manufacturing	...	Investment	51
Services	48	Exports	24
		Imports	-37

Structure of employment

	% of total		% of labour force
Agriculture	8.8	Unemployed 2015	11.0
Industry	30.4	Av. ann. rate 2005–15	11.4
Services	60.5		

Energy

	m TOE		
Total output	164.0	Net energy imports as %	
Total consumption	59.0	of energy use	-177
Consumption per head			
kg oil equivalent	1,327		

Inflation and finance

			av. ann. increase 2011–16
Consumer price			
inflation 2016	5.9%	Narrow money (M1)	6.0%
Av. ann. inflation 2011–16	6.3%	Broad money	7.0%
Treasury bill rate, Dec. 2016	1.55%		

Exchange rates

	end 2016		December 2016
AD per $	110.5	Effective rates	2010 = 100
AD per sdr	148.6	– nominal	86.7
AD per €	116.3	– real	104.2

Trade

Principal exports		Principal imports	
	$bn fob		*$bn cif*
Hydrocarbons	32.7	Capital goods	17.7
Semi-finished goods	1.7	Intermediate goods	16.0
Raw materials	0.1	Food	9.3
		Consumer goods	8.7
Total incl. others	**34.7**	Total	**51.7**

Main export destinations		Main origins of imports	
	% of total		*% of total*
Spain	17.4	China	16.0
Italy	16.3	France	10.5
France	13.0	Italy	9.4
United Kingdom	7.6	Spain	7.6

Balance of payments, reserves and debt, $bn

Visible exports fob	34.3	Change in reserves	-35.8
Visible imports fob	-52.2	Level of reserves	
Trade balance	-17.8	end Dec.	150.6
Invisibles inflows	5.6	No. months of import cover	25.9
Invisibles outflows	-17.6	Official gold holdings, m oz	5.6
Net transfers	2.5	Foreign debt	4.7
Current account balance	-27.2	– as % of GDP	2.8
– as % of GDP	-16.5	– as % of total exports	11.5
Capital balance	0.2	Debt service ratio	1.7
Overall balance	-27.4		

Health and education

Health spending, % of GDP	7.2	Education spending, % of GDP	...
Doctors per 1,000 pop.	1.2	Enrolment, %: primary	116
Hospital beds per 1,000 pop.	...	secondary	100
Improved-water source access,		tertiary	37
% of pop.	83.6		

Society

No. of households, m	7.3	Cost of living, Dec. 2016	
Av. no. per household	5.4	New York = 100	45
Marriages per 1,000 pop.	...	Cars per 1,000 pop.	87
Divorces per 1,000 pop.	...	Colour TV households, % with:	
Religion, % of pop.		cable	...
Muslim	97.9	satellite	93.1
Non-religious	1.8	Telephone lines per 100 pop.	8.0
Christian	0.2	Mobile telephone subscribers	
Hindu	<0.1	per 100 pop.	106.4
Jewish	<0.1	Broadband subs per 100 pop.	5.6
Other	<0.1	Internet users, % of pop.	38.1

ARGENTINA

Area, sq km	2,780,400	Capital	Buenos Aires
Arable as % of total land	14.3	Currency	Peso (P)

People

Population, m	43.4	Life expectancy: men	73.2 yrs
Pop. per sq km	15.6	women	80.6 yrs
Average annual growth		Adult literacy	98.1
in pop. 2015–20, %	0.9	Fertility rate (per woman)	2.2
Pop. aged 0–24, %	41.1	Urban population, 2020, %	92.4
Pop. aged 70 and over, %	7.4		per 1,000 pop.
No. of men per 100 women	95.8	Crude birth rate	16.9
Human Development Index	82.7	Crude death rate	7.5

The economy

GDP	$632bn	GDP per head	$14,553
GDP	P5,854bn	GDP per head in purchasing	
Av. ann. growth in real		power parity (USA=100)	36.3
GDP 2010–15	1.4%	Economic freedom index	50.4

Origins of GDP		**Components of GDP**	
	% of total		% of total
Agriculture	6	Private consumption	65
Industry, of which:	28	Public consumption	18
manufacturing	17	Investment	17
Services	66	Exports	11
		Imports	-12

Structure of employment

	% of total		% of labour force
Agriculture	2.0	Unemployed 2015	6.6
Industry	24.6	Av. ann. rate 2005–15	8.1
Services	72.8		

Energy

	m TOE		
Total output	67.1	Net energy imports as %	
Total consumption	94.0	of energy use	13
Consumption per head			
kg oil equivalent	2,179		

Inflation and finance

Consumer price		*av. ann. increase 2011–16*	
inflation 2016	10.6%	Narrow money (M1)	29.1%
Av. ann. inflation 2011–16	10.8%	Broad money	32.0%
Money market rate, Dec. 2016	24.66%		

Exchange rates

	end 2016		December 2016
P per $	15.9	Effective rates	2010 = 100
P per sdr	21.4	– nominal	...
P per €	16.7	– real	...

Trade

Principal exports		Principal imports	
	$bn fob		*$bn cif*
Processed agricultural products	23.3	Intermediate goods	18.1
Manufactures	18.0	Capital goods	11.8
Primary products	13.3	Consumer goods	6.8
Fuels & energy	2.3	Fuels	6.8
Total	**56.8**	Total incl. others	**59.8**

Main export destinations		Main origins of imports	
	% of total		*% of total*
Brazil	17.8	Brazil	21.9
China	9.0	China	19.7
United States	6.0	United States	12.9
Chile	4.2	Germany	5.2

Balance of payments, reserves and debt, $bn

Visible exports fob	56.8	Change in reserves	-5.9
Visible imports fob	-57.2	Level of reserves	
Trade balance	-0.4	end Dec.	25.5
Invisibles inflows	16.3	No. months of import cover	3.4
Invisibles outflows	-32.3	Official gold holdings, m oz	2.0
Net transfers	-0.4	Foreign debt	159.7
Current account balance	-16.8	– as % of GDP	25.2
– as % of GDP	-2.7	– as % of total exports	217.2
Capital balance	9.6	Debt service ratio	24.4
Overall balance	-8.4		

Health and education

Health spending, % of GDP	4.8	Education spending, % of GDP	5.5
Doctors per 1,000 pop.	3.9	Enrolment, %: primary	110
Hospital beds per 1,000 pop.	4.7	secondary	107
Improved-water source access,		tertiary	83
% of pop.	99.1		

Society

No. of households, m	13.5	Cost of living, Dec. 2016	
Av. no. per household	3.2	New York = 100	66
Marriages per 1,000 pop.	2.8	Cars per 1,000 pop.	243
Divorces per 1,000 pop.	...	Colour TV households, % with:	
Religion, % of pop.		cable	64.8
Christian	85.2	satellite	14.4
Non-religious	12.2	Telephone lines per 100 pop.	23.9
Other	1.1	Mobile telephone subscribers	
Muslim	1.0	per 100 pop.	147.0
Jewish	0.5	Broadband subs per 100 pop.	16.3
Hindu	<0.1	Internet users, % of pop.	69.4

AUSTRALIA

Area, sq km	7,741,000	Capital	Canberra
Arable as % of total land	6.1	Currency	Australian dollar (A$)

People

Population, m	24.0	Life expectancy: men	81.1 yrs
Pop. per sq km	3.1	women	85.0 yrs
Average annual growth		Adult literacy	...
in pop. 2015–20, %	1.3	Fertility rate (per woman)	1.8
Pop. aged 0–24, %	31.9	Urban population, 2020, %	90.1
Pop. aged 70 and over, %	10.1		per 1,000 pop.
No. of men per 100 women	99.9	Crude birth rate	13.0
Human Development Index	93.9	Crude death rate	6.7

The economy

GDP	$1,230bn	GDP per head	$51,238
GDP	A$ 1,634bn	GDP per head in purchasing	
Av. ann. growth in real		power parity (USA=100)	85.0
GDP 2010–15	2.7%	Economic freedom index	81.0

Origins of GDP		**Components of GDP**	
	% of total		% of total
Agriculture	3	Private consumption	57
Industry, of which:	26	Public consumption	18
manufacturing	17	Investment	27
Services	72	Exports	20
		Imports	-21

Structure of employment

	% of total		% of labour force
Agriculture	2.7	Unemployed 2015	6.1
Industry	19.5	Av. ann. rate 2005–15	5.2
Services	78.0		

Energy

	m TOE		
Total output	360.1	Net energy imports as %	
Total consumption	141.6	of energy use	-192
Consumption per head			
kg oil equivalent	5,338		

Inflation and finance

			av. ann. increase 2011–16
Consumer price			
inflation 2016	1.3%	Narrow money (M1)	5.4%
Av. ann. inflation 2011–16	4.0%	Broad money	6.8%
Money Market Rate, Dec. 2016	1.50%		

Exchange rates

	end 2016		December 2016
A$ per $	1.38	Effective rates	2010 = 100
A$ per sdr	1.86	– nominal	93.7
A$ per €	1.45	– real	95.1

Trade

Principal exports	$bn fob	Principal imports	$bn cif
Crude materials	61.3	Machinery & transport	79.8
Fuels	46.8	equipment	
Food	26.8	Miscellaneous manufactured	
Machinery & transport		articles	30.4
equipment	12.1	Manufactured goods	24.5
		Mineral fuels	21.7
Total incl. others	**187.7**	Total incl. others	**200.5**

Main export destinations	% of total	Main origins of imports	% of total
China	32.4	China	24.5
Japan	16.0	United States	11.9
South Korea	7.1	Japan	7.8
United States	5.5	South Korea	5.8

Balance of payments, reserves and aid, $bn

Visible exports fob	188.3	Overall balance	-2.3
Visible imports fob	-207.2	Change in reserves	-4.6
Trade balance	-18.8	Level of reserves	
Invisibles inflows	87.7	end Dec.	49.3
Invisibles outflows	-125.4	No. months of import cover	1.8
Net transfers	-1.4	Official gold holdings, m oz	2.6
Current account balance	-58.0	Aid given	3.5
– as % of GDP	-4.7	– as % of GDP	0.3
Capital balance	50.6		

Health and education

Health spending, % of GDP	9.4	Education spending, % of GDP	5.3
Doctors per 1,000 pop.	3.3	Enrolment, %: primary	106
Hospital beds per 1,000 pop.	3.9	secondary	138
Improved-water source access,		tertiary	90
% of pop.	100		

Society

No. of households, m	8.8	Cost of living, Dec. 2016	
Av. no. per household	2.7	New York = 100	90
Marriages per 1,000 pop.	5.2	Cars per 1,000 pop.	563
Divorces per 1,000 pop.	2.0	Colour TV households, % with:	
Religion, % of pop.		cable	24.9
Christian	67.3	satellite	33.7
Non-religious	24.2	Telephone lines per 100 pop.	38.0
Other	4.2	Mobile telephone subscribers	
Muslim	2.4	per 100 pop.	132.8
Hindu	1.4	Broadband subs per 100 pop.	28.5
Jewish	0.5	Internet users, % of pop.	84.6

AUSTRIA

Area, sq km	82,523	Capital	Vienna
Arable as % of total land	16.5	Currency	Euro (€)

People

Population, m	8.6	Life expectancy: men	79.7 yrs
Pop. per sq km	104.2	women	84.4 yrs
Average annual growth		Adult literacy	...
in pop. 2015–20, %	0.3	Fertility rate (per woman)	1.5
Pop. aged 0–24, %	25.9	Urban population, 2020, %	66.4
Pop. aged 70 and over, %	13.7		per 1,000 pop.
No. of men per 100 women	96.5	Crude birth rate	9.7
Human Development Index	89.3	Crude death rate	9.5

The economy

GDP	$377bn	GDP per head	$43,855
GDP	€340bn	GDP per head in purchasing	
Av. ann. growth in real		power parity (USA=100)	84.2
GDP 2010–15	1.0%	Economic freedom index	72.3

Origins of GDP		**Components of GDP**	
	% of total		% of total
Agriculture	1	Private consumption	53
Industry, of which:	28	Public consumption	20
manufacturing	19	Investment	24
Services	70	Exports	53
		Imports	-49

Structure of employment

	% of total		% of labour force
Agriculture	4.5	Unemployed 2015	5.7
Industry	25.8	Av. ann. rate 2005–15	5.1
Services	69.7		

Energy

	m TOE		
Total output	2.2	Net energy imports as %	
Total consumption	35.4	of energy use	62
Consumption per head			
kg oil equivalent	3,765		

Inflation and finance

Consumer price		av. ann. increase 2011–16	
inflation 2016	0.9%	Narrow money (M1)	8.1%
Av. ann. inflation 2011–16	3.7%	Broad money	3.6%
Deposit rate, Dec. 2016	0.30%		

Exchange rates

	end 2016		December 2016
€ per $	0.95	Effective rates	2010 = 100
€ per sdr	1.28	– nominal	98.5
		– real	100.4

Trade

Principal exports		Principal imports	
	$bn fob		*$bn cif*
Machinery & transport equip.	61.9	Machinery & transport equip.	55.3
Chemicals & related products	20.4	Chemicals & related products	20.9
Food, drink & tobacco	11.1	Mineral fuels & lubricants	11.7
Raw materials	4.7	Food, drink & tobacco	11.6
Total incl. others	**152.9**	Total incl. others	**156.1**

Main export destinations		Main origins of imports	
	% of total		*% of total*
Germany	29.4	Germany	41.5
Italy	6.1	Italy	6.2
United States	6.3	Switzerland	5.9
Switzerland	5.7	Czech Republic	4.2
EU28	70.1	EU28	76.8

Balance of payments, reserves and aid, $bn

Visible exports fob	142.1	Overall balance	-0.4
Visible imports fob	-140.4	Change in reserves	-2.8
Trade balance	1.7	Level of reserves	
Invisibles inflows	89.8	end Dec.	22.2
Invisibles outflows	-80.5	No. months of import cover	1.2
Net transfers	-3.8	Official gold holdings, m oz	9.0
Current account balance	7.2	Aid given	1.3
– as % of GDP	1.9	– as % of GDP	0.4
Capital balance	-7.8		

Health and education

Health spending, % of GDP	11.2	Education spending, % of GDP	5.6
Doctors per 1,000 pop.	4.8	Enrolment, %: primary	103
Hospital beds per 1,000 pop.	7.6	secondary	100
Improved-water source access,		tertiary	82
% of pop.	100		

Society

No. of households, m	3.8	Cost of living, Dec. 2016	
Av. no. per household	2.3	New York = 100	91
Marriages per 1,000 pop.	4.3	Cars per 1,000 pop.	552
Divorces per 1,000 pop.	1.9	Colour TV households, % with:	
Religion, % of pop.		cable	38.6
Christian	80.4	satellite	54.3
Non-religious	13.5	Telephone lines per 100 pop.	42.2
Muslim	5.4	Mobile telephone subscribers	
Other	0.5	per 100 pop.	157.4
Jewish	0.2	Broadband subs per 100 pop.	28.7
Hindu	<0.1	Internet users, % of pop.	83.9

BANGLADESH

Area, sq km	130,170	Capital	Dhaka
Arable as % of total land	58.9	Currency	Taka (Tk)

People

Population, m	161.0	Life expectancy: men	71.6 yrs
Pop. per sq km	1,236.8	women	74.3 yrs
Average annual growth		Adult literacy	61.5
in pop. 2015–20, %	1.1	Fertility rate (per woman)	2.4
Pop. aged 0–24, %	48.9	Urban population, 2020, %	38.0
Pop. aged 70 and over, %	3.2		per 1,000 pop.
No. of men per 100 women	102.0	Crude birth rate	18.6
Human Development Index	57.9	Crude death rate	5.3

The economy

GDP	$207bn	GDP per head	$1,284
GDP	Tk16,227bn	GDP per head in purchasing	
Av. ann. growth in real		power parity (USA=100)	6.4
GDP 2010–15	6.4%	Economic freedom index	55.0

Origins of GDP		**Components of GDP**	
	% of total		% of total
Agriculture	16	Private consumption	73
Industry, of which:	28	Public consumption	5
manufacturing	18	Investment	29
Services	56	Exports	17
		Imports	-25

Structure of employment

	% of total		% of labour force
Agriculture	47.5	Unemployed 2015	4.1
Industry	17.7	Av. ann. rate 2005–15	4.3
Services	35.3		

Energy

	m TOE		
Total output	22.6	Net energy imports as %	
Total consumption	28.4	of energy use	17
Consumption per head			
kg oil equivalent	223		

Inflation and finance

			av. ann. increase 2011–16
Consumer price			
inflation 2016	6.7%	Narrow money (M1)	13.6%
Av. ann. inflation 2011–16	7.8%	Broad money	15.8%
Treasury bill rate, Dec. 2016	3.00%		

Exchange rates

	end 2016		December 2016
Tk per $	78.7	Effective rates	2010 = 100
Tk per sdr	105.8	– nominal	...
Tk per €	82.8	– real	...

Trade

Principal exports		**Principal imports**	
	$bn fob		*$bn cif*
Clothing	20.7	Textiles & yarns	3.9
Jute goods	0.7	Fuels	3.3
Fish & fish products	0.4	Iron & steel	2.9
Leather	0.3	Capital machinery	2.7
Total incl. others	**29.9**	Total incl. others	**39.5**

Main export destinations		**Main origins of imports**	
	% of total		*% of total*
United States	13.9	China	22.4
Germany	12.9	India	14.1
United Kingdom	8.9	Singapore	5.2
France	5.0	Japan	3.9

Balance of payments, reserves and debt, $bn

Visible exports fob	31.7	Change in reserves	5.2
Visible imports fob	-37.6	Level of reserves	
Trade balance	-5.9	end Dec.	27.5
Invisibles inflows	3.2	No. months of import cover	6.9
Invisibles outflows	-10.5	Official gold holdings, m oz	0.4
Net transfers	15.9	Foreign debt	38.6
Current account balance	2.7	– as % of GDP	19.8
– as % of GDP	1.3	– as % of total exports	76.8
Capital balance	3.6	Debt service ratio	2.9
Overall balance	5.4		

Health and education

Health spending, % of GDP	2.8	Education spending, % of GDP	2.2
Doctors per 1,000 pop.	0.4	Enrolment, %: primary	120
Hospital beds per 1,000 pop.	0.6	secondary	64
Improved-water source access,		tertiary	13
% of pop.	86.9		

Society

No. of households, m	37.1	Cost of living, Dec. 2016	
Av. no. per household	4.3	New York = 100	72
Marriages per 1,000 pop.	...	Cars per 1,000 pop.	3.0
Divorces per 1,000 pop.	...	Colour TV households, % with:	
Religion, % of pop. of pop.		cable	...
Muslim	89.8	satellite	...
Hindu	9.1	Telephone lines per 100 pop.	0.5
Other	0.9	Mobile telephone subscribers	
Christian	0.2	per 100 pop.	81.9
Jewish	<0.1	Broadband subs per 100 pop.	3.1
Non-religious	<0.1	Internet users, % of pop.	14.4

BELGIUM

Area, sq km	30,280	Capital	Brussels
Arable as % of total land	27.0	Currency	Euro (€)

People

Population, m	11.3	Life expectancy: men	79.1 yrs
Pop. per sq km	373.2	women	83.7 yrs
Average annual growth		Adult literacy	...
in pop. 2015–20, %	0.6	Fertility rate (per woman)	1.8
Pop. aged 0–24, %	28.6	Urban population, 2020, %	98.0
Pop. aged 70 and over, %	12.8		per 1,000 pop.
No. of men per 100 women	96.8	Crude birth rate	11.4
Human Development Index	89.6	Crude death rate	9.7

The economy

GDP	$455bn	GDP per head	$40,295
GDP	€410bn	GDP per head in purchasing	
Av. ann. growth in real		power parity (USA=100)	78.4
GDP 2010–15	0.9%	Economic freedom index	67.8

Origins of GDP		**Components of GDP**	
	% of total		% of total
Agriculture	1	Private consumption	51
Industry, of which:	22	Public consumption	24
manufacturing	14	Investment	23
Services	77	Exports	83
		Imports	-81

Structure of employment

	% of total		% of labour force
Agriculture	1.2	Unemployed 2015	8.5
Industry	21.4	Av. ann. rate 2005–15	8.0
Services	77.4		

Energy

	m TOE		
Total output	8.3	Net energy imports as %	
Total consumption	61.2	of energy use	76
Consumption per head			
kg oil equivalent	4,699		

Inflation and finance

Consumer price			av. ann. increase 2011–16
inflation 2016	2.1%	Narrow money (M1)	8.1%
Av. ann. inflation 2011–16	3.3%	Broad money	3.60%
Treasury bill rate, Dec. 2016	-1.00%		

Exchange rates

	end 2016		December 2016
€ per $	0.95	Effective rates	2010 = 100
€ per sdr	1.28	– nominal	97.6
		– real	97.4

Trade

Principal exports		Principal imports	
	$bn fob		*$bn cif*
Chemicals & related products	120.2	Chemicals & related products	97.4
Machinery & transport equip.	85.8	Machinery & transport equip.	90.1
Food, drink & tobacco	37.2	Mineral fuels & lubricants	45.6
Mineral fuels & lubricants	33.2	Food, drink & tobacco	31.3
Total incl. others	**398.1**	Total incl. others	**375.7**

Main export destinations		Main origins of imports	
	% of total		*% of total*
Germany	16.7	Netherlands	16.7
France	15.5	Germany	12.8
Netherlands	11.4	France	9.5
United Kingdom	8.8	United States	8.7
EU28	71.9	EU28	62.8

Balance of payments, reserves and debt, $bn

Visible exports fob	254.8	Overall balance	-1.1
Visible imports fob	-251.9	Change in reserves	-1.3
Trade balance	2.8	Level of reserves	
Invisibles inflows	164.1	end Dec.	24.1
Invisibles outflows	-157.6	No. months of import cover	0.7
Net transfers	-7.4	Official gold holdings, m oz	7.3
Current account balance	1.9	Aid given	1.9
– as % of GDP	0.4	– as % of GDP	0.4
Capital balance	-4.0		

Health and education

Health spending, % of GDP	10.6	Education spending, % of GDP	6.4
Doctors per 1,000 pop.	4.9	Enrolment, %: primary	105
Hospital beds per 1,000 pop.	6.5	secondary	165
Improved-water source access,		tertiary	73
% of pop.	100		

Society

No. of households, m	4.7	Cost of living, Dec. 2016	
Av. no. per household	2.4	New York = 100	81
Marriages per 1,000 pop.	3.6	Cars per 1,000 pop.	496
Divorces per 1,000 pop.	2.5	Colour TV households, % with:	
Religion, % of pop.		cable	74.2
Christian	64.2	satellite	5.9
Non-religious	29.0	Telephone lines per 100 pop.	40.1
Muslim	5.9	Mobile telephone subscribers	
Other	0.6	per 100 pop.	115.7
Jewish	0.3	Broadband subs per 100 pop.	36.8
Hindu	<0.1	Internet users, % of pop.	85.1

BRAZIL

Area, sq km	8,516,000	Capital	Brasília
Arable as % of total land	9.6	Currency	Real (R)

People

Population, m	207.8	Life expectancy: men	71.8 yrs
Pop. per sq km	24.4	women	79.1 yrs
Average annual growth		Adult literacy	92.6
in pop. 2015–20, %	0.8	Fertility rate (per woman)	1.8
Pop. aged 0–24, %	39.5	Urban population, 2020, %	86.8
Pop. aged 70 and over, %	5.0		per 1,000 pop.
No. of men per 100 women	96.7	Crude birth rate	14.0
Human Development Index	75.4	Crude death rate	6.3

The economy

GDP	$1,801bn	GDP per head	$8,669
GDP	R6,001bn	GDP per head in purchasing	
Av. ann. growth in real		power parity (USA=100)	27.6
GDP 2010–15	1.0%	Economic freedom index	52.9

Origins of GDP		**Components of GDP**	
	% of total		% of total
Agriculture	5	Private consumption	64
Industry, of which:	22	Public consumption	20
manufacturing	12	Investment	18
Services	73	Exports	13
		Imports	-14

Structure of employment

	% of total		% of labour force
Agriculture	10.3	Unemployed 2015	8.5
Industry	22.2	Av. ann. rate 2005–15	9.0
Services	77.3		

Energy

	m TOE		
Total output	150.3	Net energy imports as %	
Total consumption	320.9	of energy use	12
Consumption per head			
kg oil equivalent	1,471		

Inflation and finance

			av. ann. increase 2011–16
Consumer price			
inflation 2016	9.0%	Narrow money (M1)	3.9%
Av. ann. inflation 2011–16	7.8%	Broad money	11.8%
Treasury bill rate, Dec. 2016	12.27%		

Exchange rates

	end 2016		December 2016
R per $	3.26	Effective rates	2010 = 100
R per sdr	4.38	– nominal	68.17
R per €	3.73	– real	84.00

Trade

Principal exports	$bn fob	Principal imports	$bn cif
Primary products	87.2	Intermediate products & raw	
Manufactured goods	72.8	materials	81.2
Semi-manufactured goods	26.5	Capital goods	37.7
		Consumer goods	30.8
		Fuels & lubricants	21.8
Total incl. others	**191.1**	Total incl. others	**171.4**

Main export destinations	% of total	Main origins of imports	% of total
China	18.6	United States	19.0
United States	12.7	China	16.5
Argentina	6.7	Argentina	6.4
Netherlands	5.3	Netherlands	6.4

Balance of payments, reserves and debt, $bn

Visible exports fob	190.1	Change in reserves	-7.1
Visible imports fob	-172.4	Level of reserves	
Trade balance	17.7	end Dec.	356.5
Invisibles inflows	45.7	No. months of import cover	14.4
Invisibles outflows	-125.0	Official gold holdings, m oz	2.2
Net transfers	2.7	Foreign debt	543.4
Current account balance	-58.9	– as % of GDP	30.2
– as % of GDP	-3.3	– as % of total exports	227.7
Capital balance	56.7	Debt service ratio	37.6
Overall balance	1.6		

Health and education

Health spending, % of GDP	8.3	Education spending, % of GDP	6.0
Doctors per 1,000 pop.	1.9	Enrolment, %: primary	111
Hospital beds per 1,000 pop.	2.3	secondary	102
Improved-water source access,		tertiary	49
% of pop.	98.1		

Society

No. of households, m	62.1	Cost of living, Dec. 2016	
Av. no. per household	3.3	New York = 100	65
Marriages per 1,000 pop.	…	Cars per 1,000 pop.	162
Divorces per 1,000 pop.	…	Colour TV households, % with:	
Religion, % of pop.		cable	11.3
Christian	88.9	satellite	16.9
Non-religious	7.9	Telephone lines per 100 pop.	21.4
Other	3.1	Mobile telephone subscribers	
Hindu	<0.1	per 100 pop.	126.6
Jewish	<0.1	Broadband subs per 100 pop.	12.2
Muslim	<0.1	Internet users, % of pop.	59.1

BULGARIA

Area, sq km	108,560	Capital	Sofia
Arable as % of total land	32.1	Currency	Lev (BGL)

People

Population, m	7.1	Life expectancy: men	71.1 yrs
Pop. per sq km	65.4	women	78.0 yrs
Average annual growth		Adult literacy	98.4
in pop. 2015–20, %	-0.8	Fertility rate (per woman)	1.5
Pop. aged 0–24, %	23.8	Urban population, 2020, %	75.5
Pop. aged 70 and over, %	13.3		per 1,000 pop.
No. of men per 100 women	94.5	Crude birth rate	9.5
Human Development Index	79.4	Crude death rate	15.6

The economy

GDP	$50bn	GDP per head	$7,070
GDP	BGL89bn	GDP per head in purchasing	
Av. ann. growth in real		power parity (USA=100)	34.7
GDP 2010–15	1.5%	Economic freedom index	67.9

Origins of GDP		**Components of GDP**	
	% of total		% of total
Agriculture	5	Private consumption	63
Industry, of which:	28	Public consumption	16
manufacturing	...	Investment	21
Services	67	Exports	64
		Imports	-64

Structure of employment

	% of total		% of labour force
Agriculture	6.9	Unemployed 2015	9.1
Industry	29.9	Av. ann. rate 2005–15	9.6
Services	63.3		

Energy

	m TOE		
Total output	9.0	Net energy imports as %	
Total consumption	19.5	of energy use	37
Consumption per head			
kg oil equivalent	2,478		

Inflation and finance

		av. ann. change 2011–16	
Consumer price			
inflation 2016	-1.6%	Narrow money (M1)	14.2%
Av. ann. inflation 2011–16	2.3%	Broad money	6.9%
Money market rate, Dec. 2016	-0.11%		

Exchange rates

	end 2016		December 2016
BGL per $	1.86	Effective rates	2010 = 100
BGL per sdr	2.49	– nominal	107.60
BGL per €	1.96	– real	98.19

Trade

Principal exports		Principal imports	
	$bn fob		$bn cif
Raw materials	10.4	Raw materials	10.7
Consumer goods	6.8	Capital goods	7.5
Capital goods	5.4	Consumer goods	6.2
Mineral fuels & lubricants	2.1	Mineral fuels & lubricants	3.6
Total incl. others	**25.5**	Total incl. others	**29.2**

Main export destinations		Main origins of imports	
	% of total		% of total
Germany	12.6	Germany	12.9
Italy	9.3	Russia	12.0
Turkey	8.6	Italy	7.6
Romania	8.2	Romania	6.8
EU28	64.9	EU28	64.3

Balance of payments, reserves and debt, $bn

Visible exports fob	24.3	Change in reserves	2.0
Visible imports fob	-27.2	Level of reserves	
Trade balance	-2.9	end Dec.	22.2
Invisibles inflows	8.8	No. months of import cover	7.6
Invisibles outflows	-7.8	Official gold holdings, m oz	1.3
Net transfers	1.8	Foreign debt	37.5
Current account balance	-0.1	– as % of GDP	74.7
– as % of GDP	-0.1	– as % of total exports	108.0
Capital balance	2.7	Debt service ratio	30.3
Overall balance	4.0		

Health and education

Health spending, % of GDP	8.4	Education spending, % of GDP	4.1
Doctors per 1,000 pop.	3.9	Enrolment, %: primary	97
Hospital beds per 1,000 pop.	6.4	secondary	99
Improved-water source access,		tertiary	74
% of pop.	99.4		

Society

No. of households, m	2.9	Cost of living, Dec. 2016	
Av. no. per household	2.4	New York = 100	54
Marriages per 1,000 pop.	3.4	Cars per 1,000 pop.	419
Divorces per 1,000 pop.	1.5	Colour TV households, % with:	
Religion, % of pop.		cable	48.2
Christian	82.1	satellite	28.8
Muslim	13.7	Telephone lines per 100 pop.	23.3
Non-religious	4.2	Mobile telephone subscribers	
Hindu	<0.1	per 100 pop.	129.3
Jewish	<0.1	Broadband subs per 100 pop.	22.7
Other	<0.1	Internet users, % of pop.	56.7

CAMEROON

Area, sq km	475,000	Capital	Yaoundé
Arable as % of total land	13.1	Currency	CFA franc (CFAfr)

People

Population, m	23.3	Life expectancy: men	55.9 yrs
Pop. per sq km	49.1	women	58.2 yrs
Average annual growth		Adult literacy	75.0
in pop. 2015–20, %	2.4	Fertility rate (per woman)	4.8
Pop. aged 0–24, %	62.8	Urban population, 2020, %	57.1
Pop. aged 70 and over, %	1.9		per 1,000 pop.
No. of men per 100 women	100.0	Crude birth rate	35.0
Human Development Index	51.8	Crude death rate	10.6

The economy

GDP	$28bn	GDP per head	$1,220
GDP	CFAfr16,807bn	GDP per head in purchasing	
Av. ann. growth in real		power parity (USA=100)	5.6
GDP 2010–15	5.2%	Economic freedom index	51.8

Origins of GDP		**Components of GDP**	
	% of total		% of total
Agriculture	23	Private consumption	78
Industry, of which:	28	Public consumption	12
manufacturing	14	Investment	21
Services	49	Exports	20
		Imports	-30

Structure of employment

	% of total		% of labour force
Agriculture	...	Unemployed 2015	4.4
Industry	...	Av. ann. rate 2005–15	3.9
Services	...		

Energy

	m TOE		
Total output	4.5	Net energy imports as %	
Total consumption	3.9	of energy use	-28
Consumption per head			
kg oil equivalent	334		

Inflation and finance

		av. ann. change 2011–16	
Consumer price			
inflation 2016	2.2%	Narrow money (M1)	8.4%
Av. ann. inflation 2011–16	4.1%	Broad money	7.6%
Deposit rate, Jun. 2016	₂.45%		

Exchange rates

	end 2016		December 2016
CFAfr per $	622.29	Effective rates	2010 = 100
CFAfr per sdr	836.56	– nominal	103.20
CFAfr per €	654.80	– real	98.16

Trade

Principal exports		Principal imports	
	$bn fob		*$bn cif*
Fuels	1.5	Manufactured products	3.2
Cocoa beans & products	0.6	Food	1.1
Timber	0.6	Fuels	1.1
Cotton	0.1		
Total incl. others	**5.2**	Total incl. others	**5.6**

Main export destinations		Main origins of imports	
	% of total		*% of total*
Netherlands	16.3	China	19.4
India	15.6	Nigeria	12.1
China	12.5	France	10.5
Portugal	7.1	Belgium	4.9

Balance of payments, reserves and debt, $bn

Visible exports fob	5.2	Change in reserves	0.4
Visible imports fob	-5.6	Level of reserves	
Trade balance	-0.4	end Dec.	3.5
Invisibles inflows	1.7	No. months of import cover	5.0
Invisibles outflows	-2.8	Official gold holdings, m oz	0.0
Net transfers	0.3	Foreign debt	6.6
Current account balance	-1.2	– as % of GDP	23.1
– as % of GDP	-4.1	– as % of total exports	91.6
Capital balance	1.9	Debt service ratio	5.9
Overall balance	0.7		

Health and education

Health spending, % of GDP	4.1	Education spending, % of GDP	3.0
Doctors per 1,000 pop.	...	Enrolment, %: primary	117
Hospital beds per 1,000 pop.	1.3	secondary	58
Improved-water source access,		tertiary	18
% of pop.	75.6		

Society

No. of households, m	4.4	Cost of living, Dec. 2016	
Av. no. per household	5.3	New York = 100	...
Marriages per 1,000 pop.	...	Cars per 1,000 pop.	11
Divorces per 1,000 pop.	...	Colour TV households, % with:	
Religion, % of pop.		cable	...
Christian	70.3	satellite	2.4
Muslim	18.3	Telephone lines per 100 pop.	4.5
Other	6.0	Mobile telephone subscribers	
Non-religious	5.3	per 100 pop.	71.8
Hindu	<0.1	Broadband subs per 100 pop.	0.1
Jewish	<0.1	Internet users, % of pop.	20.7

CANADA

Area, sq km[a]	9,985,000	Capital	Ottawa
Arable as % of total land	5.1	Currency	Canadian dollar (C$)

People

Population, m	35.9	Life expectancy: men	80.8 yrs
Pop. per sq km	3.6	women	84.4 yrs
Average annual growth		Adult literacy	...
in pop. 2015–20, %	0.9	Fertility rate (per woman)	1.6
Pop. aged 0–24, %	28.8	Urban population, 2020, %	82.7
Pop. aged 70 and over, %	10.8		per 1,000 pop.
No. of men per 100 women	98.4	Crude birth rate	10.5
Human Development Index	92.0	Crude death rate	7.5

The economy

GDP	$1,553bn	GDP per head	$43,254
GDP	C$1,986bn	GDP per head in purchasing	
Av. ann. growth in real		power parity (USA=100)	81.4
GDP 2010–15	2.1%	Economic freedom index	78.5

Origins of GDP		**Components of GDP**	
	% of total		% of total
Agriculture	2	Private consumption	58
Industry, of which:	28	Public consumption	21
manufacturing	...	Investment	23
Services	70	Exports	31
		Imports	-33

Structure of employment

	% of total		% of labour force
Agriculture	1.6	Unemployed 2015	6.9
Industry	19.9	Av. ann. rate 2005–15	7.0
Services	78.4		

Energy

	m TOE		
Total output	417.8	Net energy imports as %	
Total consumption	364.2	of energy use	-68
Consumption per head			
kg oil equivalent	7,874		

Inflation and finance

		av. ann. increase 2011–16	
Consumer price			
inflation 2016	1.6%	Narrow money (M1)	7.6%
Av. ann. inflation 2011–16	3.4%	Broad money	8.1%
Treasury bill rate, Dec. 2016	0.47%		

Exchange rates

	end 2016		December 2016
C$ per $	1.34	Effective rates	2010 = 100
C$ per sdr	1.81	– nominal	83.38
C$ per €	1.41	– real	82.64

Trade

Principal exports		Principal imports	
	$bn fob		*$bn cif*
Motor vehicles & parts	68.1	Consumer goods	91.9
Energy products	65.6	Motor vehicles & parts	78.5
Consumer goods	54.2	Electronic & electrical equip.	49.4
Metal & mineral products	45.2	Energy products	42.0
Total incl. others	**410.5**	Total incl. others	**428.5**

Main export destinations		Main origins of imports	
	% of total		*% of total*
United States	76.7	United States	53.1
China	3.9	China	12.2
United Kingdom	3.1	Mexico	5.8
Japan	1.9	Germany	3.2
EU28	7.2	EU28	11.5

Balance of payments, reserves and aid, $bn

Visible exports fob	410.7	Overall balance	8.5
Visible imports fob	-428.8	Change in reserves	5.1
Trade balance	-18.0	Level of reserves	
Invisibles inflows	151.3	end Dec.	79.8
Invisibles outflows	-183.5	No. months of import cover	1.6
Net transfers	-2.8	Official gold holdings, m oz	0.1
Current account balance	-53.1	Aid given	4.3
– as % of GDP	-3.4	– as % of GDP	0.3
Capital balance	62.2		

Health and education

Health spending, % of GDP	10.4	Education spending, % of GDP	5.3
Doctors per 1,000 pop.	2.1	Enrolment, %: primary	101
Hospital beds per 1,000 pop.	2.7	secondary	110
Improved-water source access,		tertiary	...
% of pop.	99.8		

Society

No. of households, m	14.0	Cost of living, Dec. 2016	
Av. no. per household	2.6	New York = 100	81
Marriages per 1,000 pop.	...	Cars per 1,000 pop.	612
Divorces per 1,000 pop.	...	Colour TV households, % with:	
Religion, % of pop.		cable	66.4
Christian	69.0	satellite	22.2
Non-religious	23.7	Telephone lines per 100 pop.	43.5
Other	2.8	Mobile telephone subscribers	
Muslim	2.1	per 100 pop.	83.0
Hindu	1.4	Broadband subs per 100 pop.	36.3
Jewish	1.0	Internet users, % of pop.	88.5

a Including freshwater.

CHILE

Area, sq km	743,532	Capital	Santiago
Arable as % of total land	1.7	Currency	Chilean peso (Ps)

People

Population, m	17.9	Life expectancy: men	79.8 yrs
Pop. per sq km	24.1	women	85.3 yrs
Average annual growth		Adult literacy	96.6
in pop. 2015–20, %	1.0	Fertility rate (per woman)	1.8
Pop. aged 0–24, %	35.4	Urban population, 2020, %	90.3
Pop. aged 70 and over, %	7.4		per 1,000 pop.
No. of men per 100 women	97.4	Crude birth rate	12.7
Human Development Index	84.7	Crude death rate	5.2

The economy

GDP	$243bn	GDP per head	$13,550
GDP	158.6trn pesos	GDP per head in purchasing	
Av. ann. growth in real		power parity (USA=100)	42.5
GDP 2010–15	3.9%	Economic freedom index	76.5

Origins of GDP **Components of GDP**

	% of total		% of total
Agriculture	4	Private consumption	64
Industry, of which:	33	Public consumption	13
manufacturing	12	Investment	22
Services	63	Exports	30
		Imports	-30

Structure of employment

	% of total		% of labour force
Agriculture	9.6	Unemployed 2015	6.2
Industry	23.1	Av. ann. rate 2005–15	7.3
Services	67.3		

Energy

	m TOE		
Total output	2.3	Net energy imports as %	
Total consumption	34.8	of energy use	64
Consumption per head			
kg oil equivalent	2,033		

Inflation and finance

			av. ann. increase 2011–16
Consumer price			
inflation 2016	4.0%	Narrow money (M1)	9.4%
Av. ann. inflation 2011–16	5.1%	Broad money	8.9%
Money market rate, Sep. 2016	3.50%		

Exchange rates

	end 2016		December 2016
			Effective rates	2010 = 100
Ps per $	667.29	Effective rates	2010 = 100
Ps per sdr	897.06	– nominal	98.52
Ps per €	702.16	– real	100.69

Trade

Principal exports		Principal imports	
	$bn fob		*$bn cif*
Copper	30.1	Intermediate goods	32.2
Fresh fruit	4.5	Consumer goods	18.0
Cellulose & paper products	3.2	Capital goods	12.3
Total incl. others	**62.3**	Total incl. others	**63.0**

Main export destinations		Main origins of imports	
	% of total		*% of total*
China	26.2	China	23.2
United States	13.2	United States	18.7
Japan	8.5	Brazil	7.7
South Korea	6.5	Argentina	4.0

Balance of payments, reserves and debt, $bn

Visible exports fob	62.2	Change in reserves	-1.8
Visible imports fob	-58.7	Level of reserves	
Trade balance	3.5	end Dec.	38.6
Invisibles inflows	17.1	No. months of import cover	5.4
Invisibles outflows	-27.1	Official gold holdings, m oz	0.0
Net transfers	1.8	Foreign debt	156.2
Current account balance	-4.8	– as % of GDP	64.9
– as % of GDP	-2.0	– as % of total exports	201.1
Capital balance	5.5	Debt service ratio	33.1
Overall balance	0.2		

Health and education

Health spending, % of GDP	7.8	Education spending, % of GDP	4.8
Doctors per 1,000 pop.	1.0	Enrolment, %: primary	102
Hospital beds per 1,000 pop.	2.1	secondary	101
Improved-water source access,		tertiary	89
% of pop.	99.0		

Society

No. of households, m	6.2	Cost of living, Dec. 2016	
Av. no. per household	2.9	New York = 100	65
Marriages per 1,000 pop.	3.5	Cars per 1,000 pop.	168
Divorces per 1,000 pop.	0.1	Colour TV households, % with:	
Religion, % of pop.		cable	34.2
Christian	89.4	satellite	5.2
Non-religious	8.6	Telephone lines per 100 pop.	19.2
Other	1.9	Mobile telephone subscribers	
Jewish	0.1	per 100 pop.	129.5
Hindu	<0.1	Broadband subs per 100 pop.	15.2
Muslim	<0.1	Internet users, % of pop.	64.3

CHINA

Area, sq km	9,563,000	Capital	Beijing
Arable as % of total land	11.3	Currency	Yuan

People

Population, m	1,376.0	Life expectancy: men	75.3 yrs
Pop. per sq km	143.9	women	78.1 yrs
Average annual growth		Adult literacy	96.4
in pop. 2015–20, %	0.4	Fertility rate (per woman)	1.6
Pop. aged 0–24, %	30.7	Urban population, 2020, %	61.0
Pop. aged 70 and over, %	5.8		per 1,000 pop.
No. of men per 100 women	106.3	Crude birth rate	11.4
Human Development Index	73.8	Crude death rate	7.4

The economy

GDP	$11,226bn	GDP per head	$8,159
GDP	Yuan 69,911bn	GDP per head in purchasing	
Av. ann. growth in real		power parity (USA=100)	25.5
GDP 2010–15	7.9%	Economic freedom index	57.4

Origins of GDP		**Components of GDP**	
	% of total		% of total
Agriculture	9	Private consumption	37
Industry, of which:	41	Public consumption	14
manufacturing	30	Investment	45
Services	50	Exports	22
		Imports	-18

Structure of employment

	% of total		% of labour force
Agriculture	28.3	Unemployed 2015	4.6
Industry	29.3	Av. ann. rate 2005–15	4.3
Services	42.4		

Energy

	m TOE		
Total output	2,395.7	Net energy imports as %	
Total consumption	3,072.7	of energy use	15
Consumption per head			
kg oil equivalent	2,237		

Inflation and finance

			av. ann. increase 2011–16
Consumer price			
inflation 2016	2.1%	Narrow money (M1)	10.9%
Av. ann. inflation 2011–16	4.1%	Broad money	12.7%
Treasury bill rate, Dec. 2016	0.67%		

Exchange rates

	end 2016		December 2016
Yuan per $	6.95	Effective rates	2010 = 100
Yuan per sdr	9.34	– nominal	115.39
Yuan per €	7.31	– real	122.64

Trade

Principal exports	$bn fob	Principal imports	$bn cif
Telecoms equipment	296.5	Electrical machinery	351.0
Electrical goods	292.2	Petroleum products	161.0
Office machinery	190.1	Metal ores & scrap	110.4
Clothing & apparel	174.4	Professional instruments	80.3
Total incl. others	**2,273.5**	**Total incl. others**	**1,679.6**

Main export destinations	% of total	Main origins of imports	% of total
United States	18.1	South Korea	10.4
Hong Kong	14.6	United States	8.6
Japan	6.0	Japan	8.5
South Korea	4.5	Taiwan	8.5
EU28	15.6	EU28	12.4

Balance of payments, reserves and debt, $bn

Visible exports fob	2,142.8	Change in reserves	-494.8
Visible imports fob	-1,575.8	Level of reserves	
Trade balance	567.0	end Dec.	3,405.3
Invisibles inflows	514.3	No. months of import cover	17.6
Invisibles outflows	-742.1	Official gold holdings, m oz	56.7
Net transfers	-8.7	Foreign debt	1,418.3
Current account balance	330.6	– as % of GDP	12.6
– as % of GDP	3.0	– as % of total exports	52.5
Capital balance	-485.3	Debt service ratio	4.6
Overall balance	-342.9		

Health and education

Health spending, % of GDP	5.5	Education spending, % of GDP	...
Doctors per 1,000 pop.	1.9	Enrolment, %: primary	104
Hospital beds per 1,000 pop.	3.8	secondary	94
Improved-water source access,		tertiary	43
% of pop.	95.5		

Society

No. of households, m	453.0	Cost of living, Dec. 2016	
Av. no. per household	3.0	New York = 100	79
Marriages per 1,000 pop.	9.6	Cars per 1,000 pop.	83
Divorces per 1,000 pop.	1.8	Colour TV households, % with:	
Religion, % of pop.		cable	50.0
Non-religious	52.2	satellite	...
Other	22.7	Telephone lines per 100 pop.	16.5
Buddhist	18.2	Mobile telephone subscribers	
Christian	5.1	per 100 pop.	92.2
Muslim	1.8	Broadband subs per 100 pop.	19.8
Jewish	<0.1	Internet users, % of pop.	50.3

Note: Data exclude Special Administrative Regions, ie, Hong Kong and Macau.

COLOMBIA

Area, sq km	1,142,000	Capital	Bogotá
Arable as % of total land	1.5	Currency	Colombian peso (peso)

People

Population, m	48.2	Life expectancy: men	71.2 yrs
Pop. per sq km	42.2	women	78.3 yrs
Average annual growth		Adult literacy	94.6
in pop. 2015–20, %	0.8	Fertility rate (per woman)	2.0
Pop. aged 0–24, %	41.4	Urban population, 2020, %	77.8
Pop. aged 70 and over, %	4.3		per 1,000 pop.
No. of men per 100 women	97.0	Crude birth rate	14.8
Human Development Index	72.7	Crude death rate	6.1

The economy

GDP	$292bn	GDP per head	$6,048
GDP	799trn pesos	GDP per head in purchasing	
Av. ann. growth in real		power parity (USA=100)	24.7
GDP 2010–15	4.6%	Economic freedom index	69.7

Origins of GDP		**Components of GDP**	
	% of total		% of total
Agriculture	7	Private consumption	64
Industry, of which:	34	Public consumption	18
manufacturing	12	Investment	28
Services	59	Exports	15
		Imports	-24

Structure of employment

	% of total		% of labour force
Agriculture	15.8	Unemployed 2015	9.0
Industry	19.6	Av. ann. rate 2005–15	10.8
Services	64.6		

Energy

	m TOE		
Total output	116.8	Net energy imports as %	
Total consumption	41.7	of energy use	-274
Consumption per head			
kg oil equivalent	712		

Inflation and finance

Consumer price			av. ann. increase 2011–16
inflation 2016	7.6%	Narrow money (M1)	6.0%
Av. ann. inflation 2011–16	5.0%	Broad money	10.6%
Money market rate, Dec. 2016	7.65%		

Exchange rates

	end 2016		December 2016
Peso per $	3,000.71	Effective rates	2010 = 100
Peso per sdr	4,033.94	– nominal	83.92
Peso per €	3,157.50	– real	68.51

Trade

Principal exports		Principal imports	
	$bn fob		*$bn cif*
Petroleum & products	14.2	Intermediate goods & raw	
Coal	4.6	materials	23.3
Coffee	2.5	Capital goods	18.6
Nickel	0.4	Consumer goods	12.1
Total incl. others	**35.7**	Total incl. others	**54.1**

Main export destinations		Main origins of imports	
	% of total		*% of total*
United States	27.5	United States	28.8
Panama	7.2	China	18.6
China	5.2	Mexico	7.1
Spain	4.4	Germany	4.2

Balance of payments, reserves and debt, $bn

Visible exports fob	38.1	Change in reserves	-0.6
Visible imports fob	-52.0	Level of reserves	
Trade balance	-14.0	end Dec.	46.2
Invisibles inflows	11.9	No. months of import cover	7.5
Invisibles outflows	-22.0	Official gold holdings, m oz	0.1
Net transfers	5.3	Foreign debt	111.0
Current account balance	-18.8	– as % of GDP	38.0
– as % of GDP	-6.4	– as % of total exports	203.4
Capital balance	18.7	Debt service ratio	25.6
Overall balance	0.4		

Health and education

Health spending, % of GDP	7.2	Education spending, % of GDP	4.5
Doctors per 1,000 pop.	1.5	Enrolment, %: primary	114
Hospital beds per 1,000 pop.	1.5	secondary	98
Improved-water source access,		tertiary	56
% of pop.	91.4		

Society

No. of households, m	13.3	Cost of living, Dec. 2016	
Av. no. per household	3.6	New York = 100	61
Marriages per 1,000 pop.	...	Cars per 1,000 pop.	62
Divorces per 1,000 pop.	...	Colour TV households, % with:	
Religion, % of pop.		cable	57.0
Christian	92.5	satellite	7.4
Non-religious	6.6	Telephone lines per 100 pop.	14.4
Other	0.8	Mobile telephone subscribers	
Hindu	<0.1	per 100 pop.	115.7
Jewish	<0.1	Broadband subs per 100 pop.	11.2
Muslim	<0.1	Internet users, % of pop.	55.9

CZECH REPUBLIC

Area, sq km	77,210	Capital	Prague
Arable as % of total land	40.7	Currency	Koruna (Kc)

People

Population, m	10.5	Life expectancy: men	76.3 yrs
Pop. per sq km	136.0	women	81.9 yrs
Average annual growth		Adult literacy	...
in pop. 2015–20, %	0.1	Fertility rate (per woman)	1.4
Pop. aged 0–24, %	25.1	Urban population, 2020, %	73.1
Pop. aged 70 and over, %	11.6		per 1,000 pop.
No. of men per 100 women	96.6	Crude birth rate	10.0
Human Development Index	87.8	Crude death rate	10.6

The economy

GDP	$185bn	GDP per head	$17,634
GDP	Kc4,555bn	GDP per head in purchasing	
Av. ann. growth in real		power parity (USA=100)	57.4
GDP 2010–15	1.6%	Economic freedom index	73.3

Origins of GDP		**Components of GDP**	
	% of total		% of total
Agriculture	3	Private consumption	47
Industry, of which:	38	Public consumption	20
manufacturing	27	Investment	27
Services	60	Exports	83
		Imports	-77

Structure of employment

	% of total		% of labour force
Agriculture	2.9	Unemployed 2015	5.1
Industry	38.0	Av. ann. rate 2005–15	6.4
Services	59.0		

Energy

	m TOE		
Total output	27.8	Net energy imports as %	
Total consumption	40.7	of energy use	29
Consumption per head			
kg oil equivalent	3,915		

Inflation and finance

			av. ann. increase 2011–16
Consumer price			
inflation 2016	0.6%	Narrow money (M1)	9.7%
Av. ann. inflation 2011–16	3.4%	Broad money	4.0%
Treasury bill rate, Dec. 2016	-1.19%		

Exchange rates

	end 2016		December 2016
Kc per $	25.64	Effective rates	2010 = 100
Kc per sdr	34.47	– nominal	91.10
Kc per €	26.98	– real	91.49

Trade

Principal exports		**Principal imports**	
	$bn fob		*$bn cif*
Machinery & transport equip.	87.5	Machinery & transport equip.	64.6
Semi-manufactures	25.0	Semi-manufactures	24.1
Miscellaneous manufactured		Chemicals	15.9
goods	19.4	Miscellaneous manufactured	
Chemicals	9.8	goods	15.7
Total incl. others	**157.9**	Total incl. others	**141.4**

Main export destinations		**Main origins of imports**	
	% of total		*% of total*
Germany	32.1	Germany	29.9
Slovakia	9.0	Poland	9.0
Poland	5.9	China	8.3
United Kingdom	5.3	Slovakia	6.5
EU28	83.3	EU28	77.3

Balance of payments, reserves and debt, $bn

Visible exports fob	128.2	Change in reserves	10.0
Visible imports fob	-120.5	Level of reserves	
Trade balance	7.6	end Dec.	64.5
Invisibles inflows	30.2	No. months of import cover	4.9
Invisibles outflows	-37.4	Official gold holdings, m oz	0.3
Net transfers	0.0	Foreign debt	126.3
Current account balance	0.5	– as % of GDP	68.2
– as % of GDP	0.2	– as % of total exports	77.1
Capital balance	11.3	Debt service ratio	10.0
Overall balance	14.3		

Health and education

Health spending, % of GDP	7.4	Education spending, % of GDP	...
Doctors per 1,000 pop.	3.6	Enrolment, %: primary	99
Hospital beds per 1,000 pop.	6.8	secondary	104
Improved-water source access,		tertiary	65
% of pop.	100		

Society

No. of households, m	4.4	Cost of living, Dec. 2016	
Av. no. per household	2.3	New York = 100	62
Marriages per 1,000 pop.	4.3	Cars per 1,000 pop.	461
Divorces per 1,000 pop.	2.5	Colour TV households, % with:	
Religion, % of pop.		cable	24.5
Non-religious	76.4	satellite	27.0
Christian	23.3	Telephone lines per 100 pop.	17.6
Other	0.2	Mobile telephone subscribers	
Hindu	<0.1	per 100 pop.	123.2
Jewish	<0.1	Broadband subs per 100 pop.	27.3
Muslim	<0.1	Internet users, % of pop.	81.3

DENMARK

Area, sq km	42,262	Capital	Copenhagen
Arable as % of total land	57.5	Currency	Danish krone (DKr)

People

Population, m	5.7	Life expectancy: men	78.9 yrs
Pop. per sq km	134.9	women	82.3 yrs
Average annual growth		Adult literacy	...
in pop. 2015–20, %	0.4	Fertility rate (per woman)	1.7
Pop. aged 0–24, %	30.0	Urban population, 2020, %	88.5
Pop. aged 70 and over, %	12.3		per 1,000 pop.
No. of men per 100 women	98.6	Crude birth rate	10.7
Human Development Index	92.5	Crude death rate	9.6

The economy

GDP	$301bn	GDP per head	$52,861
GDP	DKr2,027bn	GDP per head in purchasing	
Av. ann. growth in real		power parity (USA=100)	83.7
GDP 2010–15	0.6%	Economic freedom index	75.1

Origins of GDP		Components of GDP	
	% of total		% of total
Agriculture	1	Private consumption	47
Industry, of which:	23	Public consumption	26
manufacturing	15	Investment	20
Services	76	Exports	55
		Imports	-48

Structure of employment

	% of total		% of labour force
Agriculture	2.5	Unemployed 2015	6.2
Industry	19.2	Av. ann. rate 2005–15	5.8
Services	78.0		

Energy

	m TOE		
Total output	13.1	Net energy imports as %	
Total consumption	18.0	of energy use	1
Consumption per head			
kg oil equivalent	2,873		

Inflation and finance

			av. ann. increase 2011–16
Consumer price			
inflation 2016	0.4%	Narrow money (M1)	7.6%
Av. ann. inflation 2011–16	3.1%	Broad money	4.0%
Treasury bill rate, Dec. 2016	-0.49%		

Exchange rates

	end 2016		December 2016
			2010 = 100
DKr per $	7.05	Effective rates	
DKr per sdr	9.48	– nominal	98.41
DKr per €	7.42	– real	95.59

Trade

Principal exports		Principal imports	
	$bn fob		*$bn cif*
Machinery & transport equip.	25.1	Machinery & transport equip.	27.9
Chemicals & related products	19.0	Food, drink & tobacco	11.7
Food, drink & tobacco	17.3	Chemicals & related products	10.7
Mineral fuels & lubricants	5.7	Mineral fuels & lubricants	5.6
Total incl. others	**94.6**	Total incl. others	**85.3**

Main export destinations		Main origins of imports	
	% of total		*% of total*
Germany	18.1	Germany	20.5
Sweden	11.7	Sweden	12.3
United States	8.5	Netherlands	8.2
United Kingdom	6.4	China	7.3
EU28	61.3	EU28	69.5

Balance of payments, reserves and aid, $bn

Visible exports fob	102.6	Overall balance	-3.1
Visible imports fob	-87.5	Change in reserves	-10.2
Trade balance	15.1	Level of reserves	
Invisibles inflows	93.0	end Dec.	65.2
Invisibles outflows	-75.6	No. months of import cover	4.8
Net transfers	-4.8	Official gold holdings, m oz	2.1
Current account balance	27.6	Aid given	2.6
– as % of GDP	9.2	– as % of GDP	0.9
Capital balance	-24.7		

Health and education

Health spending, % of GDP	10.8	Education spending, % of GDP	8.6
Doctors per 1,000 pop.	3.5	Enrolment, %: primary	101
Hospital beds per 1,000 pop.	3.5	secondary	130
Improved-water source access,		tertiary	82
% of pop.	100		

Society

No. of households, m	2.4	Cost of living, Dec. 2016	
Av. no. per household	2.4	New York = 100	100
Marriages per 1,000 pop.	5.0	Cars per 1,000 pop.	417
Divorces per 1,000 pop.	3.4	Colour TV households, % with:	
Religion, % of pop.		cable	65.3
Christian	83.5	satellite	11.8
Non-religious	11.8	Telephone lines per 100 pop.	29.9
Muslim	4.1	Mobile telephone subscribers	
Hindu	0.4	per 100 pop.	128.3
Other	0.2	Broadband subs per 100 pop.	42.5
Jewish	<0.1	Internet users, % of pop.	96.3

EGYPT

Area, sq km	1,001,000	Capital	Cairo
Arable as % of total land	2.7	Currency	Egyptian pound (£E)

People

Population, m	91.5	Life expectancy: men	69.6 yrs
Pop. per sq km	91.4	women	74.1 yrs
Average annual growth		Adult literacy	75.8
in pop. 2015–20, %	1.9	Fertility rate (per woman)	2.8
Pop. aged 0–24, %	50.5	Urban population, 2020, %	43.8
Pop. aged 70 and over, %	3.0		*per 1,000 pop.*
No. of men per 100 women	102.1	Crude birth rate	25.1
Human Development Index	69.1	Crude death rate	5.9

The economy

GDP	$332bn	GDP per head	$3,629
GDP	£E2,444bn	GDP per head in purchasing	
Av. ann. growth in real		power parity (USA=100)	20.9
GDP 2010–15	2.5%	Economic freedom index	52.6

Origins of GDP		**Components of GDP**	
	% of total		*% of total*
Agriculture	11	Private consumption	82
Industry, of which:	36	Public consumption	12
manufacturing	17	Investment	14
Services	52	Exports	13
		Imports	-22

Structure of employment

	% of total		*% of labour force*
Agriculture	25.8	Unemployed 2015	12.8
Industry	25.1	Av. ann. rate 2005–15	11.0
Services	49.1		

Energy

	m TOE		
Total output	81.7	Net energy imports as %	
Total consumption	89.6	of energy use	-7
Consumption per head			
kg oil equivalent	835		

Inflation and finance

			av. ann. increase 2011–16
Consumer price			
inflation 2016	10.2%	Narrow money (M1)	19.6%
Av. ann. inflation 2011–16	9.7%	Broad money	20.7%
Treasury bill rate, Dec. 2016	19.03%		

Exchange rates

	end 2016		*December 2016*
£E per $	18.13	Effective rates	2010 = 100
£E per sdr	24.37	– nominal	...
£E per €	19.08	– real	...

Trade

Principal exports		Principal imports	
	$bn fob		*$bn cif*
Petroleum & products	8.9	Petroleum & products	12.4
Finished goods incl. textiles	2.0	Machinery & equip.	6.9
Chemicals	1.9	Vehicles	5.9
Food	1.8	Chemicals	5.6
Total incl. others	**19.0**	Total incl. others	**57.6**

Main export destinations		Main origins of imports	
	% of total		*% of total*
Saudi Arabia	9.1	China	13.0
Italy	7.5	Germany	7.7
Turkey	5.8	United States	5.9
United Arab Emirates	5.1	Turkey	4.5

Balance of payments, reserves and debt, $bn

Visible exports fob	19.0	Change in reserves	0.9
Visible imports fob	-50.1	Level of reserves	
Trade balance	-31.0	end Dec.	15.9
Invisibles inflows	18.8	No. months of import cover	2.6
Invisibles outflows	-22.8	Official gold holdings, m oz	2.4
Net transfers	18.2	Foreign debt	46.6
Current account balance	-16.8	– as % of GDP	15.9
– as % of GDP	-5.1	– as % of total exports	82.9
Capital balance	21.1	Debt service ratio	8.9
Overall balance	-0.4		

Health and education

Health spending, % of GDP	5.6	Education spending, % of GDP	...
Doctors per 1,000 pop.	2.8	Enrolment, %: primary	104
Hospital beds per 1,000 pop.	0.5	secondary	86
Improved-water source access,		tertiary	36
% of pop.	99.4		

Society

No. of households, m	23.4	Cost of living, Dec. 2016	
Av. no. per household	3.9	New York = 100	59
Marriages per 1,000 pop.	11.0	Cars per 1,000 pop.	47
Divorces per 1,000 pop.	2.1	Colour TV households, % with:	
Religion, % of pop.		cable	...
Muslim	94.9	satellite	71.6
Christian	5.1	Telephone lines per 100 pop.	7.4
Hindu	<0.1	Mobile telephone subscribers	
Jewish	<0.1	per 100 pop.	111.0
Non-religious	<0.1	Broadband subs per 100 pop.	4.5
Other	<0.1	Internet users, % of pop.	37.8

FINLAND

Area, sq km	303,890	Capital	Helsinki
Arable as % of total land	7.3	Currency	Euro (€)

People

Population, m	5.5	Life expectancy: men	78.8 yrs
Pop. per sq km	18.1	women	84.1 yrs
Average annual growth		Adult literacy	...
in pop. 2015–20, %	0.3	Fertility rate (per woman)	1.8
Pop. aged 0–24, %	28.2	Urban population, 2020, %	84.9
Pop. aged 70 and over, %	13.1		per 1,000 pop.
No. of men per 100 women	96.9	Crude birth rate	10.7
Human Development Index	89.5	Crude death rate	9.9

The economy

GDP	$232bn	GDP per head	$42,269
GDP	€210bn	GDP per head in purchasing	
Av. ann. growth in real		power parity (USA=100)	73.1
GDP 2010–15	0.0%	Economic freedom index	74.0

Origins of GDP		**Components of GDP**	
	% of total		% of total
Agriculture	2	Private consumption	55
Industry, of which:	27	Public consumption	24
manufacturing	17	Investment	21
Services	71	Exports	37
		Imports	-37

Structure of employment

	% of total		% of labour force
Agriculture	4.2	Unemployed 2015	9.4
Industry	21.6	Av. ann. rate 2005–15	8.0
Services	73.8		

Energy

	m TOE		
Total output	5.8	Net energy imports as %	
Total consumption	29.0	of energy use	46
Consumption per head			
kg oil equivalent	6,213		

Inflation and finance

Consumer price			av. ann. increase 2011–16
inflation 2016	0.4%	Narrow money (M1)	8.1%
Av. ann. inflation 2011–16	3.6%	Broad money	3.6%
Money market rate, Dec. 2016	-0.32%		

Exchange rates

	end 2016		December 2016
€ per $	0.95	Effective rates	2010 = 100
€ per sdr	1.28	– nominal	99.71
		– real	96.37

Trade

Principal exports	$bn fob	Principal imports	$bn cif
Machinery & transport equip.	19.0	Machinery & transport equip.	20.6
Chemicals & related products	6.3	Mineral fuels & lubricants	8.6
Raw materials	5.3	Chemicals & related products	7.7
Mineral fuels & lubricants	4.3	Food, drink & tobacco	4.8
Total incl. others	**59.7**	Total incl. others	**57.5**

Main export destinations	% of total	Main origins of imports	% of total
Germany	13.9	Germany	17.8
Sweden	10.1	Sweden	16.9
United States	7.0	Russia	11.5
Netherlands	6.6	Netherlands	9.5
EU28	58.9	EU28	73.0

Balance of payments, reserves and aid, $bn

Visible exports fob	59.6	Overall balance	-0.2
Visible imports fob	-57.5	Change in reserves	-0.7
Trade balance	2.2	Level of reserves	
Invisibles inflows	42.1	end Dec.	10.0
Invisibles outflows	-43.1	No. months of import cover	1.2
Net transfers	-2.6	Official gold holdings, m oz	1.6
Current account balance	-1.4	Aid given	1.3
– as % of GDP	-0.6	– as % of GDP	0.6
Capital balance	2.4		

Health and education

Health spending, % of GDP	9.7	Education spending, % of GDP	7.2
Doctors per 1,000 pop.	2.9	Enrolment, %: primary	102
Hospital beds per 1,000 pop.	5.5	secondary	149
Improved-water source access,		tertiary	87
% of pop.	100		

Society

No. of households, m	2.6	Cost of living, Dec. 2016	
Av. no. per household	2.1	New York = 100	92
Marriages per 1,000 pop.	4.5	Cars per 1,000 pop.	592
Divorces per 1,000 pop.	2.5	Colour TV households, % with:	
Religion, % of pop.		cable	68.5
Christian	81.6	satellite	11.1
Non-religious	17.6	Telephone lines per 100 pop.	9.8
Muslim	0.8	Mobile telephone subscribers	
Hindu	<0.1	per 100 pop.	135.4
Jewish	<0.1	Broadband subs per 100 pop.	31.7
Other	<0.1	Internet users, % of pop.	92.7

FRANCE

Area, sq km	549,000	Capital	Paris
Arable as % of total land	33.5	Currency	Euro (€)

People

Population, m	64.4	Life expectancy: men	80.0 yrs
Pop. per sq km	117.3	women	85.6 yrs
Average annual growth		Adult literacy	...
in pop. 2015–20, %	0.4	Fertility rate (per woman)	2.1
Pop. aged 0–24, %	30.1	Urban population, 2020, %	80.6
Pop. aged 70 and over, %	13.2		per 1,000 pop.
No. of men per 100 women	94.8	Crude birth rate	11.9
Human Development Index	89.7	Crude death rate	9.1

The economy

GDP	$2,420bn	GDP per head	$37,580
GDP	€2,181bn	GDP per head in purchasing	
Av. ann. growth in real		power parity (USA=100)	73.9
GDP 2010–15	0.9%	Economic freedom index	63.3

Origins of GDP		**Components of GDP**	
	% of total		% of total
Agriculture	2	Private consumption	55
Industry, of which:	20	Public consumption	24
manufacturing	11	Investment	22
Services	79	Exports	30
		Imports	-31

Structure of employment

	% of total		% of labour force
Agriculture	2.7	Unemployed 2015	10.4
Industry	20.1	Av. ann. rate 2005–15	9.3
Services	75.9		

Energy

	m TOE		
Total output	109.4	Net energy imports as %	
Total consumption	254.2	of energy use	43
Consumption per head			
kg oil equivalent	3,661		

Inflation and finance

			av. ann. increase 2011–16
Consumer price			
inflation 2016	0.3%	Narrow money (M1)	8.1%
Av. ann. inflation 2011–16	3.1%	Broad money	3.6%
Treasury bill rate, Dec. 2016	-0.85%		

Exchange rates

	end 2016		December 2016
€ per $	0.95	Effective rates	2010 = 100
€ per sdr	1.28	– nominal	96.57
		– real	92.80

Trade

Principal exports		Principal imports	
	$bn fob		*$bn cif*
Machinery & transport equip.	197.8	Machinery & transport equip.	204.6
Chemicals & related products	93.9	Chemicals & related products	79.9
Food, drink and tobacco	60.9	Mineral fuels & lubricants	59.7
Mineral fuels & lubricants	16.3	Food, drink and tobacco	51.0
Total incl. others	**505.4**	Total incl. others	**555.5**

Main export destinations		Main origins of imports	
	% of total		*% of total*
Germany	15.8	Germany	20.1
Spain	7.3	Belgium	11.2
United States	7.2	Italy	7.9
Italy	7.1	Netherlands	7.8
EU28	58.8	EU28	68.5

Balance of payments, reserves and aid, $bn

Visible exports fob	510.8	Overall balance	8.0
Visible imports fob	-537.5	Change in reserves	-5.8
Trade balance	-26.7	Level of reserves	
Invisibles inflows	419.8	end Dec.	138.2
Invisibles outflows	-352.2	No. months of import cover	1.9
Net transfers	-45.7	Official gold holdings, m oz	78.3
Current account balance	-4.9	Aid given	9.0
– as % of GDP	-0.2	– as % of GDP	0.4
Capital balance	18.6		

Health and education

Health spending, % of GDP	11.5	Education spending, % of GDP	5.5
Doctors per 1,000 pop.	3.2	Enrolment, %: primary	105
Hospital beds per 1,000 pop.	6.4	secondary	111
Improved-water source access,		tertiary	64
% of pop.	100		

Society

No. of households, m	29.3	Cost of living, Dec. 2016	
Av. no. per household	2.2	New York = 100	107
Marriages per 1,000 pop.	3.7	Cars per 1,000 pop.	492
Divorces per 1,000 pop.	1.9	Colour TV households, % with:	
Religion, % of pop.		cable	13.1
Christian	63.0	satellite	34.1
Non-religious	28.0	Telephone lines per 100 pop.	59.9
Muslim	7.5	Mobile telephone subscribers	
Other	1.0	per 100 pop.	102.6
Jewish	0.5	Broadband subs per 100 pop.	41.3
Hindu	<0.1	Internet users, % of pop.	84.7

GERMANY

Area, sq km	357,000	Capital	Berlin
Arable as % of total land	34.1	Currency	Euro (€)

People

Population, m	80.7	Life expectancy: men	79.3 yrs
Pop. per sq km	226.1	women	83.8 yrs
Average annual growth		Adult literacy	...
in pop. 2015–20, %	-0.1	Fertility rate (per woman)	1.4
Pop. aged 0–24, %	23.3	Urban population, 2020, %	76.4
Pop. aged 70 and over, %	16.1		per 1,000 pop.
No. of men per 100 women	96.6	Crude birth rate	8.7
Human Development Index	92.6	Crude death rate	11.3

The economy

GDP	$3,365bn	GDP per head	$41,701
GDP	€3,033bn	GDP per head in purchasing	
Av. ann. growth in real		power parity (USA=100)	85.3
GDP 2010–15	1.6%	Economic freedom index	73.8

Origins of GDP		**Components of GDP**	
	% of total		% of total
Agriculture	1	Private consumption	54
Industry, of which:	30	Public consumption	19
manufacturing	23	Investment	19
Services	69	Exports	47
		Imports	-39

Structure of employment

	% of total		% of labour force
Agriculture	1.4	Unemployed 2015	4.6
Industry	27.7	Av. ann. rate 2005–15	7.1
Services	70.9		

Energy

	m TOE		
Total output	72.7	Net energy imports as %	
Total consumption	321.8	of energy use	61
Consumption per head			
kg oil equivalent	3,779		

Inflation and finance

			av. ann. increase 2011–16
Consumer price			
inflation 2016	0.4%	Narrow money (M1)	8.1%
Av. ann. inflation 2011–16	3.2%	Broad money	3.6%
Deposit rate, Dec. 2016	0.23%		

Exchange rates

	end 2016		December 2016
€ per $	0.95	Effective rates	2010 = 100
€ per sdr	1.28	– nominal	98.05
		– real	94.33

Trade

Principal exports		Principal imports	
	$bn fob		*$bn cif*
Machinery & transport equip.	658.6	Machinery & transport equip.	387.5
Chemicals & related products	210.8	Chemicals & related products	145.2
Food, drink and tobacco	71.3	Mineral fuels & lubricants	98.6
Mineral fuels & lubricants	32.3	Food, drink and tobacco	79.4
Total incl. others	**1,320.7**	Total incl. others	**1,051.6**

Main export destinations		Main origins of imports	
	% of total		*% of total*
United States	9.6	Netherlands	13.6
France	8.6	France	7.6
United Kingdom	7.5	China	7.3
Netherlands	6.7	Belgium	6.0
EU28	57.9	EU28	65.6

Balance of payments, reserves and aid, $bn

Visible exports fob	1,305.7	Overall balance	-2.4
Visible imports fob	-1,017.8	Change in reserves	-19.8
Trade balance	287.9	Level of reserves	
Invisibles inflows	480.5	end Dec.	173.7
Invisibles outflows	-444.4	No. months of import cover	1.4
Net transfers	-44.0	Official gold holdings, m oz	108.7
Current account balance	280.0	Aid given	17.9
– as % of GDP	8.3	– as % of GDP	0.5
Capital balance	-252.2		

Health and education

Health spending, % of GDP	11.3	Education spending, % of GDP	4.9
Doctors per 1,000 pop.	3.9	Enrolment, %: primary	105
Hospital beds per 1,000 pop.	8.2	secondary	103
Improved-water source access,		tertiary	68
% of pop.	100		

Society

No. of households, m	41.6	Cost of living, Dec. 2016	
Av. no. per household	1.9	New York = 100	77
Marriages per 1,000 pop.	4.8	Cars per 1,000 pop.	537
Divorces per 1,000 pop.	2.1	Colour TV households, % with:	
Religion, % of pop.		cable	46.0
Christian	68.7	satellite	45.1
Non-religious	24.7	Telephone lines per 100 pop.	54.9
Muslim	5.8	Mobile telephone subscribers	
Other	0.5	per 100 pop.	116.7
Jewish	0.3	Broadband subs per 100 pop.	37.2
Hindu	<0.1	Internet users, % of pop.	87.6

GREECE

Area, sq km	128,900	Capital	Athens
Arable as % of total land	20.2	Currency	Euro (€)

People

Population, m	11.0	Life expectancy: men	78.8
Pop. per sq km	85.3	women	84.3
Average annual growth		Adult literacy	95.3
in pop. 2015–20, %	-0.2	Fertility rate (per woman)	1.4
Pop. aged 0–24, %	24.8	Urban population, 2020, %	79.5
Pop. aged 70 and over, %	15.4		per 1,000 pop.
No. of men per 100 women	95.3	Crude birth rate	8.0
Human Development Index	86.6	Crude death rate	11.3

The economy

GDP	$195bn	GDP per head	$17,723
GDP	€176bn	GDP per head in purchasing	
Av. ann. growth in real		power parity (USA=100)	46.3
GDP 2010–15	-3.9%	Economic freedom index	55.0

Origins of GDP		**Components of GDP**	
	% of total		% of total
Agriculture	4	Private consumption	70
Industry, of which:	16	Public consumption	20
manufacturing	9	Investment	10
Services	80	Exports	32
		Imports	-32

Structure of employment

	% of total		% of labour force
Agriculture	12.9	Unemployed 2015	24.9
Industry	14.9	Av. ann. rate 2005–15	16.2
Services	72.2		

Energy

	m TOE		
Total output	5.9	Net energy imports as %	
Total consumption	26.3	of energy use	62
Consumption per head			
kg oil equivalent	2,124		

Inflation and finance

			av. ann. increase 2011–16
Consumer price			
inflation 2016	-0.1%	Narrow money (M1)	8.1%
Av. ann. inflation 2011–16	1.8%	Broad money	3.6%
Treasury bill rate, Dec. 2016	-0.08%		

Exchange rates

	end 2016		December 2016
€ per $	0.95	Effective rates	2010 = 100
€ per sdr	1.28	– nominal	98.42
		– real	89.30

Trade

Principal exports		Principal imports	
	$bn fob		*$bn cif*
Mineral fuels & lubricants	8.4	Mineral fuels & lubricants	12.6
Food, drink and tobacco	5.1	Machinery & transport equip.	9.7
Chemicals & related products	3.0	Chemicals & related products	7.6
Machinery & transport equip.	2.9	Food, drink and tobacco	6.3
Total incl. others	**28.7**	Total incl. others	**48.4**

Main export destinations		Main origins of imports	
	% of total		*% of total*
Italy	11.3	Germany	10.8
Germany	7.3	Italy	8.3
Turkey	6.6	Russia	7.8
Cyprus	6.0	Iraq	6.9
EU28	54.2	EU28	52.9

Balance of payments, reserves and debt, $bn

Visible exports fob	27.5	Overall balance	10.6
Visible imports fob	-46.6	Change in reserves	-0.2
Trade balance	-19.1	Level of reserves	
Invisibles inflows	39.3	end Dec.	6.0
Invisibles outflows	-19.4	No. months of import cover	1.1
Net transfers	-0.6	Official gold holdings, m oz	3.6
Current account balance	0.2	Aid given	0.2
– as % of GDP	0.1	– as % of GDP	0.1
Capital balance	9.1		

Health and education

Health spending, % of GDP	8.1	Education spending, % of GDP	...
Doctors per 1,000 pop.	6.2	Enrolment, %: primary	98
Hospital beds per 1,000 pop.	...	secondary	107
Improved-water source access,		tertiary	114
% of pop.	100		

Society

No. of households, m	4.4	Cost of living, Dec. 2016	
Av. no. per household	2.5	New York = 100	63
Marriages per 1,000 pop.	4.9	Cars per 1,000 pop.	460
Divorces per 1,000 pop.	1.5	Colour TV households, % with:	
Religion, % of pop.		cable	0.9
Christian	88.1	satellite	13.5
Non-religious	6.1	Telephone lines per 100 pop.	47.3
Muslim	5.3	Mobile telephone subscribers	
Other	0.3	per 100 pop.	113.0
Hindu	0.1	Broadband subs per 100 pop.	30.9
Jewish	<0.1	Internet users, % of pop.	66.8

HONG KONG

Area, sq km	1,050	Capital	Victoria
Arable as % of total land	3.0	Currency	Hong Kong dollar (HK$)

People

Population, m	7.3	Life expectancy: men	81.7
Pop. per sq km	6,952.4	women	87.4
Average annual growth		Adult literacy	...
in pop. 2015–20, %	0.7	Fertility rate (per woman)	1.2
Pop. aged 0–24, %	23.2	Urban population, 2020, %	100.0
Pop. aged 70 and over, %	10.2		per 1,000 pop.
No. of men per 100 women	88.5	Crude birth rate	9.8
Human Development Index	91.7	Crude death rate	6.6

The economy

GDP	$309bn	GDP per head	$42,384
GDP	HK$2,398bn	GDP per head in purchasing	
Av. ann. growth in real		power parity (USA=100)	101.7
GDP 2010–15	2.9%	Economic freedom index	89.8

Origins of GDP		**Components of GDP**	
	% of total		% of total
Agriculture	0	Private consumption	66
Industry, of which:	7	Public consumption	10
manufacturing	1	Investment	22
Services	92	Exports	202
		Imports	-199

Structure of employment

	% of total		% of labour force
Agriculture	...	Unemployed 2015	3.3
Industry	11.4	Av. ann. rate 2005–15	4.0
Services	79.4		

Energy

	m TOE		
Total output	...	Net energy imports as %	
Total consumption	29.7	of energy use	99
Consumption per head			
kg oil equivalent	1,967		

Inflation and finance

Consumer price			av. ann. increase 2011–16
inflation 2016	2.5%	Narrow money (M1)	14.5%
Av. ann. inflation 2011–16	5.5%	Broad money	9.2%
Treasury bill rate, Dec. 2016	0.67%		

Exchange rates

	end 2016		December 2016
HK$ per $	7.75	Effective rates	2010 = 100
HK$ per sdr	10.42	– nominal	109.39
HK$ per €	8.15	– real	...

Trade

Principal exports[a]

	$bn fob
Capital goods	192.2
Semi-finished goods	159.8
Consumer goods	100.7
Foodstuffs	6.3
Total incl. others	**465.5**

Principal imports[a]

	$bn cif
Capital goods & raw materials	193.7
Raw materials & semi-manufactures	182.9
Consumer goods	111.6
Foodstuffs	22.3
Total incl. others	**522.6**

Main export destinations

	% of total
China	53.7
United States	9.5
Japan	3.4
India	2.8

Main origins of imports

	% of total
China	49.0
Taiwan	6.8
Japan	6.4
Singapore	6.1

Balance of payments, reserves and debt, $bn

Visible exports fob	501.7	Change in reserves	30.3
Visible imports fob	-524.6	Level of reserves	
Trade balance	-22.9	end Dec.	358.8
Invisibles inflows	268.8	No. months of import cover	5.7
Invisibles outflows	-232.8	Official gold holdings, m oz	0.1
Net transfers	-2.9	Foreign debt	491.9
Current account balance	10.3	– as % of GDP	159.0
– as % of GDP	3.3	– as % of total exports	63.7
Capital balance	19.8	Debt service ratio	6.3
Overall balance	36.4		

Health and education

Health spending, % of GDP	...	Education spending, % of GDP	3.3
Doctors per 1,000 pop.	...	Enrolment, %: primary	111
Hospital beds per 1,000 pop.	...	secondary	101
Improved-water source access, % of pop.	...	tertiary	68

Society

No. of households, m	2.4	Cost of living, Dec. 2016	
Av. no. per household	3.0	New York = 100	114
Marriages per 1,000 pop.	7.8	Cars per 1,000 pop.	70
Divorces per 1,000 pop.	...	Colour TV households, % with:	
Religion, % of pop.		cable	94.4
Non-religious	56.1	satellite	0.1
Christian	14.3	Telephone lines per 100 pop.	59.2
Other	14.2	Mobile telephone subscribers	
Buddhist	13.2	per 100 pop.	228.7
Muslim	1.8	Broadband subs per 100 pop.	32.1
Hindu	0.4	Internet users, % of pop.	84.9

a Including re-exports.
Note: Hong Kong became a Special Administrative Region of China on July 1 1997.

HUNGARY

Area, sq km	90,530	Capital	Budapest
Arable as % of total land	48.6	Currency	Forint (Ft)

People

Population, m	9.9	Life expectancy: men	71.9 yrs
Pop. per sq km	109.4	women	79.1 yrs
Average annual growth		Adult literacy	99.4
in pop. 2015–20, %	-0.4	Fertility rate (per woman)	1.4
Pop. aged 0–24, %	25.4	Urban population, 2020, %	73.4
Pop. aged 70 and over, %	12.4		per 1,000 pop.
No. of men per 100 women	90.8	Crude birth rate	9.4
Human Development Index	83.6	Crude death rate	13.5

The economy

GDP	$122bn	GDP per head	$12,289
GDP	Ft33,999bn	GDP per head in purchasing	
Av. ann. growth in real		power parity (USA=100)	47.1
GDP 2010–15	1.7%	Economic freedom index	65.8

Origins of GDP		**Components of GDP**	
	% of total		% of total
Agriculture	4	Private consumption	49
Industry, of which:	32	Public consumption	20
manufacturing	25	Investment	22
Services	64	Exports	91
		Imports	-82

Structure of employment

	% of total		% of labour force
Agriculture	4.9	Unemployed 2015	6.8
Industry	30.3	Av. ann. rate 2005–15	8.9
Services	64.7		

Energy

	m TOE		
Total output	7.7	Net energy imports as %	
Total consumption	23.7	of energy use	56
Consumption per head			
kg oil equivalent	2,314		

Inflation and finance

Consumer price		av. ann. increase 2011–16	
inflation 2016	0.4%	Narrow money (M1)	17.3%
Av. ann. inflation 2011–16	3.7%	Broad money	4.0%
Treasury bill rate, Dec. 2016	0.16%		

Exchange rates

	end 2016		December 2016
			2010 = 100
Ft per $	293.69	Effective rates	
Ft per sdr	394.82	– nominal	87.96
Ft per €	309.04	– real	89.68

Trade

Trade

Principal exports		Principal imports	
	$bn fob		*$bn cif*
Machinery & equipment	57.4	Machinery & equipment	45.0
Manufactured goods	31.2	Manufactured goods	32.4
Food, drink & tobacco	7.3	Fuels & energy	7.4
Raw materials	2.3	Food, drink & tobacco	4.7
Total incl. others	**100.3**	Total incl. others	**90.7**

Main export destinations		Main origins of imports	
	% of total		*% of total*
Germany	27.5	Germany	26.4
Romania	5.4	Austria	6.7
Slovakia	5.0	China	6.3
Austria	4.9	Poland	5.5
EU28	81.3	EU28	76.6

Balance of payments, reserves and debt, $bn

Visible exports fob	88.3	Change in reserves	-8.9
Visible imports fob	-83.4	Level of reserves	
Trade balance	4.9	end Dec.	33.1
Invisibles inflows	34.0	No. months of import cover	3.4
Invisibles outflows	-33.7	Official gold holdings, m oz	0.1
Net transfers	-1.2	Foreign debt	127.4
Current account balance	4.0	– as % of GDP	104.8
– as % of GDP	3.3	– as % of total exports	104.1
Capital balance	-7.2	Debt service ratio	25.9
Overall balance	-5.4		

Health and education

Health spending, % of GDP	7.4	Education spending, % of GDP	4.2
Doctors per 1,000 pop.	3.1	Enrolment, %: primary	102
Hospital beds per 1,000 pop.	7.2	secondary	105
Improved-water source access,		tertiary	51
% of pop.	100		

Society

No. of households, m	4.2	Cost of living, Dec. 2016	
Av. no. per household	2.4	New York = 100	56
Marriages per 1,000 pop.	3.9	Cars per 1,000 pop.	314
Divorces per 1,000 pop.	2.0	Colour TV households, % with:	
Religion, % of pop.		cable	56.4
Christian	81.0	satellite	28.5
Non-religious	18.6	Telephone lines per 100 pop.	31.2
Other	0.2	Mobile telephone subscribers	
Jewish	0.1	per 100 pop.	118.9
Hindu	<0.1	Broadband subs per 100 pop.	27.4
Muslim	<0.1	Internet users, % of pop.	72.8

INDIA

Area, sq km	3,287,000	Capital	New Delhi
Arable as % of total land	52.6	Currency	Indian rupee (Rs)

People

Population, m	1,311.1	Life expectancy: men	67.7 yrs
Pop. per sq km	398.9	women	70.6 yrs
Average annual growth		Adult literacy	72.2
in pop. 2015–20, %	1.2	Fertility rate (per woman)	2.5
Pop. aged 0–24, %	47.2	Urban population, 2020, %	34.8
Pop. aged 70 and over, %	3.4		per 1,000 pop.
No. of men per 100 women	107.6	Crude birth rate	19.1
Human Development Index	62.4	Crude death rate	7.3

The economy

GDP	$2,088bn	GDP per head	$1,593
GDP	Rs136trn	GDP per head in purchasing	
Av. ann. growth in real		power parity (USA=100)	10.9
GDP 2010–15	6.7%	Economic freedom index	52.6

Origins of GDP		**Components of GDP**	
	% of total		% of total
Agriculture	17	Private consumption	59
Industry, of which:	30	Public consumption	10
manufacturing	17	Investment	33
Services	53	Exports	20
		Imports	-22

Structure of employment

	% of total		% of labour force
Agriculture	49.7	Unemployed 2015	3.5
Industry	21.5	Av. ann. rate 2005–15	3.8
Services	28.7		

Energy

	m TOE		
Total output	354.6	Net energy imports as %	
Total consumption	622.5	of energy use	34
Consumption per head			
kg oil equivalent	637		

Inflation and finance

			av. ann. increase 2011–16
Consumer price			
inflation 2016	5.5%	Narrow money (M1)	3.3%
Av. ann. inflation 2011–16	8.4%	Broad money	10.8%
Money market rate, Dec. 2016	6.00%		

Exchange rates

	end 2016		December 2016
Rs per $	67.95	Effective rates	2010 = 100
Rs per sdr	91.35	– nominal	...
Rs per €	71.50	– real	...

Trade

Principal exports		Principal imports	
	$bn fob		*$bn cif*
Engineering products	60.6	Petroleum & products	82.9
Gems & jewellery	39.5	Electronic goods	40.0
Petroleum & products	30.4	Gold & silver	35.3
Agricultural products	26.4	Machinery	29.5
Total incl. others	**262.0**	Total incl. others	**380.4**

Main export destinations		Main origins of imports	
	% of total		*% of total*
United States	15.4	China	16.2
United Arab Emirates	11.6	Saudi Arabia	5.6
Hong Kong	4.7	Switzerland	5.5
China	3.7	United States	5.4

Balance of payments, reserves and debt, $bn

Visible exports fob	272.4	Change in reserves	28.2
Visible imports fob	-409.2	Level of reserves	
Trade balance	-136.9	end Dec.	353.3
Invisibles inflows	170.8	No. months of import cover	8.0
Invisibles outflows	-120.5	Official gold holdings, m oz	17.9
Net transfers	64.2	Foreign debt	479.6
Current account balance	-22.5	– as % of GDP	23.0
– as % of GDP	-1.1	– as % of total exports	93.7
Capital balance	67.7	Debt service ratio	9.4
Overall balance	44.1		

Health and education

Health spending, % of GDP	4.7	Education spending, % of GDP	3.8
Doctors per 1,000 pop.	0.7	Enrolment, %: primary	108
Hospital beds per 1,000 pop.	0.7	secondary	74
Improved-water source access,		tertiary	26
% of pop.	94.1		

Society

No. of households, m	268.6	Cost of living, Dec. 2016	
Av. no. per household	4.9	New York = 100	47
Marriages per 1,000 pop.	...	Cars per 1,000 pop.	17
Divorces per 1,000 pop.	...	Colour TV households, % with:	
Religion, % of pop.		cable	62.5
Hindu	79.5	satellite	17.1
Muslim	14.4	Telephone lines per 100 pop.	2.0
Other	3.6	Mobile telephone subscribers	
Christian	2.5	per 100 pop.	78.1
Jewish	<0.1	Broadband subs per 100 pop.	1.3
Non-religious	<0.1	Internet users, % of pop.	26.0

INDONESIA

Area, sq km	1,911,000	Capital	Jakarta
Arable as % of total land	13.0	Currency	Rupiah (Rp)

People

Population, m	257.6	Life expectancy: men	67.4 yrs
Pop. per sq km	134.8	women	71.7 yrs
Average annual growth		Adult literacy	95.4
in pop. 2015–20, %	1.1	Fertility rate (per woman)	2.2
Pop. aged 0–24, %	44.8	Urban population, 2020, %	57.2
Pop. aged 70 and over, %	3.1		per 1,000 pop.
No. of men per 100 women	101.4	Crude birth rate	18.5
Human Development Index	68.9	Crude death rate	7.2

The economy

GDP	$861bn	GDP per head	$3,343
GDP	Rs11,531trn	GDP per head in purchasing	
Av. ann. growth in real		power parity (USA=100)	19.7
GDP 2010–15	5.5%	Economic freedom index	61.9

Origins of GDP		**Components of GDP**	
	% of total		% of total
Agriculture	14	Private consumption	55
Industry, of which:	40	Public consumption	10
manufacturing	21	Investment	35
Services	46	Exports	21
		Imports	-21

Structure of employment

	% of total		% of labour force
Agriculture	32.9	Unemployed 2015	6.0
Industry	22.2	Av. ann. rate 2005–15	7.8
Services	44.9		

Energy

	m TOE		
Total output	380.2	Net energy imports as %	
Total consumption	184.6	of energy use	-103
Consumption per head			
kg oil equivalent	886		

Inflation and finance

Consumer price		*av. ann. increase 2011–16*	
inflation 2016	3.7%	Narrow money (M1)	11.4%
Av. ann. inflation 2011–16	7.0%	Broad money	11.7%
Money market rate, Nov. 2016	4.17%		

Exchange rates

	end 2016		December 2016
Rp per $	13,436	Effective rates	2010 = 100
Rp per sdr	18,062	– nominal	...
Rp per €	14,138	– real	...

Trade

Principal exports		Principal imports	
	$bn fob		*$bn cif*
Manufactured goods	106.2	Raw materials & auxiliary	
Mining & other sector products	34.4	materials	98.0
Agricultural goods	5.8	Capital goods	24.9
Unclassified exports	1.3	Consumer goods	18.5
Total incl. others	**150.4**	Total incl. others	**142.7**

Main export destinations		Main origins of imports	
	% of total		*% of total*
Japan	12.0	China	20.6
United States	10.8	Singapore	12.6
China	10.0	Japan	9.3
Singapore	8.4	Malaysia	6.0

Balance of payments, reserves and debt, $bn

Visible exports fob	149.1	Change in reserves	-5.9
Visible imports fob	-135.1	Level of reserves	
Trade balance	14.0	end Dec.	105.9
Invisibles inflows	25.0	No. months of import cover	6.4
Invisibles outflows	-62.1	Official gold holdings, m oz	2.5
Net transfers	5.5	Foreign debt	308.5
Current account balance	-17.5	– as % of GDP	35.8
– as % of GDP	-2.0	– as % of total exports	167.8
Capital balance	16.9	Debt service ratio	30.3
Overall balance	-1.1		

Health and education

Health spending, % of GDP	2.8	Education spending, % of GDP	3.3
Doctors per 1,000 pop.	0.2	Enrolment, %: primary	106
Hospital beds per 1,000 pop.	0.9	secondary	82
Improved-water source access,		tertiary	31
% of pop.	87.4		

Society

No. of households, m	65.3	Cost of living, Dec. 2016	
Av. no. per household	3.9	New York = 100	66
Marriages per 1,000 pop.	...	Cars per 1,000 pop.	50
Divorces per 1,000 pop.	...	Colour TV households, % with:	
Religion, % of pop.		cable	6.0
Muslim	87.2	satellite	25.5
Christian	9.9	Telephone lines per 100 pop.	8.8
Hindu	1.7	Mobile telephone subscribers	
Other	1.1	per 100 pop.	132.3
Jewish	<0.1	Broadband subs per 100 pop.	1.1
Non-religious	<0.1	Internet users, % of pop.	22.0

IRAN

Area, sq km	1,745,000	Capital	Tehran
Arable as % of total land	9.0	Currency	Rial (IR)

People

Population, m	79.1	Life expectancy: men	74.7 yrs
Pop. per sq km	45.3	women	77.1 yrs
Average annual growth		Adult literacy	87.2
in pop. 2015–20, %	1.1	Fertility rate (per woman)	1.8
Pop. aged 0–24, %	39.5	Urban population, 2020, %	75.7
Pop. aged 70 and over, %	3.2		per 1,000 pop.
No. of men per 100 women	101.4	Crude birth rate	15.6
Human Development Index	77.4	Crude death rate	4.6

The economy

GDP	$374bn	GDP per head	$4,732
GDP	IR11,096trn	GDP per head in purchasing	
Av. ann. growth in real		power parity (USA=100)	30.4
GDP 2010–15	-0.1%	Economic freedom index	50.5

Origins of GDP		**Components of GDP**	
	% of total		% of total
Agriculture	11	Private consumption	50
Industry, of which:	33	Public consumption	12
manufacturing	...	Investment	36
Services	56	Exports	20
		Imports	-19

Structure of employment

	% of total		% of labour force
Agriculture	18.0	Unemployed 2015	11.1
Industry	32.5	Av. ann. rate 2005–15	11.5
Services	49.4		

Energy

	m TOE		
Total output	334.0	Net energy imports as %	
Total consumption	264.7	of energy use	-33
Consumption per head			
kg oil equivalent	3,034		

Inflation and finance

			av. ann. increase 2011–16
Consumer price			
inflation 2016	7.4%	Narrow money (M1)	14.9%
Av. ann. inflation 2011–16	20.6%	Broad money	29.5%
Deposit rate, Dec. 2016	12.90%		

Exchange rates

	end 2016		December 2016
IR per $	32,376	Effective rates	2010 = 100
IR per sdr	43,524	– nominal	39.56
IR per €	34,067	– real	109.43

Trade

Principal exports		**Principal imports**	
	$bn fob		$bn cif
Oil & gas	33.6	Machinery & transport equip.[a]	14.1
Petrochemicals[a]	9.8	Intermediate goods[a]	8.2
Fresh & dry fruits[a]	1.5	Chemicals[a]	6.2
Carpets[a]	0.4		
Total incl. others	**64.6**	Total incl. others	**52.4**

Main export destinations		**Main origins of imports**	
	% of total		% of total
China	38.1	United Arab Emirates	27.6
India	14.8	China	15.4
Turkey	14.5	Turkey	6.2
Japan	7.7	South Korea	4.9

Balance of payments[b], reserves and debt, $bn

Visible exports fob	64.6	Change in reserves	...
Visible imports fob	-52.4	Level of reserves	
Trade balance	12.2	end Dec.	...
Invisibles inflows	12.3	No. months of import cover	...
Invisibles outflows	-16.0	Official gold holdings, m oz	...
Net transfers	0.5	Foreign debt	6.3
Current account balance	9.0	– as % of GDP	1.5
– as % of GDP	2.4	– as % of total exports	8.1
Capital balance	-2.5	Debt service ratio	1.1
Overall balance	2.2		

Health and education

Health spending, % of GDP	6.9	Education spending, % of GDP	2.9
Doctors per 1,000 pop.	...	Enrolment, %: primary	109
Hospital beds per 1,000 pop.	0.1	secondary	89
Improved-water source access,		tertiary	72
% of pop.	96.2		

Society

No. of households, m	24.3	Cost of living, Dec. 2016	
Av. no. per household	3.3	New York = 100	50
Marriages per 1,000 pop.	9.3	Cars per 1,000 pop.	153
Divorces per 1,000 pop.	2.1	Colour TV households, % with:	
Religion, % of pop.		cable	...
Muslim	99.5	satellite	37.0
Christian	0.2	Telephone lines per 100 pop.	38.3
Other	0.2	Mobile telephone subscribers	
Non-religious	0.1	per 100 pop.	93.4
Hindu	<0.1	Broadband subs per 100 pop.	10.9
Jewish	<0.1	Internet users, % of pop.	45.3

a Estimate.   b Iranian year ending March 19th 2016.

IRELAND

Area, sq km	69,797	Capital	Dublin
Arable as % of total land	15.4	Currency	Euro (€)

People

Population, m	4.7	Life expectancy: men	79.5 yrs
Pop. per sq km	67.3	women	83.5 yrs
Average annual growth		Adult literacy	...
in pop. 2015–20, %	0.8	Fertility rate (per woman)	2.0
Pop. aged 0–24, %	32.9	Urban population, 2020, %	64.8
Pop. aged 70 and over, %	8.6		per 1,000 pop.
No. of men per 100 women	99.6	Crude birth rate	13.3
Human Development Index	92.3	Crude death rate	6.6

The economy

GDP	$283bn	GDP per head	$60,303
GDP	€256bn	GDP per head in purchasing	
Av. ann. growth in real		power parity (USA=100)	115.7
GDP 2010–15	6.5%	Economic freedom index	76.7

Origins of GDP		**Components of GDP**	
	% of total		% of total
Agriculture	1	Private consumption	34
Industry, of which:	42	Public consumption	13
manufacturing	37	Investment	22
Services	57	Exports	124
		Imports	-92

Structure of employment

	% of total		% of labour force
Agriculture	5.6	Unemployed 2015	9.4
Industry	19.0	Av. ann. rate 2005–15	9.9
Services	75.0		

Energy

	m TOE		
Total output	0.1	Net energy imports as %	
Total consumption	14.1	of energy use	84
Consumption per head			
kg oil equivalent	2,766		

Inflation and finance

		av. ann. increase 2011–16	
Consumer price			
inflation 2016	0.3%	Narrow money (M1)	8.1%
Av. ann. inflation 2011–16	2.8%	Broad money	3.6%
Money market rate, Dec. 2016	-0.37%		

Exchange rates

	end 2016		December 2016
€ per $	0.95	Effective rates	2010 = 100
€ per sdr	1.28	– nominal	93.23
		– real	88.06

Trade

Principal exports		Principal imports	
	$bn fob		*$bn cif*
Chemicals & related products	71.2	Machinery & transport equip.	30.2
Machinery & transport equip.	18.4	Chemicals & related products	15.3
Food, drink and tobacco	12.3	Food, drink and tobacco	8.4
Raw materials	2.0	Mineral fuels & lubricants	5.7
Total incl. others	**124.7**	Total incl. others	**77.7**

Main export destinations		Main origins of imports	
	% of total		*% of total*
United States	23.8	United Kingdom	31.2
United Kingdom	13.6	United States	14.5
Belgium	12.9	France	11.0
Germany	6.5	Germany	9.0
EU28	53.1	EU28	66.1

Balance of payments, reserves and aid, $bn

Visible exports fob	216.9	Overall balance	11.8
Visible imports fob	-94.3	Change in reserves	0.5
Trade balance	122.6	Level of reserves	
Invisibles inflows	203.2	end Dec.	2.2
Invisibles outflows	-293.3	No. months of import cover	0.1
Net transfers	-3.5	Official gold holdings, m oz	0.2
Current account balance	29.0	Aid given	0.7
– as % of GDP	10.2	– as % of GDP	0.3
Capital balance	-14.9		

Health and education

Health spending, % of GDP	7.8	Education spending, % of GDP	5.3
Doctors per 1,000 pop.	2.7	Enrolment, %: primary	102
Hospital beds per 1,000 pop.	2.9	secondary	127
Improved-water source access,		tertiary	78
% of pop.	97.9		

Society

No. of households, m	1.7	Cost of living, Dec. 2016	
Av. no. per household	2.8	New York = 100	88
Marriages per 1,000 pop.	4.8	Cars per 1,000 pop.	411
Divorces per 1,000 pop.	0.6	Colour TV households, % with:	
Religion, % of pop.		cable	31.7
Christian	92.0	satellite	47.6
Non-religious	6.2	Telephone lines per 100 pop.	40.9
Muslim	1.1	Mobile telephone subscribers	
Other	0.4	per 100 pop.	103.7
Hindu	0.2	Broadband subs per 100 pop.	27.7
Jewish	<0.1	Internet users, % of pop.	80.1

ISRAEL

Area, sq km	22,072	Capital	Jerusalem[a]
Arable as % of total land	13.9	Currency	New Shekel (NIS)

People

Population, m	8.1	Life expectancy: men	81.3 yrs
Pop. per sq km	367.0	women	84.6 yrs
Average annual growth		Adult literacy	...
in pop. 2015–20, %	1.6	Fertility rate (per woman)	2.7
Pop. aged 0–24, %	42.7	Urban population, 2020, %	52.7
Pop. aged 70 and over, %	7.4		per 1,000 pop.
No. of men per 100 women	98.4	Crude birth rate	19.6
Human Development Index	89.9	Crude death rate	5.2

The economy

GDP	$299bn	GDP per head	$36,965
GDP	NIS1,164bn	GDP per head in purchasing	
Av. ann. growth in real		power parity (USA=100)	62.8
GDP 2010–15	3.5%	Economic freedom index	69.7

Origins of GDP		**Components of GDP**	
	% of total		% of total
Agriculture	2	Private consumption	55
Industry, of which:	27	Public consumption	22
manufacturing	20	Investment	20
Services	69	Exports	31
		Imports	-28

Structure of employment

	% of total		% of labour force
Agriculture	1.0	Unemployed 2015	5.3
Industry	17.4	Av. ann. rate 2005–15	8.0
Services	79.8		

Energy

	m TOE		
Total output	7.2	Net energy imports as %	
Total consumption	23.2	of energy use	67
Consumption per head			
kg oil equivalent	2,763		

Inflation and finance

			av. ann. increase 2011–16
Consumer price			
inflation 2016	-0.6%	Narrow money (M1)	22.9%
Av. ann. inflation 2011–16	2.9%	Broad money	9.2%
Treasury bill rate, Dec. 2016	0.15%		

Exchange rates

	end 2016		December 2016
NIS per $	3.85	Effective rates	2010 = 100
NIS per sdr	5.17	– nominal	115.8
NIS per €	4.05	– real	107.3

Trade

Principal exports		Principal imports	
	$bn fob		$bn cif
Chemicals & chemical products	14.0	Fuel	7.4
Communications, medical &		Diamonds	6.3
scientific equipment	8.2	Machinery & equipment	5.7
Polished diamonds	7.2	Chemicals	4.6
Electronic components &			
computers	7.1		
Total incl. others	**53.5**	Total incl. others	**61.3**

Main export destinations		Main origins of imports	
	% of total		% of total
United States	33.9	United States	13.2
Hong Kong	9.9	China	9.4
United Kingdom	7.5	Switzerland	7.2
China	6.1	Germany	6.2

Balance of payments, reserves and debt, $bn

Visible exports fob	56.3	Change in reserves	4.5
Visible imports fob	-59.7	Level of reserves	
Trade balance	-3.4	end Dec.	90.6
Invisibles inflows	45.1	No. months of import cover	11.2
Invisibles outflows	-37.1	Official gold holdings, m oz	0.0
Net transfers	9.0	Foreign debt	89.1
Current account balance	13.6	– as % of GDP	29.8
– as % of GDP	4.6	– as % of total exports	87.0
Capital balance	-6.4	Debt service ratio	16.8
Overall balance	7.3		

Health and education

Health spending, % of GDP	7.8	Education spending, % of GDP	5.9
Doctors per 1,000 pop.	3.3	Enrolment, %: primary	104
Hospital beds per 1,000 pop.	3.3	secondary	102
Improved-water source access,		tertiary	66
% of pop.	100		

Society

No. of households, m	2.3	Cost of living, Dec. 2016	
Av. no. per household	3.5	New York = 100	99
Marriages per 1,000 pop.	6.5	Cars per 1,000 pop.	317
Divorces per 1,000 pop.	1.8	Colour TV households, % with:	
Religion, % of pop.		cable	77.8
Jewish	75.6	satellite	19.2
Muslim	18.6	Telephone lines per 100 pop.	43.1
Non-religious	3.1	Mobile telephone subscribers	
Christian	2.0	per 100 pop.	133.5
Other	0.6	Broadband subs per 100 pop.	27.4
Hindu	<0.1	Internet users, % of pop.	77.4

a Sovereignty over the city is disputed.

ITALY

Area, sq km	301,000	Capital	Rome
Arable as % of total land	22.9	Currency	Euro (€)

People

Population, m	59.8	Life expectancy: men	81.3 yrs
Pop. per sq km	198.7	women	86.0 yrs
Average annual growth		Adult literacy	99.0
in pop. 2015–20, %	0.0	Fertility rate (per woman)	1.4
Pop. aged 0–24, %	23.3	Urban population, 2020, %	69.8
Pop. aged 70 and over, %	16.3		per 1,000 pop.
No. of men per 100 women	94.6	Crude birth rate	8.3
Human Development Index	88.7	Crude death rate	10.2

The economy

GDP	$1,826bn	GDP per head	$30,532
GDP	€1,645bn	GDP per head in purchasing	
Av. ann. growth in real		power parity (USA=100)	65.2
GDP 2010–15	-0.7%	Economic freedom index	62.5

Origins of GDP		**Components of GDP**	
	% of total		% of total
Agriculture	2	Private consumption	61
Industry, of which:	24	Public consumption	19
manufacturing	16	Investment	17
Services	74	Exports	30
		Imports	-27

Structure of employment

	% of total		% of labour force
Agriculture	3.8	Unemployed 2015	11.9
Industry	26.6	Av. ann. rate 2005–15	9.0
Services	69.7		

Energy

	m TOE		
Total output	12.5	Net energy imports as %	
Total consumption	160.3	of energy use	75
Consumption per head			
kg oil equivalent	2,414		

Inflation and finance

Consumer price		av. ann. increase 2011–16	
inflation 2016	-0.1%	Narrow money (M1)	8.1%
Av. ann. inflation 2011–16	3.3%	Broad money	3.6%
Treasury bill rate, Dec. 2016	-0.27%		

Exchange rates

	end 2016		December 2016
€ per $	0.95	Effective rates	2010 = 100
€ per sdr	1.28	– nominal	98.10
		– real	94.92

Trade

Principal exports

	$bn fob
Machinery & transport equip.	166.9
Chemicals & related products	55.9
Food, drink and tobacco	37.1
Mineral fuels & lubricants	15.7
Total incl. others	**457.0**

Principal imports

	$bn cif
Machinery & transport equip.	111.6
Chemicals & related products	65.4
Mineral fuels & lubricants	52.3
Food, drink and tobacco	39.3
Total incl. others	**410.9**

Main export destinations

	% of total
Germany	12.3
France	10.4
United States	8.7
United Kingdom	5.4
EU28	54.8

Main origins of imports

	% of total
Germany	15.5
France	8.7
China	7.6
Netherlands	5.6
EU28	58.7

Balance of payments, reserves and aid, $bn

Visible exports fob	449.3	Overall balance	0.6
Visible imports fob	-391.4	Change in reserves	-12.2
Trade balance	57.9	Level of reserves	
Invisibles inflows	157.0	end Dec.	130.6
Invisibles outflows	-169.0	No. months of import cover	2.8
Net transfers	-16.5	Official gold holdings, m oz	78.8
Current account balance	29.3	Aid given	4.0
– as % of GDP	1.6	– as % of GDP	0.2
Capital balance	-24.4		

Health and education

Health spending, % of GDP	9.2	Education spending, % of GDP	4.2
Doctors per 1,000 pop.	3.8	Enrolment, %: primary	102
Hospital beds per 1,000 pop.	3.4	secondary	103
Improved-water source access,		tertiary	63
% of pop.	100		

Society

No. of households, m	27.3	Cost of living, Dec. 2016	
Av. no. per household	2.2	New York = 100	82
Marriages per 1,000 pop.	3.1	Cars per 1,000 pop.	607
Divorces per 1,000 pop.	0.9	Colour TV households, % with:	
Religion, % of pop.		cable	1.1
Christian	83.3	satellite	29.0
Non-religious	12.4	Telephone lines per 100 pop.	33.1
Muslim	3.7	Mobile telephone subscribers	
Other	0.4	per 100 pop.	142.1
Hindu	0.1	Broadband subs per 100 pop.	24.4
Jewish	<0.1	Internet users, % of pop.	65.6

IVORY COAST

Area, sq km	322,463	Capital	Yamoussoukro
Arable as % of total land	9.1	Currency	CFA franc (CFAfr)

People

Population, m	22.7	Life expectancy: men	52.0 yrs
Pop. per sq km	70.4	women	53.7 yrs
Average annual growth		Adult literacy	43.3
in pop. 2015–20, %	2.4	Fertility rate (per woman)	3.5
Pop. aged 0–24, %	62.8	Urban population, 2020, %	57.5
Pop. aged 70 and over, %	1.7		per 1,000 pop.
No. of men per 100 women	103.5	Crude birth rate	36.2
Human Development Index	47.4	Crude death rate	12.8

The economy

GDP	$33bn	GDP per head	$1,443
GDP	CFAfr19,368bn	GDP per head in purchasing	
Av. ann. growth in real		power parity (USA=100)	6.3
GDP 2010–15	6.2%	Economic freedom index	63.0

Origins of GDP		**Components of GDP**	
	% of total		% of total
Agriculture	23	Private consumption	62
Industry, of which:	29	Public consumption	14
manufacturing	14	Investment	21
Services	49	Exports	39
		Imports	-36

Structure of employment

	% of total		% of labour force
Agriculture	48.3	Unemployed 2015	9.3
Industry	6.2	Av. ann. rate 2005–15	9.3
Services	45.5		

Energy

	m TOE		
Total output	3.7	Net energy imports as %	
Total consumption	4.1	of energy use	7
Consumption per head			
kg oil equivalent	626		

Inflation and finance

		av. ann. increase 2011–16	
Consumer price			
inflation 2016	1.0%	Narrow money (M1)	12.7%
Av. ann. inflation 2011–16	3.4%	Broad money	12.1%
Money market rate, Dec. 2016	4.87%		

Exchange rates

	end 2016		December 2016
			2010 = 100
CFAfr per $	622.29	Effective rates	
CFAfr per sdr	856.56	– nominal	100.28
CFAfr per €	654.80	– real	96.29

Trade

Principal exports		**Principal imports**	
	$bn fob		*$bn cif*
Cocoa beans & butter	5.1	Fuels & lubricants	2.1
Petroleum products	1.9	Capital equip.	2.0
Coffee beans & products	1.6	Foodstuffs	1.9
Gold	0.8	Raw materials & intermediate	
		goods	1.8
Total incl. others	**11.9**	Total incl. others	**9.8**

Main export destinations		**Main origins of imports**	
	% of total		*% of total*
Netherlands	12.0	Nigeria	14.8
United States	8.1	France	13.5
Belgium	6.5	China	12.6
France	6.4	United States	4.3

Balance of payments, reserves and debt, $bn

Visible exports fob	11.7	Change in reserves	0.2
Visible imports fob	-8.6	Level of reserves	
Trade balance	3.2	end Dec.	4.7
Invisibles inflows	1.0	No. months of import cover	4.5
Invisibles outflows	-4.0	Official gold holdings, m oz	0.0
Net transfers	-0.3	Foreign debt	10.0
Current account balance	-0.2	– as % of GDP	31.6
– as % of GDP	-0.6	– as % of total exports	81.7
Capital balance	0.7	Debt service ratio	6.7
Overall balance	0.4		

Health and education

Health spending, % of GDP	5.1	Education spending, % of GDP	4.7
Doctors per 1,000 pop.	0.1	Enrolment, %: primary	94
Hospital beds per 1,000 pop.	...	secondary	44
Improved-water source access,		tertiary	9
% of pop.	81.9		

Society

No. of households, m	3.7	Cost of living, Dec. 2016	
Av. no. per household	6.1	New York = 100	59
Marriages per 1,000 pop.	...	Cars per 1,000 pop.	20
Divorces per 1,000 pop.	...	Colour TV households, % with:	
Religion, % of pop.	...	cable	...
		satellite	...
		Telephone lines per 100 pop.	1.3
		Mobile telephone subscribers	
		per 100 pop.	119.3
		Broadband subs per 100 pop.	0.5
		Internet users, % of pop.	21.0

JAPAN

Area, sq km	377,930	Capital	Tokyo
Arable as % of total land	11.6	Currency	Yen (¥)

People

Population, m	126.6	Life expectancy: men	80.8 yrs
Pop. per sq km	335.0	women	87.3 yrs
Average annual growth		Adult literacy	...
in pop. 2015–20, %	-0.2	Fertility rate (per woman)	1.4
Pop. aged 0–24, %	22.4	Urban population, 2020, %	95.3
Pop. aged 70 and over, %	18.9		per 1,000 pop.
No. of men per 100 women	94.7	Crude birth rate	8.1
Human Development Index	90.3	Crude death rate	10.9

The economy

GDP	$4,382bn	GDP per head	$34,616
GDP	¥530trn	GDP per head in purchasing	
Av. ann. growth in real		power parity (USA=100)	72.1
GDP 2010–15	0.6%	Economic freedom index	69.6

Origins of GDP		**Components of GDP**	
	% of total		% of total
Agriculture	1	Private consumption	57
Industry, of which:	30	Public consumption	20
manufacturing	...	Investment	24
Services	69	Exports	18
		Imports	-18

Structure of employment

	% of total		% of labour force
Agriculture	3.6	Unemployed 2015	3.4
Industry	25.5	Av. ann. rate 2005–15	4.2
Services	69.4		

Energy

	m TOE		
Total output	5.4	Net energy imports as %	
Total consumption	476.7	of energy use	94
Consumption per head			
kg oil equivalent	3,475		

Inflation and finance

		av. ann. increase 2011–16	
Consumer price			
inflation 2016	-0.2%	Narrow money (M1)	4.9%
Av. ann. inflation 2011–16	3.1%	Broad money	2.9%
Treasury bill rate, Dec. 2016	-0.41%		

Exchange rates

	end 2016		December 2016
¥ per $	116.80	Effective rates	2010 = 100
¥ per sdr	157.02	– nominal	83.20
¥ per €	122.90	– real	76.08

Trade

Principal exports	$bn fob	Principal imports	$bn cif
Capital equipment	315.4	Industrial supplies	299.0
Industrial supplies	150.8	Capital equipment	179.1
Consumer durable goods	104.5	Food & direct consumer goods	58.1
Consumer non-durable goods	4.6	Consumer durable goods	48.9
Total incl. others	**624.9**	Total incl. others	**648.1**

Main export destinations	% of total	Main origins of imports	% of total
United States	20.2	China	24.8
China	17.5	United States	10.5
South Korea	7.0	Australia	5.4
Taiwan	5.9	South Korea	4.1

Balance of payments, reserves and aid, $bn

Visible exports fob	622.0	Overall balance	5.1
Visible imports fob	-629.4	Change in reserves	-27.6
Trade balance	-7.3	Level of reserves	
Invisibles inflows	409.3	end Dec.	1,233.1
Invisibles outflows	-251.6	No. months of import cover	16.8
Net transfers	-16.3	Official gold holdings, m oz	24.6
Current account balance	134.1	Aid given	9.2
– as % of GDP	3.1	– as % of GDP	0.2
Capital balance	-175.7		

Health and education

Health spending, % of GDP	10.2	Education spending, % of GDP	3.8
Doctors per 1,000 pop.	2.3	Enrolment, %: primary	101
Hospital beds per 1,000 pop.	13.7	secondary	102
Improved-water source access,		tertiary	63
% of pop.	100		

Society

No. of households, m	53.0	Cost of living, Dec. 2016	
Av. no. per household	2.4	New York = 100	110
Marriages per 1,000 pop.	5.1	Cars per 1,000 pop.	478
Divorces per 1,000 pop.	1.7	Colour TV households, % with:	
Religion, % of pop.		cable	52.7
Non-religious	57.0	satellite	42.3
Buddhist	36.2	Telephone lines per 100 pop.	50.2
Other	5.0	Mobile telephone subscribers	
Christian	1.6	per 100 pop.	126.5
Muslim	0.2	Broadband subs per 100 pop.	30.7
Jewish	<0.1	Internet users, % of pop.	91.1

KENYA

Area, sq km	580,000	Capital	Nairobi
Arable as % of total land	10.2	Currency	Kenyan shilling (KSh)

People

Population, m	46.1	Life expectancy: men	61.1 yrs
Pop. per sq km	79.5	women	65.5 yrs
Average annual growth		Adult literacy	78.0
in pop. 2015–20, %	2.5	Fertility rate (per woman)	3.3
Pop. aged 0–24, %	61.4	Urban population, 2020, %	27.9
Pop. aged 70 and over, %	1.6		per 1,000 pop.
No. of men per 100 women	99.9	Crude birth rate	32.8
Human Development Index	55.5	Crude death rate	7.6

The economy

GDP	$64bn	GDP per head	$1,380
GDP	KSh6,224bn	GDP per head in purchasing	
Av. ann. growth in real		power parity (USA=100)	5.5
GDP 2010–15	5.5%	Economic freedom index	53.5

Origins of GDP		**Components of GDP**	
	% of total		% of total
Agriculture	33	Private consumption	78
Industry, of which:	20	Public consumption	14
manufacturing	11	Investment	21
Services	48	Exports	16
		Imports	-29

Structure of employment

	% of total		% of labour force
Agriculture	...	Unemployed 2015	11.3
Industry	...	Av. ann. rate 2005–15	11.8
Services	...		

Energy

	m TOE		
Total output	...	Net energy imports as %	
Total consumption	6.7	of energy use	17
Consumption per head			
kg oil equivalent	527		

Inflation and finance

			av. ann. increase 2011–16
Consumer price			
inflation 2016	6.2%	Narrow money (M1)	16.0%
Av. ann. inflation 2011–16	8.1%	Broad money	12.3%
Treasury bill rate, Dec. 2016	8.44%		

Exchange rates

	end 2016		December 2016
KSh per $	116.80	Effective rates	2010 = 100
KSh per sdr	157.02	– nominal	83.20
KSh per €	122.90	– real	76.08

Trade

Principal exports		Principal imports	
	$bn fob		*$bn cif*
Tea	1.3	Industrial supplies	5.0
Horticultural products	1.2	Machinery & other capital equip.	3.2
Coffee	0.4	Transport equipment	2.0
Fish products	0.1	Food & beverages	1.2
Total incl. others	**6.5**	Total incl. others	**15.6**

Main export destinations		Main origins of imports	
	% of total		*% of total*
Uganda	11.4	India	20.8
Tanzania	8.6	China	11.9
United States	7.5	United Arab Emirates	6.8
Netherlands	7.1	United Kingdom	6.7

Balance of payments[a], reserves[a] and debt, $bn

Visible exports fob	6.2	Change in reserves	1.3
Visible imports fob	-17.6	Level of reserves	
Trade balance	-11.4	end Dec.	7.9
Invisibles inflows	5.1	No. months of import cover	4.4
Invisibles outflows	-3.8	Official gold holdings, m oz	0.0
Net transfers	3.8	Foreign debt	19.1
Current account balance	-6.3	– as % of GDP	30.2
– as % of GDP	-10.0	– as % of total exports	155.6
Capital balance	6.9	Debt service ratio	6.1
Overall balance	1.4		

Health and education

Health spending, % of GDP	5.7	Education spending, % of GDP	5.4
Doctors per 1,000 pop.	0.2	Enrolment, %: primary	109
Hospital beds per 1,000 pop.	1.4	secondary	68
Improved-water source access,		tertiary	...
% of pop.	63.2		

Society

No. of households, m	10.5	Cost of living, Dec. 2016	
Av. no. per household	4.3	New York = 100	69
Marriages per 1,000 pop.	...	Cars per 1,000 pop.	17
Divorces per 1,000 pop.	...	Colour TV households, % with:	
Religion, % of pop.		cable	2.4
Christian	84.8	satellite	3.4
Muslim	9.7	Telephone lines per 100 pop.	0.2
Other	3.0	Mobile telephone subscribers	
Non-religious	2.5	per 100 pop.	80.7
Hindu	0.1	Broadband subs per 100 pop.	0.3
Jewish	<0.1	Internet users, % of pop.	45.6

MALAYSIA

Area, sq km	331,000	Capital	Kuala Lumpur
Arable as % of total land	2.9	Currency	Malaysian dollar/ringgit (M$)

People

Population, m	30.3	Life expectancy: men	73.0 yrs
Pop. per sq km	91.5	women	77.7 yrs
Average annual growth		Adult literacy	94.6
in pop. 2015–20, %	1.3	Fertility rate (per woman)	2.6
Pop. aged 0–24, %	43.2	Urban population, 2020, %	77.7
Pop. aged 70 and over, %	3.4		per 1,000 pop.
No. of men per 100 women	98.2	Crude birth rate	16.6
Human Development Index	78.9	Crude death rate	5.2

The economy

GDP	$296bn	GDP per head	$9,778
GDP	M$1,157bn	GDP per head in purchasing	
Av. ann. growth in real		power parity (USA=100)	48.1
GDP 2010–15	5.3%	Economic freedom index	73.8

Origins of GDP		**Components of GDP**	
	% of total		% of total
Agriculture	8	Private consumption	54
Industry, of which:	36	Public consumption	13
manufacturing	23	Investment	25
Services	55	Exports	71
		Imports	-63

Structure of employment

	% of total		% of labour force
Agriculture	12.5	Unemployed 2015	3.1
Industry	27.5	Av. ann. rate 2005–15	3.2
Services	60.0		

Energy

	m TOE		
Total output	95.2	Net energy imports as %	
Total consumption	87.0	of energy use	-6
Consumption per head			
kg oil equivalent	3,000		

Inflation and finance

Consumer price			av. ann. increase 2011–16
inflation 2016	2.1%	Narrow money (M1)	8.1%
Av. ann. inflation 2011–16	4.1%	Broad money	5.6%
Treasury bill rate, Dec. 2016	3.12%		

Exchange rates

	end 2016		December 2016
M$ per $	4.49	Effective rates	2010 = 100
M$ per SDR	6.03	– nominal	81.98
M$ per €	4.72	– real	84.58

Trade

Principal exports		Principal imports	
	$bn fob		*$bn cif*
Machinery & transport equip.	83.5	Machinery & transport equip.	76.1
Mineral fuels	32.9	Manufactured goods	23.0
Manufactured goods	19.2	Mineral fuels	21.7
Chemicals	15.5	Chemicals	17.9
Total incl. others	**199.2**	Total incl. others	**176.0**

Main export destinations		Main origins of imports	
	% of total		*% of total*
Singapore	14.0	China	18.8
China	13.0	Singapore	12.0
Japan	9.5	United States	8.1
United States	9.5	Japan	7.8

Balance of payments, reserves and debt, $bn

Visible exports fob	175.7	Change in reserves	-20.7
Visible imports fob	-147.7	Level of reserves	
Trade balance	28.1	end Dec.	95.3
Invisibles inflows	47.3	No. months of import cover	5.5
Invisibles outflows	-60.7	Official gold holdings, m oz	1.2
Net transfers	-5.6	Foreign debt	191.0
Current account balance	9.0	– as % of GDP	64.4
– as % of GDP	3.0	– as % of total exports	85.0
Capital balance	-13.6	Debt service ratio	6.0
Overall balance	0.3		

Health and education

Health spending, % of GDP	4.2	Education spending, % of GDP	5.0
Doctors per 1,000 pop.	1.2	Enrolment, %: primary	102
Hospital beds per 1,000 pop.	1.9	secondary	78
Improved-water source access,		tertiary	26
% of pop.	98.2		

Society

No. of households, m	7.3	Cost of living, Dec. 2016	
Av. no. per household	4.2	New York = 100	61
Marriages per 1,000 pop.	...	Cars per 1,000 pop.	365
Divorces per 1,000 pop.	...	Colour TV households, % with:	
Religion, % of pop.		cable	12.7
Muslim	63.7	satellite	56.2
Buddhist	17.7	Telephone lines per 100 pop.	14.6
Christian	9.4	Mobile telephone subscribers	
Hindu	6.0	per 100 pop.	143.9
Other	2.5	Broadband subs per 100 pop.	10.0
Non-religious	0.7	Internet users, % of pop.	71.1

MEXICO

Area, sq km	1,964,375	Capital	Mexico City
Arable as % of total land	11.8	Currency	Mexican peso (PS)

People

Population, m	127.0	Life expectancy: men	75.2 yrs
Pop. per sq km	64.7	women	79.9 yrs
Average annual growth		Adult literacy	94.5
in pop. 2015–20, %	1.2	Fertility rate (per woman)	2.3
Pop. aged 0–24, %	45.9	Urban population, 2020, %	80.6
Pop. aged 70 and over, %	4.3		per 1,000 pop.
No. of men per 100 women	99.0	Crude birth rate	17.7
Human Development Index	76.2	Crude death rate	4.9

The economy

GDP	$1,151bn	GDP per head	$9,063
GDP	PS18,242bn	GDP per head in purchasing	
Av. ann. growth in real		power parity (USA=100)	31.4
GDP 2010–15	2.8%	Economic freedom index	63.6

Origins of GDP		**Components of GDP**	
	% of total		% of total
Agriculture	4	Private consumption	67
Industry, of which:	33	Public consumption	12
manufacturing	18	Investment	23
Services	64	Exports	35
		Imports	-37

Structure of employment

	% of total		% of labour force
Agriculture	13.5	Unemployed 2015	4.3
Industry	24.9	Av. ann. rate 2005–15	4.5
Services	61.1		

Energy

	m TOE		
Total output	195.9	Net energy imports as %	
Total consumption	187.9	of energy use	-11
Consumption per head			
kg oil equivalent	1,499		

Inflation and finance

			av. ann. increase 2011–16
Consumer price			
inflation 2016	2.8%	Narrow money (M1)	13.2%
Av. ann. inflation 2011–16	5.3%	Broad money	10.2%
Treasury bill rate, Dec. 2016	5.61%		

Exchange rates

	end 2016		December 2016
PS per $	20.73	Effective rates	2010 = 100
PS per sdr	27.87	– nominal	66.1
PS per €	21.81	– real	73.8

Trade

Principal exports		**Principal imports**	
	$bn fob		*$bn cif*
Manufactured goods	340.0	Intermediate goods	297.3
Crude oil & products	23.2	Consumer goods	56.3
Agricultural products	13.0	Capital goods	41.7
Mining products	4.5		
Total	**380.6**	Total	**395.2**

Main export destinations		**Main origins of imports**	
	% of total		*% of total*
United States	81.2	United States	50.1
Canada	2.8	China	18.8
China	1.3	Japan	4.7
Colombia	1.0	South Korea	3.9

Balance of payments, reserves and debt, $bn

Visible exports fob	381.0	Change in reserves	-18.1
Visible imports fob	-395.6	Level of reserves	
Trade balance	-14.5	end Dec.	177.6
Invisibles inflows	30.8	No. months of import cover	4.5
Invisibles outflows	-73.9	Official gold holdings, m oz	3.9
Net transfers	24.3	Foreign debt	426.3
Current account balance	-33.3	– as % of GDP	37.0
– as % of GDP	-2.9	– as % of total exports	97.6
Capital balance	35.2	Debt service ratio	12.4
Overall balance	-15.4		

Health and education

Health spending, % of GDP	6.3	Education spending, % of GDP	5.2
Doctors per 1,000 pop.	2.1	Enrolment, %: primary	103
Hospital beds per 1,000 pop.	1.5	secondary	91
Improved-water source access,		tertiary	30
% of pop.	96.1		

Society

No. of households, m	32.8	Cost of living, Dec. 2016	
Av. no. per household	3.9	New York = 100	66
Marriages per 1,000 pop.	4.8	Cars per 1,000 pop.	206
Divorces per 1,000 pop.	0.9	Colour TV households, % with:	
Religion, % of pop.		cable	21.4
Christian	95.1	satellite	23.5
Non-religious	4.7	Telephone lines per 100 pop.	15.9
Hindu	<0.1	Mobile telephone subscribers	
Jewish	<0.1	per 100 pop.	86.0
Muslim	<0.1	Broadband subs per 100 pop.	11.6
Other	<0.1	Internet users, % of pop.	57.4

MOROCCO

Area, sq km	447,400	Capital	Rabat
Arable as % of total land	18.2	Currency	Dirham (Dh)

People

Population, m	34.4	Life expectancy: men	73.8 yrs
Pop. per sq km	76.9	women	76.0 yrs
Average annual growth		Adult literacy	71.7
in pop. 2015–20, %	1.2	Fertility rate (per woman)	2.4
Pop. aged 0–24, %	44.9	Urban population, 2020, %	62.6
Pop. aged 70 and over, %	4.1		per 1,000 pop.
No. of men per 100 women	97.7	Crude birth rate	19.1
Human Development Index	64.7	Crude death rate	5.7

The economy

GDP	$101bn	GDP per head	$2,924
GDP	Dh982bn	GDP per head in purchasing	
Av. ann. growth in real		power parity (USA=100)	14.2
GDP 2010–15	4.0%	Economic freedom index	61.5

Origins of GDP		**Components of GDP**	
	% of total		% of total
Agriculture	14	Private consumption	58
Industry, of which:	29	Public consumption	19
manufacturing	18	Investment	30
Services	56	Exports	34
		Imports	-42

Structure of employment

	% of total		% of labour force
Agriculture	37.2	Unemployed 2015	9.7
Industry	17.7	Av. ann. rate 2005–15	9.5
Services	44.9		

Energy

	m TOE		
Total output	0.1	Net energy imports as %	
Total consumption	20.5	of energy use	91
Consumption per head			
kg oil equivalent	560		

Inflation and finance

			av. ann. increase 2011–16
Consumer price			
inflation 2016	1.3%	Narrow money (M1)	5.1%
Av. ann. inflation 2011–16	3.3%	Broad money	4.8%
Money market rate, Dec. 2016	2.25%		

Exchange rates

	end 2016		December 2016
Dh per $	10.10	Effective rates	2010 = 100
Dh per sdr	13.57	– nominal	105.62
Dh per €	10.63	– real	100.95

Trade

Principal exports		Principal imports	
	$bn fob		*$bn cif*
Electric cables & wires	2.3	Capital goods	9.6
Clothing & textiles	2.1	Semi-finished goods	8.8
Fertilisers & chemicals	1.9	Consumer goods	7.2
Phosphoric acid	1.7	Fuel & lubricants	6.8
Total incl. others	**22.4**	Total incl. others	**38.2**

Main export destinations		Main origins of imports	
	% of total		*% of total*
Spain	22.1	Spain	13.9
France	19.7	France	12.4
India	4.9	China	8.5
United States	4.3	United States	6.5

Balance of payments, reserves and debt, $bn

Visible exports fob	18.6	Change in reserves	2.5
Visible imports fob	-33.3	Level of reserves	
Trade balance	-14.7	end Dec.	23.0
Invisibles inflows	15.2	No. months of import cover	6.3
Invisibles outflows	-10.3	Official gold holdings, m oz	0.7
Net transfers	7.6	Foreign debt	43.0
Current account balance	-2.2	– as % of GDP	42.6
– as % of GDP	-2.1	– as % of total exports	105.6
Capital balance	5.8	Debt service ratio	8.7
Overall balance	4.3		

Health and education

Health spending, % of GDP	5.9	Education spending, % of GDP	...
Doctors per 1,000 pop.	0.6	Enrolment, %: primary	115
Hospital beds per 1,000 pop.	0.9	secondary	69
Improved-water source access,		tertiary	28
% of pop.	85.4		

Society

No. of households, m	7.5	Cost of living, Dec. 2016	
Av. no. per household	4.6	New York = 100	57
Marriages per 1,000 pop.	...	Cars per 1,000 pop.	72
Divorces per 1,000 pop.	...	Colour TV households, % with:	
Religion, % of pop.		cable	...
Muslim	99.9	satellite	92.0
Christian	<0.1	Telephone lines per 100 pop.	6.5
Hindu	<0.1	Mobile telephone subscribers	
Jewish	<0.1	per 100 pop.	126.9
Non-religious	<0.1	Broadband subs per 100 pop.	3.4
Other	<0.1	Internet users, % of pop.	57.1

NETHERLANDS

Area, sq km^a	37,354	Capital	Amsterdam
Arable as % of total land	31.0	Currency	Euro (€)

People

Population, m	16.9	Life expectancy: men	80.3 yrs
Pop. per sq km	452.4	women	83.7 yrs
Average annual growth		Adult literacy	...
in pop. 2015–20, %	0.3	Fertility rate (per woman)	1.8
Pop. aged 0–24, %	28.4	Urban population, 2020, %	92.8
Pop. aged 70 and over, %	12.0		per 1,000 pop.
No. of men per 100 women	98.5	Crude birth rate	10.5
Human Development Index	92.4	Crude death rate	8.8

The economy

GDP	$751bn	GDP per head	$44,420
GDP	€677bn	GDP per head in purchasing	
Av. ann. growth in real		power parity (USA=100)	88.7
GDP 2010–15	0.8%	Economic freedom index	75.8

Origins of GDP		**Components of GDP**	
	% of total		% of total
Agriculture	2	Private consumption	45
Industry, of which:	20	Public consumption	25
manufacturing	12	Investment	19
Services	78	Exports	82
		Imports	-72

Structure of employment

	% of total		% of labour force
Agriculture	2.1	Unemployed 2015	6.9
Industry	15.2	Av. ann. rate 2005–15	5.0
Services	74.9		

Energy

	m TOE		
Total output	58.4	Net energy imports as %	
Total consumption	96.2	of energy use	20
Consumption per head			
kg oil equivalent	4,326		

Inflation and finance

			av. ann. increase 2011–16
Consumer price			
inflation 2016	0.1%	Narrow money (M1)	8.1%
Av. ann. inflation 2011–16	3.5%	Broad money	3.6%
Deposit rate, Dec. 2016	1.75%		

Exchange rates

	end 2016		December 2016
€ per $	0.95	Effective rates	2010 = 100
€ per sdr	1.28	– nominal	97.35
		– real	96.69

Trade

Principal exports		**Principal imports**	
	$bn fob		*$bn cif*
Machinery & transport equip.	183.2	Machinery & transport equip.	171.3
Chemicals & related products	95.7	Mineral fuels & lubricants	82.3
Mineral fuels & lubricants	74.3	Chemicals & related products	67.5
Food, drink & tobacco	73.5	Food, drink & tobacco	50.8
Total incl. others	**474.1**	Total incl. others	**425.0**

Main export destinations		**Main origins of imports**	
	% of total		*% of total*
Germany	29.5	Germany	17.8
Belgium	13.4	China	17.4
United Kingdom	11.2	Belgium	10.0
France	10.1	United States	9.6
EU28	75.7	EU28	45.9

Balance of payments, reserves and aid, $bn

Visible exports fob	474.1	Overall balance	-0.5
Visible imports fob	-389.6	Change in reserves	-4.8
Trade balance	84.5	Level of reserves	
Invisibles inflows	400.2	end Dec.	38.2
Invisibles outflows	-406.4	No. months of import cover	0.6
Net transfers	-12.2	Official gold holdings, m oz	19.7
Current account balance	66.2	Aid given	5.7
– as % of GDP	8.8	– as % of GDP	0.8
Capital balance	-63.2		

Health and education

Health spending, % of GDP	10.9	Education spending, % of GDP	5.6
Doctors per 1,000 pop.	2.9	Enrolment, %: primary	104
Hospital beds per 1,000 pop.	...	secondary	132
Improved-water source access,		tertiary	79
% of pop.	100		

Society

No. of households, m	7.7	Cost of living, Dec. 2016	
Av. no. per household	2.2	New York = 100	75
Marriages per 1,000 pop.	3.9	Cars per 1,000 pop.	488
Divorces per 1,000 pop.	2.1	Colour TV households, % with:	
Religion, % of pop.		cable	69.3
Christian	50.6	satellite	7.2
Non-religious	42.1	Telephone lines per 100 pop.	41.3
Muslim	6.0	Mobile telephone subscribers	
Other	0.6	per 100 pop.	123.5
Hindu	0.5	Broadband subs per 100 pop.	41.7
Jewish	0.2	Internet users, % of pop.	93.1

a Includes water.

NEW ZEALAND

Area, sq km	268,107	Capital	Wellington
Arable as % of total land	2.2	Currency	New Zealand dollar (NZ$)

People

Population, m	4.5	Life expectancy: men	80.8 yrs
Pop. per sq km	16.8	women	84.0 yrs
Average annual growth		Adult literacy	...
in pop. 2015–20, %	0.9	Fertility rate (per woman)	2.0
Pop. aged 0–24, %	34.1	Urban population, 2020, %	86.5
Pop. aged 70 and over, %	9.8		per 1,000 pop.
No. of men per 100 women	95.6	Crude birth rate	12.9
Human Development Index	91.5	Crude death rate	6.9

The economy

GDP	$173bn	GDP per head	$38,501
GDP	NZ$247bn	GDP per head in purchasing	
Av. ann. growth in real		power parity (USA=100)	66.6
GDP 2010–15	2.5%	Economic freedom index	83.7

Origins of GDP		**Components of GDP**	
	% of total		% of total
Agriculture	4	Private consumption	58
Industry, of which:	26	Public consumption	19
manufacturing	...	Investment	23
Services	70	Exports	28
		Imports	-27

Structure of employment

	% of total		% of labour force
Agriculture	6.1	Unemployed 2015	5.4
Industry	21.9	Av. ann. rate 2005–15	5.1
Services	71.5		

Energy

	m TOE		
Total output	9.5	Net energy imports as %	
Total consumption	22.5	of energy use	17
Consumption per head			
kg oil equivalent	4,560		

Inflation and finance

			av. ann. increase 2011–16
Consumer price			
inflation 2016	0.7%	Narrow money (M1)	8.2%
Av. ann. inflation 2011–16	3.1%	Broad money	6.3%
Treasury bill rate, Dec. 2016	1.79%		

Exchange rates

	end 2016		December 2016
NZ$ per $	1.44	Effective rates	2010 = 100
NZ$ per sdr	1.93	– nominal	116.96
NZ$ per €	1.52	– real	114.34

Trade

Principal exports	$bn fob	Principal imports	$bn cif
Dairy produce	8.1	Machinery & electrical equip.	7.9
Meat	4.8	Transport equipment	6.4
Forestry products	2.5	Mineral fuels	3.7
Wool	0.6		
Total incl. others	**34.4**	Total incl. others	**36.6**

Main export destinations	% of total	Main origins of imports	% of total
China	17.5	China	19.5
Australia	16.9	Australia	11.9
United States	11.8	United States	11.7
Japan	6.0	Japan	6.6

Balance of payments, reserves and aid, $bn

Visible exports fob	34.4	Overall balance	-0.5
Visible imports fob	-35.8	Change in reserves	-1.2
Trade balance	-1.4	Level of reserves	
Invisibles inflows	19.7	end Dec.	14.7
Invisibles outflows	-23.6	No. months of import cover	3.0
Net transfers	-0.3	Official gold holdings, m oz	0.0
Current account balance	-5.5	Aid given	0.4
– as % of GDP	-3.2	– as % of GDP	0.3
Capital balance	-1.9		

Health and education

Health spending, % of GDP	11.0	Education spending, % of GDP	6.4
Doctors per 1,000 pop.	…	Enrolment, %: primary	99
Hospital beds per 1,000 pop.	2.3	secondary	118
Improved-water source access,		tertiary	81
% of pop.	100		

Society

No. of households, m	1.5	Cost of living, Dec. 2016	
Av. no. per household	3.0	New York = 100	92
Marriages per 1,000 pop.	4.5	Cars per 1,000 pop.	648
Divorces per 1,000 pop.	1.8	Colour TV households, % with:	
Religion, % of pop.		cable	5.9
Christian	57.0	satellite	40.7
Non-religious	36.6	Telephone lines per 100 pop.	40.2
Other	2.8	Mobile telephone subscribers	
Hindu	2.1	per 100 pop.	121.8
Muslim	1.2	Broadband subs per 100 pop.	31.6
Jewish	0.2	Internet users, % of pop.	88.2

NIGERIA

Area, sq km	923,768	Capital	Abuja
Arable as % of total land	37.3	Currency	Naira (N)

People

Population, m	182.2	Life expectancy: men	53.3 yrs
Pop. per sq km	197.2	women	54.0 yrs
Average annual growth		Adult literacy	59.6
in pop. 2015–20, %	2.5	Fertility rate (per woman)	5.2
Pop. aged 0–24, %	63.0	Urban population, 2020, %	51.7
Pop. aged 70 and over, %	1.4		per 1,000 pop.
No. of men per 100 women	103.8	Crude birth rate	37.9
Human Development Index	52.7	Crude death rate	12.2

The economy

GDP	$494bn	GDP per head	$2,710
GDP	N95,178bn	GDP per head in purchasing	
Av. ann. growth in real		power parity (USA=100)	10.7
GDP 2010–15	4.7%	Economic freedom index	57.1

Origins of GDP		**Components of GDP**	
	% of total		% of total
Agriculture	21	Private consumption	78
Industry, of which:	20	Public consumption	7
manufacturing	10	Investment	15
Services	59	Exports	11
		Imports	-11

Structure of employment

	% of total		% of labour force
Agriculture	...	Unemployed 2015	4.3
Industry	...	Av. ann. rate 2005–15	6.7
Services	...		

Energy

	m TOE		
Total output	170.6	Net energy imports as %	
Total consumption	33.2	of energy use	-93
Consumption per head			
kg oil equivalent	759		

Inflation and finance

		av. ann. increase 2011–16	
Consumer price			
inflation 2016	15.4%	Narrow money (M1)	5.9%
Av. ann. inflation 2011–16	9.9%	Broad money	9.4%
Treasury bill rate, Dec. 2016	13.96%		

Exchange rates

	end 2016		December 2016
N per $	305.00	Effective rates	2010 = 100
N per sdr	410.02	– nominal	61.11
N per €	320.94	– real	101.61

Trade

Principal exports		**Principal imports**[a]	
	$bn fob		*$bn cif*
Crude oil	35.4	Machinery & transport equip.	11.3
Gas	6.8	Mineral fuels	6.4
Food, drink & tobacco	0.9	Food & live animals	5.2
Vegetable products	0.5	Manufactured goods	4.8
Total incl. others	**49.8**	Total incl. others	**34.8**

Main export destinations		**Main origins of imports**	
	% of total		*% of total*
India	40.5	China	21.8
Brazil	11.2	United States	12.2
Netherlands	8.2	Belgium	5.8
Spain	7.5	United Kingdom	4.4

Balance of payments, reserves and debt, $bn

Visible exports fob	46.9	Change in reserves	-6.2
Visible imports fob	-53.4	Level of reserves	
Trade balance	-6.6	end Dec.	31.3
Invisibles inflows	4.2	No. months of import cover	4.3
Invisibles outflows	-34.0	Official gold holdings, m oz	0.7
Net transfers	20.6	Foreign debt	29.0
Current account balance	-15.8	– as % of GDP	5.9
– as % of GDP	-3.2	– as % of total exports	40.9
Capital balance	-7.0	Debt service ratio	2.1
Overall balance	-6.0		

Health and education

Health spending, % of GDP	3.7	Education spending, % of GDP	...
Doctors per 1,000 pop.	0.4	Enrolment, %: primary	94
Hospital beds per 1,000 pop.	...	secondary	56
Improved-water source access,		tertiary	...
% of pop.	68.5		

Society

No. of households, m	38.3	Cost of living, Dec. 2016	
Av. no. per household	4.8	New York = 100	39
Marriages per 1,000 pop.	...	Cars per 1,000 pop.	16
Divorces per 1,000 pop.	...	Colour TV households, % with:	
Religion, % of pop.		cable	1.9
Christian	49.3	satellite	...
Muslim	48.8	Telephone lines per 100 pop.	0.1
Other	1.4	Mobile telephone subscribers	
Non-religious	0.4	per 100 pop.	82.2
Hindu	<0.1	Broadband subs per 100 pop.	0.0
Jewish	<0.1	Internet users, % of pop.	47.4

a   2012

NORWAY

Area, sq km	385,000	Capital	Oslo
Arable as % of total land	2.2	Currency	Norwegian krone (Nkr)

People

Population, m	5.2	Life expectancy: men	80.2 yrs
Pop. per sq km	13.5	women	84.0 yrs
Average annual growth		Adult literacy	...
in pop. 2015–20, %	1.1	Fertility rate (per woman)	1.9
Pop. aged 0–24, %	31.1	Urban population, 2020, %	81.7
Pop. aged 70 and over, %	10.6		per 1,000 pop.
No. of men per 100 women	101.5	Crude birth rate	11.9
Human Development Index	94.9	Crude death rate	7.9

The economy

GDP	$387bn	GDP per head	$74,342
GDP	Nkr3,117bn	GDP per head in purchasing	
Av. ann. growth in real		power parity (USA=100)	122.2
GDP 2010–15	1.7%	Economic freedom index	74.0

Origins of GDP		**Components of GDP**	
	% of total		% of total
Agriculture	2	Private consumption	43
Industry, of which:	35	Public consumption	23
manufacturing	8	Investment	28
Services	64	Exports	37
		Imports	-32

Structure of employment

	% of total		% of labour force
Agriculture	2.0	Unemployed 2015	4.3
Industry	20.1	Av. ann. rate 2005–15	3.7
Services	77.7		

Energy

	m TOE		
Total output	195.3	Net energy imports as %	
Total consumption	47.8	of energy use	-583
Consumption per head			
kg oil equivalent	5,596		

Inflation and finance

			av. ann. increase 2011–16
Consumer price			
inflation 2016	3.2%	Narrow money (M1)	17.4%
Av. ann. inflation 2011–16	3.7%	Broad money	4.5%
Central bank policy rate Dec. 2016	0.50%		

Exchange rates

	end 2016		December 2016
Nkr per $	8.62	Effective rates	2010 = 100
Nkr per sdr	11.59	– nominal	86.05
Nkr per €	9.07	– real	88.80

Trade

Principal exports		**Principal imports**	
	$bn fob		*$bn cif*
Mineral fuels & lubricants	60.0	Machinery & transport equip.	31.1
Machinery & transport equip.	12.3	Miscellaneous manufactured	
Food & beverages	9.6	goods	12.2
Manufactured goods	9.6	Manufactured goods	10.8
		Chemicals & mineral products	7.4
Total incl. others	**103.9**	Total incl. others	**76.4**

Main export destinations		**Main origins of imports**	
	% of total		*% of total*
United Kingdom	22.1	Sweden	11.5
Germany	17.8	Germany	11.3
Netherlands	10.1	China	10.4
France	6.6	United Kingdom	6.7
EU28	79.4	EU28	60.9

Balance of payments, reserves and aid, $bn

Visible exports fob	103.4	Overall balance	-5.0
Visible imports fob	-75.4	Change in reserves	-7.3
Trade balance	27.9	Level of reserves	
Invisibles inflows	83.0	end Dec.	57.5
Invisibles outflows	-70.3	No. months of import cover	4.7
Net transfers	-6.9	Official gold holdings, m oz	0.0
Current account balance	33.7	Aid given	4.3
– as % of GDP	8.7	– as % of GDP	1.1
Capital balance	-17.3		

Health and education

Health spending, % of GDP	9.4	Education spending, % of GDP	7.4
Doctors per 1,000 pop.	4.3	Enrolment, %: primary	100
Hospital beds per 1,000 pop.	3.3	secondary	113
Improved-water source access,		tertiary	77
% of pop.	100		

Society

No. of households, m	2.3	Cost of living, Dec. 2016	
Av. no. per household	2.3	New York = 100	99
Marriages per 1,000 pop.	4.6	Cars per 1,000 pop.	498
Divorces per 1,000 pop.	1.9	Colour TV households, % with:	
Religion, % of pop.		cable	44.5
Christian	84.7	satellite	38.5
Non-religious	10.1	Telephone lines per 100 pop.	18.4
Muslim	3.7	Mobile telephone subscribers	
Other	0.9	per 100 pop.	111.1
Hindu	0.5	Broadband subs per 100 pop.	39.7
Jewish	<0.1	Internet users, % of pop.	96.8

PAKISTAN

Area, sq km	796,095	Capital	Islamabad
Arable as % of total land	39.5	Currency	Pakistan rupee (PRs)

People

Population, m	188.9	Life expectancy: men	65.8 yrs
Pop. per sq km	237.3	women	67.8 yrs
Average annual growth		Adult literacy	56.4
in pop. 2015–20, %	2.0	Fertility rate (per woman)	2.8
Pop. aged 0–24, %	54.9	Urban population, 2020, %	41.2
Pop. aged 70 and over, %	2.8		per 1,000 pop.
No. of men per 100 women	105.6	Crude birth rate	27.6
Human Development Index	55.0	Crude death rate	7.2

The economy

GDP	$271bn	GDP per head	$1,435
GDP	PRs27,493bn	GDP per head in purchasing	
Av. ann. growth in real		power parity (USA=100)	8.8
GDP 2010–15	3.8%	Economic freedom index	52.8

Origins of GDP		**Components of GDP**	
	% of total		% of total
Agriculture	25	Private consumption	80
Industry, of which:	20	Public consumption	11
manufacturing	13	Investment	15
Services	55	Exports	11
		Imports	-17

Structure of employment

	% of total		% of labour force
Agriculture	43.5	Unemployed 2015	5.9
Industry	22.5	Av. ann. rate 2005–15	5.9
Services	34.0		

Energy

	m TOE		
Total output	37.4	Net energy imports as %	
Total consumption	66.3	of energy use	24
Consumption per head			
kg oil equivalent	486		

Inflation and finance

			av. ann. increase 2011–16
Consumer price			
inflation 2016	2.9%	Narrow money (M1)	16.6%
Av. ann. inflation 2011–16	8.7%	Broad money	13.6%
Treasury bill rate, Dec. 2016	5.98%		

Exchange rates

	end 2016		December 2016
PRs per $	104.81	Effective rates	2010 = 100
PRs per sdr	140.90	– nominal	95.05
PRs per €	110.29	– real	127.49

Trade

Principal exports		Principal imports	
	$bn fob		*$bn cif*
Cotton fabrics	2.2	Petroleum products	6.5
Knitwear	2.1	Crude oil	3.7
Rice	1.8	Palm oil	1.8
Cotton yard & thread	1.6	Telecoms equipment	1.4
Total incl. others	**21.9**	Total incl. others	**43.9**

Main export destinations		Main origins of imports	
	% of total		*% of total*
United States	16.7	China	25.1
China	8.8	United Arab Emirates	13.1
Afghanistan	7.9	Saudi Arabia	6.8
United Kingdom	7.2	Indonesia	4.7

Balance of payments, reserves and debt, $bn

Visible exports fob	22.7	Change in reserves	5.7
Visible imports fob	-39.3	Level of reserves	
Trade balance	-16.6	end Dec.	20.0
Invisibles inflows	6.4	No. months of import cover	4.5
Invisibles outflows	-13.6	Official gold holdings, m oz	2.1
Net transfers	22.1	Foreign debt	65.5
Current account balance	-1.6	– as % of GDP	24.2
– as % of GDP	-0.6	– as % of total exports	135.1
Capital balance	6.0	Debt service ratio	7.7
Overall balance	3.9		

Health and education

Health spending, % of GDP	2.6	Education spending, % of GDP	2.7
Doctors per 1,000 pop.	0.8	Enrolment, %: primary	93
Hospital beds per 1,000 pop.	0.6	secondary	45
Improved-water source access,		tertiary	10
% of pop.	91.4		

Society

No. of households, m	28.1	Cost of living, Dec. 2016	
Av. no. per household	6.7	New York = 100	44
Marriages per 1,000 pop.	...	Cars per 1,000 pop.	13
Divorces per 1,000 pop.	...	Colour TV households, % with:	
Religion, % of pop.		cable	1.3
Muslim	96.4	satellite	15.4
Hindu	1.9	Telephone lines per 100 pop.	1.9
Christian	1.6	Mobile telephone subscribers	
Jewish	<0.1	per 100 pop.	66.9
Non-religious	<0.1	Broadband subs per 100 pop.	1.0
Other	<0.1	Internet users, % of pop.	18.0

PERU

Area, sq km	1,285,216	Capital	Lima
Arable as % of total land	3.2	Currency	Nuevo Sol (new Sol)

People

Population, m	31.4	Life expectancy: men	72.9 yrs
Pop. per sq km	24.4	women	78.1 yrs
Average annual growth		Adult literacy	94.4
in pop. 2015–20, %	1.2	Fertility rate (per woman)	2.2
Pop. aged 0–24, %	45.7	Urban population, 2020, %	80.1
Pop. aged 70 and over, %	4.5		per 1,000 pop.
No. of men per 100 women	99.8	Crude birth rate	18.7
Human Development Index	74.0	Crude death rate	5.6

The economy

GDP	$192bn	GDP per head	$6,127
GDP	New Soles 613bn	GDP per head in purchasing	
Av. ann. growth in real		power parity (USA=100)	21.9
GDP 2010–15	4.8%	Economic freedom index	68.9

Origins of GDP		**Components of GDP**	
	% of total		% of total
Agriculture	8	Private consumption	65
Industry, of which:	33	Public consumption	13
manufacturing	15	Investment	24
Services	59	Exports	21
		Imports	-24

Structure of employment

	% of total		% of labour force
Agriculture	...	Unemployed 2015	4.4
Industry	22.8	Av. ann. rate 2005–15	5.2
Services	76.1		

Energy

	m TOE		
Total output	22.9	Net energy imports as %	
Total consumption	26.4	of energy use	0.15
Consumption per head			
kg oil equivalent	768		

Inflation and finance

			av. ann. increase 2011–16
Consumer price			
inflation 2016	3.6%	Narrow money (M1)	8.6%
Av. ann. inflation 2011–16	5.0%	Broad money	10.0%
Money market rate, Dec. 2016	4.37%		

Exchange rates

	end 2016		December 2016
New Soles per $	3.36	Effective rates	2010 = 100
New Soles per sdr	4.51	– nominal	...
New Soles per €	3.54	– real	...

Trade

Principal exports		**Principal imports**	
	$bn fob		*$bn cif*
Copper	8.2	Intermediate goods	15.9
Gold	6.7	Capital goods	12.0
Zinc	1.5	Consumer goods	8.8
Fishmeal	1.4		
Total incl. others	**34.2**	Total incl. others	**37.4**

Main export destinations		**Main origins of imports**	
	% of total		*% of total*
China	21.5	China	24.4
United States	14.8	United States	22.2
Switzerland	7.8	Brazil	5.4
Canada	6.8	Mexico	4.8

Balance of payments, reserves and debt, $bn

Visible exports fob	34.2	Change in reserves	-0.9
Visible imports fob	-37.0	Level of reserves	
Trade balance	-2.8	end Dec.	61.6
Invisibles inflows	6.9	No. months of import cover	13.8
Invisibles outflows	-16.6	Official gold holdings, m oz	1.1
Net transfers	3.3	Foreign debt	65.9
Current account balance	-9.2	– as % of GDP	34.3
– as % of GDP	-4.8	– as % of total exports	150.4
Capital balance	10.1	Debt service ratio	10.8
Overall balance	-0.8		

Health and education

Health spending, % of GDP	5.5	Education spending, % of GDP	3.9
Doctors per 1,000 pop.	1.1	Enrolment, %: primary	102
Hospital beds per 1,000 pop.	1.5	secondary	96
Improved-water source access,		tertiary	...
% of pop.	86.7		

Society

No. of households, m	7.8	Cost of living, Dec. 2016	
Av. no. per household	4.0	New York = 100	65
Marriages per 1,000 pop.	3.1	Cars per 1,000 pop.	45
Divorces per 1,000 pop.	0.4	Colour TV households, % with:	
Religion, % of pop.		cable	32.5
Christian	95.5	satellite	0.2
Non-religious	3.0	Telephone lines per 100 pop.	9.3
Other	1.5	Mobile telephone subscribers	
Hindu	<0.1	per 100 pop.	109.9
Jewish	<0.1	Broadband subs per 100 pop.	6.4
Muslim	<0.1	Internet users, % of pop.	40.9

PHILIPPINES

Area, sq km	300,000	Capital	Manila
Arable as % of total land	18.7	Currency	Philippine peso (P)

People

Population, m	100.7	Life expectancy: men	65.4 yrs
Pop. per sq km	335.7	women	72.4 yrs
Average annual growth		Adult literacy	96.6
in pop. 2015–20, %	1.5	Fertility rate (per woman)	3.1
Pop. aged 0–24, %	51.5	Urban population, 2020, %	44.3
Pop. aged 70 and over, %	2.6		per 1,000 pop.
No. of men per 100 women	101.9	Crude birth rate	22.7
Human Development Index	68.2	Crude death rate	6.8

The economy

GDP	$292bn	GDP per head	$2,904
GDP	P13,307bn	GDP per head in purchasing	
Av. ann. growth in real		power parity (USA=100)	13.2
GDP 2010–15	5.9%	Economic freedom index	65.6

Origins of GDP		**Components of GDP**	
	% of total		% of total
Agriculture	10	Private consumption	75
Industry, of which:	31	Public consumption	11
manufacturing	20	Investment	21
Services	59	Exports	28
		Imports	-35

Structure of employment

	% of total		% of labour force
Agriculture	29.2	Unemployed 2015	6.3
Industry	16.2	Av. ann. rate 2005–15	7.2
Services	54.7		

Energy

	m TOE		
Total output	9.7	Net energy imports as %	
Total consumption	34.8	of energy use	46
Consumption per head			
kg oil equivalent	481		

Inflation and finance

			av. ann. increase 2011–16
Consumer price			
inflation 2016	2.0%	Narrow money (M1)	15.5%
Av. ann. inflation 2011–16	4.7%	Broad money	14.0%
Treasury bill rate, Dec. 2016	1.56%		

Exchange rates

	end 2016		December 2016
P per $	49.81	Effective rates	2010 = 100
P per sdr	66.97	– nominal	103.14
P per €	52.41	– real	112.11

Trade

Principal exports		**Principal imports**	
	$bn fob		*$bn cif*
Electrical & electronic equip.	28.6	Raw materials & intermediate	
Machinery & transport equip.	5.2	goods	30.5
Agricultural products	3.7	Capital goods	19.6
Mineral products	2.9	Consumer goods	11.4
		Mineral fuels & lubricants	9.2
Total incl. others	**58.6**	Total incl. others	**74.8**

Main export destinations		**Main origins of imports**	
	% of total		*% of total*
Japan	21.1	China	15.9
United States	15.0	United States	10.6
China	10.9	Japan	9.4
Hong Kong	10.6	Taiwan	7.7

Balance of payments, reserves and debt, $bn

Visible exports fob	43.2	Change in reserves	1.0
Visible imports fob	-66.5	Level of reserves	
Trade balance	-23.3	end Dec.	80.6
Invisibles inflows	38.6	No. months of import cover	9.9
Invisibles outflows	-31.3	Official gold holdings, m oz	6.3
Net transfers	23.3	Foreign debt	77.7
Current account balance	7.3	– as % of GDP	26.6
– as % of GDP	2.5	– as % of total exports	69.5
Capital balance	-2.2	Debt service ratio	7.2
Overall balance	2.6		

Health and education

Health spending, % of GDP	4.7	Education spending, % of GDP	...
Doctors per 1,000 pop.	...	Enrolment, %: primary	117
Hospital beds per 1,000 pop.	1.0	secondary	88
Improved-water source access,		tertiary	36
% of pop.	91.8		

Society

No. of households, m	22.9	Cost of living, Dec. 2016	
Av. no. per household	4.4	New York = 100	63
Marriages per 1,000 pop.	...	Cars per 1,000 pop.	31
Divorces per 1,000 pop.	...	Colour TV households, % with:	
Religion, % of pop.		cable	52.5
Christian	92.6	satellite	0.6
Muslim	5.5	Telephone lines per 100 pop.	3.2
Other	1.7	Mobile telephone subscribers	
Non-religious	0.1	per 100 pop.	116.0
Hindu	<0.1	Broadband subs per 100 pop.	4.8
Jewish	<0.1	Internet users, % of pop.	40.7

POLAND

Area, sq km	312,888	Capital	Warsaw
Arable as % of total land	35.7	Currency	Zloty (Zl)

People

Population, m	38.6	Life expectancy: men	74.1 yrs
Pop. per sq km	123.4	women	81.8 yrs
Average annual growth		Adult literacy	99.8
in pop. 2015–20, %	-0.1	Fertility rate (per woman)	1.3
Pop. aged 0–24, %	26.5	Urban population, 2020, %	60.7
Pop. aged 70 and over, %	10.2		per 1,000 pop.
No. of men per 100 women	93.7	Crude birth rate	9.5
Human Development Index	85.5	Crude death rate	10.4

The economy

GDP	$477bn	GDP per head	$12,359
GDP	Zl1,798bn	GDP per head in purchasing	
Av. ann. growth in real		power parity (USA=100)	46.8
GDP 2010–15	2.9%	Economic freedom index	68.3

Origins of GDP		**Components of GDP**	
	% of total		% of total
Agriculture	3	Private consumption	58
Industry, of which:	34	Public consumption	18
manufacturing	20	Investment	20
Services	63	Exports	50
		Imports	-46

Structure of employment

	% of total		% of labour force
Agriculture	11.5	Unemployed 2015	7.5
Industry	30.4	Av. ann. rate 2005–15	10.2
Services	57.8		

Energy

	m TOE		
Total output	54.7	Net energy imports as %	
Total consumption	98.0	of energy use	28
Consumption per head			
kg oil equivalent	2,473		

Inflation and finance

Consumer price		*av. ann. increase 2011–16*	
inflation 2016	-0.6%	Narrow money (M1)	11.7%
Av. ann. inflation 2011–16	3.0%	Broad money	7.5%
Money market rate, Dec. 2016	1.47%		

Exchange rates

	end 2016		December 2016
Zl per $	4.18	Effective rates	2010 = 100
Zl per sdr	5.62	– nominal	91.51
Zl per €	4.40	– real	88.18

Trade

Principal exports		Principal imports	
	$bn fob		*$bn cif*
Machinery & transport equip.	77.0	Machinery & transport equip.	71.0
Manufactured goods	37.6	Manufactured goods	34.0
Foodstuffs & live animals	21.4	Chemicals & mineral products	27.4
Total incl. others	**199.4**	Total incl. others	**195.2**

Main export destinations		Main origins of imports	
	% of total		*% of total*
Germany	27.1	Germany	27.8
United Kingdom	6.7	China	7.4
Czech Republic	6.6	Russia	7.2
France	5.5	Netherlands	5.9
EU28	79.3	EU28	70.7

Balance of payments, reserves and debt, $bn

Visible exports fob	191.0	Change in reserves	-5.5
Visible imports fob	-188.6	Level of reserves	
Trade balance	2.5	end Dec.	94.9
Invisibles inflows	57.5	No. months of import cover	4.5
Invisibles outflows	-62.0	Official gold holdings, m oz	3.3
Net transfers	-1.0	Foreign debt	331.4
Current account balance	-2.9	– as % of GDP	69.5
– as % of GDP	-0.6	– as % of total exports	131.2
Capital balance	10.9	Debt service ratio	12.2
Overall balance	1.1		

Health and education

Health spending, % of GDP	6.4	Education spending, % of GDP	4.9
Doctors per 1,000 pop.	2.2	Enrolment, %: primary	101
Hospital beds per 1,000 pop.	6.5	secondary	109
Improved-water source access,		tertiary	71
% of pop.	98.3		

Society

No. of households, m	14.1	Cost of living, Dec. 2016	
Av. no. per household	2.7	New York = 100	58
Marriages per 1,000 pop.	5.0	Cars per 1,000 pop.	523
Divorces per 1,000 pop.	1.7	Colour TV households, % with:	
Religion, % of pop.		cable	33.8
Christian	94.3	satellite	62.8
Non-religious	5.6	Telephone lines per 100 pop.	23.7
Hindu	<0.1	Mobile telephone subscribers	
Jewish	<0.1	per 100 pop.	142.7
Muslim	<0.1	Broadband subs per 100 pop.	19.0
Other	<0.1	Internet users, % of pop.	68.0

PORTUGAL

Area, sq km	92,225	Capital	Lisbon
Arable as % of total land	12.4	Currency	Euro (€)

People

Population, m	10.3	Life expectancy: men	78.8 yrs
Pop. per sq km	111.7	women	84.4 yrs
Average annual growth		Adult literacy	95.4
in pop. 2015–20, %	-0.4	Fertility rate (per woman)	1.5
Pop. aged 0–24, %	24.5	Urban population, 2020, %	66.1
Pop. aged 70 and over, %	15.0		per 1,000 pop.
No. of men per 100 women	89.9	Crude birth rate	7.6
Human Development Index	84.3	Crude death rate	10.7

The economy

GDP	$199bn	GDP per head	$19,342
GDP	€180bn	GDP per head in purchasing	
Av. ann. growth in real		power parity (USA=100)	50.4
GDP 2010–15	-0.9%	Economic freedom index	62.6

Origins of GDP		**Components of GDP**	
	% of total		% of total
Agriculture	2	Private consumption	66
Industry, of which:	22	Public consumption	18
manufacturing	14	Investment	15
Services	75	Exports	41
		Imports	-40

Structure of employment

	% of total		% of labour force
Agriculture	7.5	Unemployed 2015	12.4
Industry	24.4	Av. ann. rate 2005–15	11.1
Services	68.1		

Energy

	m TOE		
Total output	...	Net energy imports as %	
Total consumption	25.6	of energy use	72
Consumption per head			
kg oil equivalent	2,035		

Inflation and finance

			av. ann. increase 2011–16
Consumer price			
inflation 2016	0.7%	Narrow money (M1)	8.1%
Av. ann. inflation 2011–16	3.0%	Broad money	3.6%
Deposit rate, Dec. 2016	0.32%		

Exchange rates

	end 2016		December 2016
€ per $	0.95	Effective rates	2010 = 100
€ per sdr	1.28	– nominal	98.14
		– real	97.21

Trade

Principal exports	$bn fob	Principal imports	$bn cif
Machinery & transport equip.	14.3	Machinery & transport equip.	18.6
Food, drink & tobacco	6.2	Chemicals & related products	9.5
Chemicals & related products	4.9	Food, drink & tobacco	8.8
Mineral fuels & lubricants	4.3	Mineral fuels & lubricants	8.8
Total incl. others	**55.3**	Total incl. others	**66.9**

Main export destinations	% of total	Main origins of imports	% of total
Spain	25.0	Spain	33.0
France	12.1	Germany	12.9
Germany	11.8	France	7.4
United Kingdom	6.7	Italy	5.4
EU28	72.8	EU28	76.5

Balance of payments, reserves and debt, $bn

Visible exports fob	54.5	Overall balance	10.8
Visible imports fob	-64.7	Change in reserves	-0.3
Trade balance	-10.3	Level of reserves	
Invisibles inflows	37.0	end Dec.	19.4
Invisibles outflows	-28.3	No. months of import cover	2.5
Net transfers	1.7	Official gold holdings, m oz	12.3
Current account balance	0.1	Aid given	0.3
– as % of GDP	0.1	– as % of GDP	0.2
Capital balance	11.0		

Health and education

Health spending, % of GDP	9.5	Education spending, % of GDP	5.3
Doctors per 1,000 pop.	4.1	Enrolment, %: primary	109
Hospital beds per 1,000 pop.	3.4	secondary	116
Improved-water source access,		tertiary	66
% of pop.	100		

Society

No. of households, m	4.1	Cost of living, Dec. 2016	
Av. no. per household	2.5	New York = 100	64
Marriages per 1,000 pop.	3.0	Cars per 1,000 pop.	421
Divorces per 1,000 pop.	2.2	Colour TV households, % with:	
Religion, % of pop.		cable	56.1
Christian	93.8	satellite	20.1
Non-religious	4.4	Telephone lines per 100 pop.	44.1
Other	1.0	Mobile telephone subscribers	
Muslim	0.6	per 100 pop.	110.4
Hindu	0.1	Broadband subs per 100 pop.	29.6
Jewish	<0.1	Internet users, % of pop.	68.6

ROMANIA

Area, sq km	238,391	Capital	Bucharest
Arable as % of total land	38.2	Currency	Leu (RON)

People

Population, m	19.5	Life expectancy: men	71.6 yrs
Pop. per sq km	81.8	women	78.7 yrs
Average annual growth		Adult literacy	98.8
in pop. 2015–20, %	-0.7	Fertility rate (per woman)	1.3
Pop. aged 0–24, %	26.0	Urban population, 2020, %	55.6
Pop. aged 70 and over, %	11.8		*per 1,000 pop.*
No. of men per 100 women	93.9	Crude birth rate	9.0
Human Development Index	80.2	Crude death rate	13.7

The economy

GDP	$178bn	GDP per head	$9,104
GDP	RON711bn	GDP per head in purchasing	
Av. ann. growth in real		power parity (USA=100)	38.1
GDP 2010–15	2.4%	Economic freedom index	69.7

Origins of GDP		**Components of GDP**	
	% of total		*% of total*
Agriculture	5	Private consumption	61
Industry, of which:	35	Public consumption	14
manufacturing	24	Investment	26
Services	60	Exports	41
		Imports	-42

Structure of employment

	% of total		*% of labour force*
Agriculture	25.6	Unemployed 2015	6.8
Industry	28.5	Av. ann. rate 2005–15	6.8
Services	46.0		

Energy

	m TOE		
Total output	21.3	Net energy imports as %	
Total consumption	33.2	of energy use	17
Consumption per head			
kg oil equivalent	1,592		

Inflation and finance

			av. ann. increase 2011–16
Consumer price			
inflation 2016	-1.5%	Narrow money (M1)	16.0%
Av. ann. inflation 2011–16	3.9%	Broad money	7.8%
Treasury bill rate, Dec. 2016	2.43%		

Exchange rates

	end 2016		*December 2016*
Lei per $	4.30	Effective rates	2010 = 100
Lei per sdr	5.79	– nominal	94.81
Lei per €	4.52	– real	94.98

Trade

Principal exports

	$bn fob
Machinery & transport equip.	26.9
Basic metals & products	5.2
Textiles & apparel	4.4
Minerals, fuels & lubricants	2.7
Total incl. others	**60.6**

Principal imports

	$bn cif
Machinery & transport equip.	26.3
Chemical products	7.0
Minerals, fuels & lubricants	4.9
Textiles & products	4.7
Total incl. others	**69.9**

Main export destinations

	% of total
Germany	19.7
Italy	12.5
France	6.8
Hungary	5.4
EU28	73.7

Main origins of imports

	% of total
Germany	19.8
Italy	10.9
Hungary	7.9
France	5.6
EU28	77.1

Balance of payments, reserves and debt, $bn

Visible exports fob	54.5	Change in reserves	-4.5
Visible imports fob	-63.1	Level of reserves	
Trade balance	-8.6	end Dec.	38.7
Invisibles inflows	21.1	No. months of import cover	5.7
Invisibles outflows	-17.7	Official gold holdings, m oz	3.3
Net transfers	3.1	Foreign debt	96.0
Current account balance	-2.2	– as % of GDP	53.9
– as % of GDP	-1.2	– as % of total exports	121.9
Capital balance	2.7	Debt service ratio	30.1
Overall balance	0.9		

Health and education

Health spending, % of GDP	5.6	Education spending, % of GDP	2.9
Doctors per 1,000 pop.	2.4	Enrolment, %: primary	90
Hospital beds per 1,000 pop.	6.1	secondary	92
Improved-water source access,		tertiary	53
% of pop.	100		

Society

No. of households, m	7.0	Cost of living, Dec. 2016	
Av. no. per household	2.8	New York = 100	47
Marriages per 1,000 pop.	5.9	Cars per 1,000 pop.	227
Divorces per 1,000 pop.	1.4	Colour TV households, % with:	
Religion, % of pop.		cable	45.9
Christian	99.5	satellite	37.4
Muslim	0.3	Telephone lines per 100 pop.	19.8
Non-religious	0.1	Mobile telephone subscribers	
Hindu	<0.1	per 100 pop.	107.1
Jewish	<0.1	Broadband subs per 100 pop.	19.8
Other	<0.1	Internet users, % of pop.	55.8

RUSSIA

Area, sq km	17,098,246	Capital	Moscow
Arable as % of total land	7.5	Currency	Rouble (Rb)

People

Population, m	143.5	Life expectancy: men	64.7 yrs
Pop. per sq km	8.4	women	76.1 yrs
Average annual growth		Adult literacy	99.7
in pop. 2015–20, %	-0.1	Fertility rate (per woman)	1.6
Pop. aged 0–24, %	27.4	Urban population, 2020, %	74.6
Pop. aged 70 and over, %	9.3		per 1,000 pop.
No. of men per 100 women	86.8	Crude birth rate	12.3
Human Development Index	80.4	Crude death rate	14.3

The economy

GDP	$1,366bn	GDP per head	$9,518
GDP	Rb83,233bn	GDP per head in purchasing	
Av. ann. growth in real		power parity (USA=100)	46.7
GDP 2010–15	1.1%	Economic freedom index	57.1

Origins of GDP		**Components of GDP**	
	% of total		% of total
Agriculture	5	Private consumption	52
Industry, of which:	33	Public consumption	19
manufacturing	14	Investment	21
Services	63	Exports	30
		Imports	-21

Structure of employment

	% of total		% of labour force
Agriculture	6.7	Unemployed 2015	5.6
Industry	27.2	Av. ann. rate 2005–15	6.4
Services	66.1		

Energy

	m TOE		
Total output	1,350.3	Net energy imports as %	
Total consumption	772.0	of energy use	-84
Consumption per head			
kg oil equivalent	4,943		

Inflation and finance

			av. ann. increase 2011–16
Consumer price			
inflation 2016	7.2%	Narrow money (M1)	6.7%
Av. ann. inflation 2011–16	9.4%	Broad money	12.3%
Money market rate, Dec. 2016	10.16%		

Exchange rates

	end 2016		December 2016
Rb per $	60.66	Effective rates	2010 = 100
Rb per sdr	81.54	– nominal	68.80
Rb per €	63.83	– real	90.83

Trade

Principal exports[a]

	$bn fob
Fuels	350.8
Ores & metals	52.3
Chemicals	29.2
Machinery & equipment	26.4
Total incl.others	**497.8**

Principal imports[a]

	$bn cif
Machinery & equipment	136.3
Chemicals	46.5
Food & agricultural products	39.9
Metals	20.5
Total incl.others	**286.7**

Main export destinations

	% of total
Netherlands	11.9
China	8.3
Germany	7.4
Italy	6.5
EU28	39.8

Main origins of imports

	% of total
China	19.1
Germany	11.2
United States	6.3
Belarus	5.1
EU28	35.8

Balance of payments, reserves and debt, $bn

Visible exports fob	341.5	Change in reserves	-18.2
Visible imports fob	-193.0	Level of reserves	
Trade balance	148.5	end Dec.	368.0
Invisibles inflows	89.0	No. months of import cover	12.4
Invisibles outflows	-162.8	Official gold holdings, m oz	45.5
Net transfers	-5.7	Foreign debt	467.7
Current account balance	68.9	– as % of GDP	34.2
– as % of GDP	5.0	– as % of total exports	106.9
Capital balance	-70.3	Debt service ratio	23.0
Overall balance	1.7		

Health and education

Health spending, % of GDP	7.1	Education spending, % of GDP	4.3
Doctors per 1,000 pop.	4.3	Enrolment, %: primary	99
Hospital beds per 1,000 pop.	...	secondary	101
Improved-water source access,		tertiary	79
% of pop.	96.9		

Society

No. of households, m	56.5	Cost of living, Dec. 2016	
Av. no. per household	2.5	New York = 100	90
Marriages per 1,000 pop.	8.5	Cars per 1,000 pop.	304
Divorces per 1,000 pop.	4.5	Colour TV households, % with:	
Religion, % of pop.		cable	32.9
Christian	73.3	satellite	24.7
Non-religious	16.2	Telephone lines per 100 pop.	25.0
Muslim	10.0	Mobile telephone subscribers	
Jewish	0.2	per 100 pop.	160.0
Hindu	<0.1	Broadband subs per 100 pop.	18.9
Other	<0.1	Internet users, % of pop.	70.1

a 2014

SAUDI ARABIA

Area, sq km	2,150,000	Capital	Riyadh
Arable as % of total land	1.6	Currency	Riyal (SR)

People

Population, m	31.5	Life expectancy: men	73.5 yrs
Pop. per sq km	14.7	women	76.3 yrs
Average annual growth		Adult literacy	94.8
in pop. 2015–20, %	1.7	Fertility rate (per woman)	2.1
Pop. aged 0–24, %	42.2	Urban population, 2020, %	84.1
Pop. aged 70 and over, %	1.7		per 1,000 pop.
No. of men per 100 women	130.1	Crude birth rate	18.5
Human Development Index	84.7	Crude death rate	3.5

The economy

GDP	$652bn	GDP per head	$20,691
GDP	SR2,444bn	GDP per head in purchasing	
Av. ann. growth in real		power parity (USA=100)	96.5
GDP 2010–15	5.0%	Economic freedom index	64.4

Origins of GDP		**Components of GDP**	
	% of total		% of total
Agriculture	2	Private consumption	41
Industry, of which:	46	Public consumption	30
manufacturing	12	Investment	35
Services	52	Exports	34
		Imports	-39

Structure of employment

	% of total		% of labour force
Agriculture	6.1	Unemployed 2015	5.6
Industry	22.7	Av. ann. rate 2005–15	5.7
Services	71.2		

Energy

	m TOE		
Total output	689.7	Net energy imports as %	
Total consumption	255.2	of energy use	-192
Consumption per head			
kg oil equivalent	6,913		

Inflation and finance

			av. ann. increase 2011–16
Consumer price			
inflation 2016	4.0%	Narrow money (M1)	8.5%
Av. ann. inflation 2011–16	4.6%	Broad money	7.9%
Treasury bill rate, Dec. 2016	0.87%		

Exchange rates

	end 2016		December 2016
			2010 = 100
SR per $	3.75	Effective rates	
SR per sdr	5.04	– nominal	123.53
SR per €	3.95	– real	127.57

Trade

Principal exports		**Principal imports**	
	$bn fob		*$bn cif*
Crude oil	128.0	Machinery & transport equip.	79.7
Refined petroleum products	27.9	Foodstuffs	24.5
		Chemical & metal products	14.7
Total incl. others	**203.5**	Total incl. others	**174.6**

Main export destinations		**Main origins of imports**	
	% of total		*% of total*
China	14.1	China	14.5
Japan	11.7	United States	13.3
United States	10.3	Germany	7.1
India	9.9	Japan	5.9

Balance of payments, reserves and aid, $bn

Visible exports fob	203.5	Change in reserves	-117.5
Visible imports fob	-159.3	Level of reserves	
Trade balance	44.3	end Dec.	627.0
Invisibles inflows	40.1	No. months of import cover	29.4
Invisibles outflows	-96.3	Official gold holdings, m oz	10.4
Net transfers	-44.7	Foreign debt	171.5
Current account balance	-56.7	– as % of GDP	26.3
– as % of GDP	-8.7	– as % of total exports	70.4
Capital balance	-43.9	Debt service ratio	5.4
Overall balance	-115.4		

Health and education

Health spending, % of GDP	4.7	Education spending, % of GDP	...
Doctors per 1,000 pop.	2.5	Enrolment, %: primary	109
Hospital beds per 1,000 pop.	2.1	secondary	108
Improved-water source access,		tertiary	63
% of pop.	97.0		

Society

No. of households, m	5.0	Cost of living, Dec. 2016	
Av. no. per household	6.3	New York = 100	54
Marriages per 1,000 pop.	...	Cars per 1,000 pop.	140
Divorces per 1,000 pop.	...	Colour TV households, % with:	
Religion, % of pop.		cable	0.3
Muslim	93.0	satellite	99.5
Christian	4.4	Telephone lines per 100 pop.	12.5
Hindu	1.1	Mobile telephone subscribers	
Other	0.9	per 100 pop.	176.6
Non-religious	0.7	Broadband subs per 100 pop.	11.9
Jewish	<0.1	Internet users, % of pop.	69.6

SINGAPORE

Area, sq km	718	Capital	Singapore
Arable as % of total land	0.8	Currency	Singapore dollar (S$)

People

Population, m	5.6	Life expectancy: men	80.6 yrs
Pop. per sq km	7,799.4	women	86.7 yrs
Average annual growth		Adult literacy	96.8
in pop. 2015–20, %	1.4	Fertility rate (per woman)	1.0
Pop. aged 0–24, %	28.7	Urban population, 2020, %	100.0
Pop. aged 70 and over, %	7.1		per 1,000 pop.
No. of men per 100 women	97.4	Crude birth rate	8.7
Human Development Index	92.5	Crude death rate	5.1

The economy

GDP	$297bn	GDP per head	$53,006
GDP	S$408bn	GDP per head in purchasing	
Av. ann. growth in real		power parity (USA=100)	151.9
GDP 2010–15	4.0%	Economic freedom index	88.6

Origins of GDP		**Components of GDP**	
	% of total		% of total
Agriculture	0	Private consumption	36
Industry, of which:	26	Public consumption	10
manufacturing	20	Investment	26
Services	74	Exports	176
		Imports	-150

Structure of employment

	% of total		% of labour force
Agriculture	1.0	Unemployed 2015	1.7
Industry	16.3	Av. ann. rate 2005–15	3.5
Services	82.7		

Energy

	m TOE		
Total output	...	Net energy imports as %	
Total consumption	82.3	of energy use	99
Consumption per head			
kg oil equivalent	5,122		

Inflation and finance

Consumer price		av. ann. increase 2011–16	
inflation 2016	-0.3%	Narrow money (M1)	5.8%
Av. ann. inflation 2011–16	3.8%	Broad money	4.9%
Money market rate, Dec. 2016	0.46%		

Exchange rates

	end 2016		December 2016
S$ per $	1.45	Effective rates	2010 = 100
S$ per sdr	1.94	– nominal	109.86
S$ per €	1.53	– real	108.01

Trade

Principal exports	
	$bn fob
Mineral fuels	59.5
Electronic components & parts	48.5
Chemicals & chemical products	47.7
Manufactured products	30.5
Total incl.others	**357.8**

Principal imports	
	$bn cif
Machinery & transport equip.	141.5
Mineral fuels	64.6
Misc. manufactured articles	26.0
Manufactured products	20.5
Total incl.others	**307.7**

Main export destinations	
	% of total
China	13.5
Hong Kong	11.3
Malaysia	10.6
Indonesia	8.1

Main origins of imports	
	% of total
China	13.7
Malaysia	10.8
United States	10.8
Taiwan	8.0

Balance of payments, reserves and debt, $bn

Visible exports fob	379.6	Change in reserves	-9.7
Visible imports fob	-296.7	Level of reserves	
Trade balance	82.8	end Dec.	251.9
Invisibles inflows	211.5	No. months of import cover	5.7
Invisibles outflows	-230.6	Official gold holdings, m oz	4.1
Net transfers	-10.0	Foreign debt	465.5
Current account balance	53.8	– as % of GDP	156.8
– as % of GDP	18.1	– as % of total exports	78.7
Capital balance	-51.5	Debt service ratio	7.3
Overall balance	1.1		

Health and education

Health spending, % of GDP	4.9	Education spending, % of GDP	2.9
Doctors per 1,000 pop.	2.0	Enrolment, %: primary	...
Hospital beds per 1,000 pop.	2.0	secondary	...
Improved-water source access,		tertiary	70
% of pop.	100		

Society

No. of households, m	1.6	Cost of living, Dec. 2016	
Av. no. per household	3.5	New York = 100	120
Marriages per 1,000 pop.	7.3	Cars per 1,000 pop.	118
Divorces per 1,000 pop.	1.8	Colour TV households, % with:	
Religion, % of pop.		cable	55.8
Buddhist	33.9	satellite	...
Christian	18.2	Telephone lines per 100 pop.	35.9
Non-religious	16.4	Mobile telephone subscribers	
Muslim	14.3	per 100 pop.	146.5
Other	12.0	Broadband subs per 100 pop.	26.4
Hindu	5.2	Internet users, % of pop.	82.1

SLOVAKIA

Area, sq km	49,035	Capital	Bratislava
Arable as % of total land	29.0	Currency	Euro (€)

People

Population, m	5.4	Life expectancy: men	73.0 yrs
Pop. per sq km	110.1	women	80.3 yrs
Average annual growth		Adult literacy	...
in pop. 2015–20, %	0.0	Fertility rate (per woman)	1.4
Pop. aged 0–24, %	27.0	Urban population, 2020, %	53.2
Pop. aged 70 and over, %	9.0		per 1,000 pop.
No. of men per 100 women	94.1	Crude birth rate	10.4
Human Development Index	84.5	Crude death rate	10.2

The economy

GDP	$87bn	GDP per head	$16,169
GDP	€79bn	GDP per head in purchasing	
Av. ann. growth in real		power parity (USA=100)	53.7
GDP 2010–15	2.4%	Economic freedom index	65.7

Origins of GDP		**Components of GDP**	
	% of total		% of total
Agriculture	4	Private consumption	55
Industry, of which:	35	Public consumption	19
manufacturing	22	Investment	23
Services	62	Exports	93
		Imports	-91

Structure of employment

	% of total		% of labour force
Agriculture	3.2	Unemployed 2015	11.5
Industry	36.1	Av. ann. rate 2005–15	13.0
Services	60.7		

Energy

	m TOE		
Total output	4.9	Net energy imports as %	
Total consumption	17.0	of energy use	59
Consumption per head			
kg oil equivalent	2,943		

Inflation and finance

			av. ann. increase 2011–16
Consumer price			
inflation 2016	-0.2%	Narrow money (M1)	8.1%
Av. ann. inflation 2011–16	3.3%	Broad money	3.6%
Deposit rate, Dec. 2016	1.90%		

Exchange rates

	end 2016		December 2016
€ per $	0.95	Effective rates	2010 = 100
€ per sdr	1.28	– nominal	99.91
		– real	97.52

Trade

Principal exports		Principal imports	
	$bn fob		*$bn cif*
Machinery & transport equip.	44.4	Machinery & transport equip.	34.6
Chemicals & related products	3.6	Chemicals & related products	6.4
Mineral fuels & lubricants	2.8	Mineral fuels & lubricants	5.8
Food, drink & tobacco	2.7	Food, drink & tobacco	3.9
Total incl. others	**75.3**	Total incl. others	**83.4**

Main export destinations		Main origins of imports	
	% of total		*% of total*
Germany	22.4	Germany	16.9
Czech Republic	12.5	Czech Republic	15.2
Poland	8.5	Austria	8.1
Austria	6.0	Poland	5.6
EU28	85.5	EU28	78.7

Balance of payments, reserves and debt, $bn

Visible exports fob	73.3	Overall balance	0.3
Visible imports fob	-71.0	Change in reserves	0.3
Trade balance	2.2	Level of reserves	
Invisibles inflows	12.3	end Dec.	2.9
Invisibles outflows	-13.0	No. months of import cover	0.4
Net transfers	-1.4	Official gold holdings, m oz	1.0
Current account balance	0.2	Aid given	0.09
– as % of GDP	0.2	– as % of GDP	0.1
Capital balance	2.4		

Health and education

Health spending, % of GDP	8.1	Education spending, % of GDP	...
Doctors per 1,000 pop.	3.3	Enrolment, %: primary	101
Hospital beds per 1,000 pop.	6.0	secondary	92
Improved-water source access,		tertiary	53
% of pop.	100		

Society

No. of households, m	1.8	Cost of living, Dec. 2016	
Av. no. per household	3.0	New York = 100	...
Marriages per 1,000 pop.	4.9	Cars per 1,000 pop.	355
Divorces per 1,000 pop.	1.9	Colour TV households, % with:	
Religion, % of pop.		cable	43.0
Christian	85.3	satellite	49.6
Non-religious	14.3	Telephone lines per 100 pop.	15.9
Muslim	0.2	Mobile telephone subscribers	
Other	0.1	per 100 pop.	122.9
Hindu	<0.1	Broadband subs per 100 pop.	23.3
Jewish	<0.1	Internet users, % of pop.	77.6

SLOVENIA

Area, sq km	20,273	Capital	Ljubljana
Arable as % of total land	9.1	Currency	Euro (€)

People

Population, m	2.1	Life expectancy: men	78.1 yrs
Pop. per sq km	103.6	women	83.9 yrs
Average annual growth		Adult literacy	99.7
in pop. 2015–20, %	0.1	Fertility rate (per woman)	1.3
Pop. aged 0–24, %	24.4	Urban population, 2020, %	49.8
Pop. aged 70 and over, %	13.0		per 1,000 pop.
No. of men per 100 women	98.3	Crude birth rate	10.1
Human Development Index	89.0	Crude death rate	10.0

The economy

GDP	$43bn	GDP per head	$20,380
GDP	€39bn	GDP per head in purchasing	
Av. ann. growth in real		power parity (USA=100)	54.2
GDP 2010–15	0.4%	Economic freedom index	59.2

Origins of GDP		**Components of GDP**	
	% of total		% of total
Agriculture	2	Private consumption	52
Industry, of which:	33	Public consumption	19
manufacturing	23	Investment	20
Services	65	Exports	78
		Imports	-69

Structure of employment

	% of total		% of labour force
Agriculture	7.0	Unemployed 2015	9.0
Industry	31.6	Av. ann. rate 2005–15	7.3
Services	60.2		

Energy

	m TOE		
Total output	2.2	Net energy imports as %	
Total consumption	7.0	of energy use	44
Consumption per head			
kg oil equivalent	3,136		

Inflation and finance

Consumer price			av. ann. increase 2011–16
inflation 2016	-0.3%	Narrow money (M1)	8.1%
Av. ann. inflation 2011–16	3.1%	Broad money	3.6%
Money market rate, Dec. 2016	-0.37%		

Exchange rates

	end 2016		December 2016
€ per $	0.95	Effective rates	2010 = 100
€ per sdr	1.28	– nominal	...
		– real	...

Trade

Principal exports		**Principal imports**	
	$bn fob		*$bn cif*
Machinery & transport equip.	12.4	Machinery & transport equip.	10.1
Manufactures	9.9	Manufactures	8.5
Chemicals	5.0	Chemicals	4.2
Miscellaneous manufactures	4.6	Mineral fuels & lubricants	2.8
Total incl. others	**32.0**	Total incl. others	**29.7**

Main export destinations		**Main origins of imports**	
	% of total		*% of total*
Germany	19.0	Germany	16.5
Italy	10.6	Italy	13.8
Austria	8.0	Austria	10.2
Croatia	6.7	China	5.4
EU28	76.0	EU28	70.0

Balance of payments, reserves and debt, $bn

Visible exports fob	26.7	Overall balance	-0.1
Visible imports fob	-25.0	Change in reserves	-0.2
Trade balance	1.7	Level of reserves	
Invisibles inflows	8.5	end Dec.	0.9
Invisibles outflows	-7.3	No. months of import cover	0.3
Net transfers	-0.6	Official gold holdings, m oz	0.1
Current account balance	2.2	Aid given	0.06
– as % of GDP	5.2	– as % of GDP	0.2
Capital balance	-1.7		

Health and education

Health spending, % of GDP	9.2	Education spending, % of GDP	5.5
Doctors per 1,000 pop.	2.5	Enrolment, %: primary	99
Hospital beds per 1,000 pop.	4.6	secondary	111
Improved-water source access,		tertiary	83
% of pop.	99.5		

Society

No. of households, m	0.9	Cost of living, Dec. 2016	
Av. no. per household	2.3	New York = 100	...
Marriages per 1,000 pop.	3.2	Cars per 1,000 pop.	513
Divorces per 1,000 pop.	1.2	Colour TV households, % with:	
Religion, % of pop.		cable	70.7
Christian	78.4	satellite	9.1
Non-religious	18.0	Telephone lines per 100 pop.	36.2
Muslim	3.6	Mobile telephone subscribers	
Hindu	<0.1	per 100 pop.	113.2
Jewish	<0.1	Broadband subs per 100 pop.	27.6
Other	<0.1	Internet users, % of pop.	73.1

SOUTH AFRICA

Area, sq km	1,219,000	Capital	Pretoria
Arable as % of total land	10.3	Currency	Rand (R)

People

Population, m	54.5	Life expectancy: men	55.7 yrs
Pop. per sq km	44.7	women	59.3 yrs
Average annual growth		Adult literacy	94.6
in pop. 2015–20, %	0.8	Fertility rate (per woman)	2.3
Pop. aged 0–24, %	48.6	Urban population, 2020, %	67.2
Pop. aged 70 and over, %	3.2		per 1,000 pop.
No. of men per 100 women	96.8	Crude birth rate	19.8
Human Development Index	66.6	Crude death rate	12.6

The economy

GDP	$315bn	GDP per head	$5,775
GDP	R4,014bn	GDP per head in purchasing	
Av. ann. growth in real		power parity (USA=100)	23.8
GDP 2010–15	2.1%	Economic freedom index	62.3

Origins of GDP		**Components of GDP**	
	% of total		% of total
Agriculture	2	Private consumption	60
Industry, of which:	29	Public consumption	21
manufacturing	13	Investment	21
Services	69	Exports	31
		Imports	-32

Structure of employment

	% of total		% of labour force
Agriculture	5.6	Unemployed 2015	25.2
Industry	23.9	Av. ann. rate 2005–15	24.0
Services	70.5		

Energy

	m TOE		
Total output	137.8	Net energy imports as %	
Total consumption	142.0	of energy use	-14
Consumption per head			
kg oil equivalent	2,714		

Inflation and finance

			av. ann. increase 2011–16
Consumer price			
inflation 2016	6.4%	Narrow money (M1)	11.10%
Av. ann. inflation 2011–16	6.8%	Broad money	6.9%
Treasury bill rate, Dec. 2016	7.61%		

Exchange rates

	end 2016		December 2016
		Effective rates	2010 = 100
R per $	13.68	Effective rates	2010 = 100
R per sdr	18.40	– nominal	63.48
R per €	14.39	– real	80.01

Trade

Principal exports		Principal imports	
	$bn fob		*$bn cif*
Mineral products	16.6	Machinery & equipment	21.3
Precious metals	14.8	Mineral products	13.8
Vehicles, aircraft & vessels	10.2	Vehicles, aircraft & vessels	8.9
Iron & steel products	9.8	Chemicals	8.8
Total incl. others	**81.5**	Total incl. others	**85.7**

Main export destinations		Main origins of imports	
	% of total		*% of total*
China	9.2	China	19.4
United States	7.6	Germany	11.9
Germany	6.2	United States	7.5
Namibia	4.8	India	5.3

Balance of payments, reserves and debt, $bn

Visible exports fob	81.6	Change in reserves	-3.2
Visible imports fob	-84.6	Level of reserves	
Trade balance	-3.0	end Dec.	45.9
Invisibles inflows	23.0	No. months of import cover	4.8
Invisibles outflows	-31.2	Official gold holdings, m oz	4.0
Net transfers	-2.6	Foreign debt	137.9
Current account balance	-13.9	– as % of GDP	43.8
– as % of GDP	-4.4	– as % of total exports	131.3
Capital balance	15.1	Debt service ratio	7.7
Overall balance	-0.8		

Health and education

Health spending, % of GDP	8.8	Education spending, % of GDP	6.1
Doctors per 1,000 pop.	0.8	Enrolment, %: primary	100
Hospital beds per 1,000 pop.	...	secondary	92
Improved-water source access,		tertiary	19
% of pop.	93.2		

Society

No. of households, m	15.3	Cost of living, Dec. 2016	
Av. no. per household	3.6	New York = 100	51
Marriages per 1,000 pop.	...	Cars per 1,000 pop.	120
Divorces per 1,000 pop.	...	Colour TV households, % with:	
Religion, % of pop.		cable	...
Christian	81.2	satellite	8.9
Non-religious	14.9	Telephone lines per 100 pop.	7.7
Muslim	1.7	Mobile telephone subscribers	
Hindu	1.1	per 100 pop.	164.5
Other	0.9	Broadband subs per 100 pop.	2.6
Jewish	0.1	Internet users, % of pop.	51.9

SOUTH KOREA

Area, sq km	100,266	Capital	Seoul
Arable as % of total land	15.1	Currency	Won (W)

People

Population, m	50.3	Life expectancy: men	79.5 yrs
Pop. per sq km	501.7	women	85.7 yrs
Average annual growth		Adult literacy	...
in pop. 2015–20, %	0.4	Fertility rate (per woman)	1.3
Pop. aged 0–24, %	27.5	Urban population, 2020, %	83.1
Pop. aged 70 and over, %	8.9		per 1,000 pop.
No. of men per 100 women	98.8	Crude birth rate	9.1
Human Development Index	90.1	Crude death rate	6.1

The economy

GDP	$1,383bn	GDP per head	$27,490
GDP	W1,564trn	GDP per head in purchasing	
Av. ann. growth in real		power parity (USA=100)	65.8
GDP 2010–15	3.0%	Economic freedom index	74.3

Origins of GDP		**Components of GDP**	
	% of total		% of total
Agriculture	2	Private consumption	50
Industry, of which:	38	Public consumption	15
manufacturing	30	Investment	29
Services	60	Exports	46
		Imports	-39

Structure of employment

	% of total		% of labour force
Agriculture	5.2	Unemployed 2015	3.6
Industry	25.1	Av. ann. rate 2005–15	3.4
Services	69.7		

Energy

	m TOE		
Total output	37.6	Net energy imports as %	
Total consumption	280.6	of energy use	82
Consumption per head			
kg oil equivalent	5,323		

Inflation and finance

			av. ann. increase 2011–16
Consumer price			
inflation 2016	1.0%	Narrow money (M1)	12.5%
Av. ann. inflation 2011–16	3.4%	Broad money	6.6%
Money market rate, Dec. 2016	1.23%		

Exchange rates

	end 2016		December 2016
W per $	1,208.50	Effective rates	2010 = 100
W per sdr	1,624.62	– nominal	...
W per €	1,271.64	– real	...

Trade

Principal exports	$bn fob	Principal imports	$bn cif
Machinery & transport equip.	310.6	Machinery & transport equip.	145.4
Manufactured goods	67.2	Mineral fuels & lubricants	103.4
Chemicals & related products	58.9	Manufactured goods	50.4
Miscellaneous manufactured articles	44.1	Chemicals & related products	43.5
Total incl. others	**526.9**	Total incl. others	**436.1**

Main export destinations	% of total	Main origins of imports	% of total
China	26.0	China	20.7
United States	13.3	Japan	10.5
Hong Kong	5.8	United States	10.1
Vietnam	5.3	Germany	4.8

Balance of payments, reserves and debt, $bn

Visible exports fob	542.9	Change in reserves	3.9
Visible imports fob	-420.6	Level of reserves	
Trade balance	122.3	end Dec.	366.7
Invisibles inflows	121.6	No. months of import cover	7.9
Invisibles outflows	-132.9	Official gold holdings, m oz	3.4
Net transfers	-5.0	Foreign debt	376.6
Current account balance	105.9	– as % of GDP	27.3
– as % of GDP	7.7	– as % of total exports	56.7
Capital balance	-94.3	Debt service ratio	6.4
Overall balance	12.1		

Health and education

Health spending, % of GDP	7.4	Education spending, % of GDP	4.6
Doctors per 1,000 pop.	2.1	Enrolment, %: primary	99
Hospital beds per 1,000 pop.	...	secondary	98
Improved-water source access, % of pop.	97.6	tertiary	95

Society

No. of households, m	18.7	Cost of living, Dec. 2016	
Av. no. per household	2.7	New York = 100	108
Marriages per 1,000 pop.	5.9	Cars per 1,000 pop.	318
Divorces per 1,000 pop.	2.1	Colour TV households, % with:	
Religion, % of pop.		cable	81.8
Non-religious	46.4	satellite	13.5
Christian	29.4	Telephone lines per 100 pop.	58.1
Buddhist	22.9	Mobile telephone subscribers	
Other	1.0	per 100 pop.	118.5
Muslim	0.2	Broadband subs per 100 pop.	40.2
Jewish	<0.1	Internet users, % of pop.	89.6

SPAIN

Area, sq km	505,992	Capital	Madrid
Arable as % of total land	24.5	Currency	Euro (€)

People

Population, m	46.1	Life expectancy: men	80.5 yrs
Pop. per sq km	91.1	women	85.8 yrs
Average annual growth		Adult literacy	98.1
in pop. 2015–20, %	0.0	Fertility rate (per woman)	1.5
Pop. aged 0–24, %	24.3	Urban population, 2020, %	80.7
Pop. aged 70 and over, %	13.7		per 1,000 pop.
No. of men per 100 women	96.3	Crude birth rate	8.6
Human Development Index	88.4	Crude death rate	9.1

The economy

GDP	$1,194bn	GDP per head	$25,891
GDP	€1,076bn	GDP per head in purchasing	
Av. ann. growth in real		power parity (USA=100)	62.4
GDP 2010–15	-0.2%	Economic freedom index	63.6

Origins of GDP		**Components of GDP**	
	% of total		% of total
Agriculture	3	Private consumption	58
Industry, of which:	24	Public consumption	19
manufacturing	14	Investment	20
Services	74	Exports	33
		Imports	-31

Structure of employment

	% of total		% of labour force
Agriculture	4.1	Unemployed 2015	22.1
Industry	19.9	Av. ann. rate 2005–15	17.6
Services	76.0		

Energy

	m TOE		
Total output	15.4	Net energy imports as %	
Total consumption	136.9	of energy use	69
Consumption per head			
kg oil equivalent	2,465		

Inflation and finance

			av. ann. increase 2011–16
Consumer price			
inflation 2016	-0.3%	Narrow money (M1)	8.1%
Av. ann. inflation 2011–16	2.9%	Broad money	3.6%
Treasury bill rate, Dec. 2016	-0.24%		

Exchange rates

	end 2016		December 2016
€ per $	0.95	Effective rates	2010 = 100
€ per sdr	1.28	– nominal	97.94
		– real	92.59

Trade

Principal exports	$bn fob	Principal imports	$bn cif
Machinery & transport equip.	96.1	Machinery & transport equip.	98.6
Food, drink & tobacco	42.2	Chemicals & related products	46.9
Chemicals & related products	38.3	Mineral fuels & lubricants	42.8
Mineral fuels & lubricants	18.8	Food, drink & tobacco	30.9
Total incl. others	**277.1**	Total incl. others	**304.9**

Main export destinations	% of total	Main origins of imports	% of total
France	15.9	Germany	14.8
Germany	11.1	France	12.1
Italy	7.5	China	7.2
United Kingdom	7.5	Italy	6.6
EU28	65.1	EU28	60.7

Balance of payments, reserves and aid, $bn

Visible exports fob	277.4	Overall balance	5.7
Visible imports fob	-301.5	Change in reserves	3.6
Trade balance	-24.1	Level of reserves	
Invisibles inflows	176.4	end Dec.	54.0
Invisibles outflows	-124.0	No. months of import cover	1.5
Net transfers	-12.1	Official gold holdings, m oz	9.1
Current account balance	16.2	Aid given	1.4
– as % of GDP	1.4	– as % of GDP	0.1
Capital balance	-14.4		

Health and education

Health spending, % of GDP	9.0	Education spending, % of GDP	4.3
Doctors per 1,000 pop.	4.9	Enrolment, %: primary	105
Hospital beds per 1,000 pop.	3.1	secondary	130
Improved-water source access,		tertiary	90
% of pop.	100		

Society

No. of households, m	18.8	Cost of living, Dec. 2016	
Av. no. per household	2.5	New York = 100	80
Marriages per 1,000 pop.	3.4	Cars per 1,000 pop.	468
Divorces per 1,000 pop.	2.2	Colour TV households, % with:	
Religion, % of pop.		cable	13.9
Christian	78.6	satellite	12.7
Non-religious	19.0	Telephone lines per 100 pop.	41.5
Muslim	2.1	Mobile telephone subscribers	
Jewish	0.1	per 100 pop.	108.2
Other	0.1	Broadband subs per 100 pop.	28.7
Hindu	<0.1	Internet users, % of pop.	78.7

SWEDEN

Area, sq km	447,000	Capital	Stockholm
Arable as % of total land	6.4	Currency	Swedish krona (Skr)

People

Population, m	9.8	Life expectancy: men	81.1 yrs
Pop. per sq km	21.9	women	84.4 yrs
Average annual growth		Adult literacy	...
in pop. 2015–20, %	0.7	Fertility rate (per woman)	1.9
Pop. aged 0–24, %	29.6	Urban population, 2020, %	86.6
Pop. aged 70 and over, %	13.4		per 1,000 pop.
No. of men per 100 women	99.9	Crude birth rate	12.2
Human Development Index	91.3	Crude death rate	9.0

The economy

GDP	$496bn	GDP per head	$50,581
GDP	Skr4,181bn	GDP per head in purchasing	
Av. ann. growth in real		power parity (USA=100)	86.6
GDP 2010–15	2.0%	Economic freedom index	74.9

Origins of GDP		**Components of GDP**	
	% of total		% of total
Agriculture	1	Private consumption	45
Industry, of which:	26	Public consumption	26
manufacturing	17	Investment	24
Services	72	Exports	46
		Imports	-41

Structure of employment

	% of total		% of labour force
Agriculture	2.0	Unemployed 2015	7.4
Industry	18.2	Av. ann. rate 2005–15	7.6
Services	79.2		

Energy

	m TOE		
Total output	15.7	Net energy imports as %	
Total consumption	52.8	of energy use	28
Consumption per head			
kg oil equivalent	5,132		

Inflation and finance

			av. ann. increase 2011–16
Consumer price			
inflation 2016	1.1%	Narrow money (M1)	9.2%
Av. ann. inflation 2011–16	2.8%	Broad money	3.6%
Treasury bill rate, Dec. 2016	-0.79%		

Exchange rates

	end 2016		December 2016
Skr per $	9.06	Effective rates	2010 = 100
Skr per sdr	12.18	– nominal	96.58
Skr per €	9.53	– real	91.29

Trade

Principal exports

	$bn fob
Machinery & transport equip.	55.1
Chemicals & related products	17.9
Mineral fuels & lubricants	9.2
Raw materials	8.9
Total incl. others	**140.0**

Principal imports

	$bn cif
Machinery & transport equip.	53.4
Chemicals & related products	16.2
Food, drink & tobacco	14.7
Mineral fuels & lubricants	13.5
Total incl. others	**138.3**

Main export destinations

	% of total
Norway	10.3
Germany	10.2
United States	7.7
United Kingdom	7.2
EU28	58.5

Main origins of imports

	% of total
Germany	17.8
Netherlands	8.1
Norway	7.8
Denmark	7.7
EU28	70.0

Balance of payments, reserves and aid, $bn

Visible exports fob	152.1	Overall balance	1.3
Visible imports fob	-138.5	Change in reserves	-4.5
Trade balance	13.5	Level of reserves	
Invisibles inflows	121.4	end Dec.	58.1
Invisibles outflows	-103.4	No. months of import cover	2.9
Net transfers	-8.2	Official gold holdings, m oz	4.0
Current account balance	23.3	Aid given	7.1
– as % of GDP	4.7	– as % of GDP	1.4
Capital balance	-10.1		

Health and education

Health spending, % of GDP	11.9	Education spending, % of GDP	7.7
Doctors per 1,000 pop.	3.9	Enrolment, %: primary	121
Hospital beds per 1,000 pop.	2.7	secondary	133
Improved-water source access,		tertiary	62
% of pop.	100		

Society

No. of households, m	5.1	Cost of living, Dec. 2016	
Av. no. per household	1.9	New York = 100	80
Marriages per 1,000 pop.	5.5	Cars per 1,000 pop.	478
Divorces per 1,000 pop.	2.7	Colour TV households, % with:	
Religion, % of pop.		cable	57.5
Christian	67.2	satellite	20.1
Non-religious	27.0	Telephone lines per 100 pop.	36.7
Muslim	4.6	Mobile telephone subscribers	
Other	0.8	per 100 pop.	130.4
Hindu	0.2	Broadband subs per 100 pop.	36.1
Jewish	0.1	Internet users, % of pop.	90.6

SWITZERLAND

Area, sq km	41,285	Capital	Berne
Arable as % of total land	10.1	Currency	Swiss franc (SFr)

People

Population, m	8.3	Life expectancy: men	81.6 yrs
Pop. per sq km	201.0	women	85.5 yrs
Average annual growth		Adult literacy	...
in pop. 2015–20, %	0.8	Fertility rate (per woman)	1.6
Pop. aged 0–24, %	26.2	Urban population, 2020, %	74.4
Pop. aged 70 and over, %	12.7		per 1,000 pop.
No. of men per 100 women	98.1	Crude birth rate	10.5
Human Development Index	93.9	Crude death rate	8.0

The economy

GDP	$671bn	GDP per head	$80,802
GDP	SFr645bn	GDP per head in purchasing	
Av. ann. growth in real		power parity (USA=100)	103.9
GDP 2010–15	1.5%	Economic freedom index	81.5

Origins of GDP		**Components of GDP**	
	% of total		% of total
Agriculture	1	Private consumption	54
Industry, of which:	26	Public consumption	11
manufacturing	18	Investment	23
Services	74	Exports	63
		Imports	-51

Structure of employment

	% of total		% of labour force
Agriculture	3.2	Unemployed 2015	4.6
Industry	19.3	Av. ann. rate 2005–15	4.2
Services	74.9		

Energy

	m TOE		
Total output	6.8	Net energy imports as %	
Total consumption	30.9	of energy use	47
Consumption per head			
kg oil equivalent	3,060		

Inflation and finance

		av. ann. increase 2011–16	
Consumer price			
inflation 2016	-0.4%	Narrow money (M1)	4.2%
Av. ann. inflation 2011–16	1.9%	Broad money	3.6%
Treasury bill rate, Dec. 2016	-0.91%		

Exchange rates

	end 2016		December 2016
			2010 = 100
SFr per $	1.02	Effective rates	
SFr per sdr	1.37	– nominal	124.67
SFr per €	1.07	– real	110.64

Trade

Principal exports		**Principal imports**	
	$bn fob		*$bn cif*
Chemicals	88.0	Chemicals	40.3
Precision instruments, watches		Machinery, equipment &	
& jewellery	48.6	electronics	29.6
Machinery, equipment &		Precision instruments, watches	
electronics	32.3	& jewellery	21.7
Metals & metal manufactures	12.3	Motor vehicles	17.5
Total incl. others	**210.8**	Total incl. others	**172.8**

Main export destinations		**Main origins of imports**	
	% of total		*% of total*
Germany	19.6	Germany	30.1
United States	14.5	United Kingdom	18.6
Hong Kong	11.9	United States	11.8
India	10.1	Italy	11.3
EU28	43.4	EU28	64.5

Balance of payments, reserves and aid, $bn

Visible exports fob	303.1	Overall balance	98.8
Visible imports fob	-249.5	Change in reserves	56.6
Trade balance	53.6	Level of reserves	
Invisibles inflows	268.3	end Dec.	602.4
Invisibles outflows	-231.2	No. months of import cover	15.0
Net transfers	-13.3	Official gold holdings, m oz	33.4
Current account balance	77.4	Aid given	3.6
– as % of GDP	11.5	– as % of GDP	0.5
Capital balance	-12.7		

Health and education

Health spending, % of GDP	11.7	Education spending, % of GDP	5.1
Doctors per 1,000 pop.	4.0	Enrolment, %: primary	103
Hospital beds per 1,000 pop.	5.0	secondary	100
Improved-water source access,		tertiary	57
% of pop.	100		

Society

No. of households, m	3.7	Cost of living, Dec. 2016	
Av. no. per household	2.2	New York = 100	107
Marriages per 1,000 pop.	5.1	Cars per 1,000 pop.	535
Divorces per 1,000 pop.	2.1	Colour TV households, % with:	
Religion, % of pop.		cable	82.4
Christian	81.3	satellite	16.0
Non-religious	11.9	Telephone lines per 100 pop.	50.3
Muslim	5.5	Mobile telephone subscribers	
Other	0.6	per 100 pop.	136.5
Hindu	0.4	Broadband subs per 100 pop.	45.1
Jewish	0.3	Internet users, % of pop.	87.5

TAIWAN

Area, sq km	36,179	Capital	Taipei
Arable as % of total land	...	Currency	Taiwan dollar (T$)

People

Population, m	23.4	Life expectancy: men	77.0 yrs
Pop. per sq km	646.8	women	83.5 yrs
Average annual growth		Adult literacy	...
in pop. 2015–20, %	0.2	Fertility rate (per woman)	1.1
Pop. aged 0–24, %	26.9	Urban population, 2020, %	78.0
Pop. aged 70 and over, %	8.5		per 1,000 pop.
No. of men per 100 women	99.0	Crude birth rate	8.0
Human Development Index	...	Crude death rate	7.3

The economy

GDP	$525bn	GDP per head	$22,446
GDP	T$16,759bn	GDP per head in purchasing	
Av. ann. growth in real		power parity (USA=100)	84.0
GDP 2010–15	2.5%	Economic freedom index	76.5

Origins of GDP		**Components of GDP**	
	% of total		% of total
Agriculture	2	Private consumption	51
Industry, of which:	35	Public consumption	14
manufacturing	30	Investment	23
Services	63	Exports	63
		Imports	-50

Structure of employment

	% of total		% of labour force
Agriculture	4.9	Unemployed 2015	3.4
Industry	35.9	Av. ann. rate 2005–15	...
Services	59.2		

Energy

	m TOE		
Total output	10.4	Net energy imports as %	
Total consumption	115.1	of energy use	...
Consumption per head			
kg oil equivalent	...		

Inflation and finance

			av. ann. increase 2011–16
Consumer price			
inflation 2016	1.1%	Narrow money (M1)	6.5%
Av. ann. inflation 2011–16	3.0%	Broad money	4.9%
Treasury bill rate, Dec. 2016	...		

Exchange rates

	end 2016		December 2016
T$ per $	32.43	Effective rates	2010 = 100
T$ per sdr	...	– nominal	...
T$ per €	34.12	– real	...

Trade

Principal exports		Principal imports	
	$bn fob		*$bn cif*
Machinery & electrical equip.	150.4	Machinery & electrical equip.	84.1
Basic metals & articles	25.5	Minerals	41.6
Plastic & rubber articles	21.1	Chemicals & related products	25.6
Chemicals	18.2	Basic metals & articles	19.2
Total incl. others	**263.2**	Total incl. others	**236.4**

Main export destinations		Main origins of imports	
	% of total		*% of total*
China	27.9	China	19.1
Hong Kong	14.9	Japan	16.4
United States	13.1	United States	12.3
Japan	7.4	South Korea	5.7

Balance of payments, reserves and debt, $bn

Visible exports fob	284.9	Change in reserves	5.1
Visible imports fob	-231.6	Level of reserves	
Trade balance	53.3	end Dec.	440.5
Invisibles inflows	86.5	No. months of import cover	18.1
Invisibles outflows	-60.3	Official gold holdings, m oz	13.6
Net transfers	-3.4	Foreign debt	159.0
Current account balance	76.2	– as % of GDP	30.3
– as % of GDP	14.5	– as % of total exports	39.0
Capital balance	68.0	Debt service ratio	2.9
Overall balance	151.1		

Health and education

Health spending, % of GDP	...	Education spending, % of GDP	...
Doctors per 1,000 pop.	...	Enrolment, %: primary	...
Hospital beds per 1,000 pop.	...	secondary	...
Improved-water source access,		tertiary	...
% of pop.	...		

Society

No. of households, m	7.8	Cost of living, Dec. 2016	
Av. no. per household	3.0	New York = 100	75
Marriages per 1,000 pop.	...	Cars per 1,000 pop.	274
Divorces per 1,000 pop.	...	Colour TV households, % with:	
Religion, % of pop.		cable	84.6
Other	60.5	satellite	0.4
Buddhist	21.3	Telephone lines per 100 pop.	59.7
Non-religious	12.7	Mobile telephone subscribers	
Christian	5.5	per 100 pop.	127.3
Hindu	<0.1	Broadband subs per 100 pop.	24.3
Jewish	<0.1	Internet users, % of pop.	78.0

THAILAND

Area, sq km	513,120	Capital	Bangkok
Arable as % of total land	32.9	Currency	Baht (Bt)

People

Population, m	68.0	Life expectancy: men	71.8 yrs
Pop. per sq km	132.5	women	78.5 yrs
Average annual growth		Adult literacy	94.0
in pop. 2015–20, %	0.2	Fertility rate (per woman)	1.5
Pop. aged 0–24, %	30.9	Urban population, 2020, %	55.8
Pop. aged 70 and over, %	6.7		per 1,000 pop.
No. of men per 100 women	97.2	Crude birth rate	9.9
Human Development Index	74.0	Crude death rate	8.4

The economy

GDP	$399bn	GDP per head	$5,871
GDP	Bt13,673bn	GDP per head in purchasing	
Av. ann. growth in real		power parity (USA=100)	29.2
GDP 2010–15	2.9%	Economic freedom index	66.2

Origins of GDP		**Components of GDP**	
	% of total		% of total
Agriculture	9	Private consumption	47
Industry, of which:	36	Public consumption	17
manufacturing	27	Investment	24
Services	55	Exports	69
		Imports	-58

Structure of employment

	% of total		% of labour force
Agriculture	32.3	Unemployed 2015	0.7
Industry	23.7	Av. ann. rate 2005–15	1.0
Services	43.9		

Energy

	m TOE		
Total output	62.5	Net energy imports as %	
Total consumption	129.0	of energy use	42
Consumption per head			
kg oil equivalent	1,990		

Inflation and finance

			av. ann. increase 2011–16
Consumer price			
inflation 2016	0.3%	Narrow money (M1)	5.7%
Av. ann. inflation 2011–16	3.5%	Broad money	6.2%
Treasury bill rate, Dec. 2016	1.50%		

Exchange rates

	end 2016		December 2016
Bt per $	35.83	Effective rates	2010 = 100
Bt per sdr	48.17	– nominal	...
Bt per €	37.70	– real	...

Trade

Principal exports[a]

	$bn fob
Machinery, equip. & supplies	94.4
Food	26.7
Manufactured goods	26.5
Chemicals	20.5
Total incl. others	**211.0**

Principal imports[a]

	$bn cif
Machinery, equip. & supplies	76.2
Manufactured goods	34.5
Fuel & lubricants	30.1
Chemicals	21.6
Total incl. others	**201.9**

Main export destinations

	% of total
United States	11.2
China	11.1
Japan	9.4
Hong Kong	5.5

Main origins of imports

	% of total
Japan	20.3
China	15.4
United States	6.9
Malaysia	5.9

Balance of payments, reserves and debt, $bn

Visible exports fob	214.1	Change in reserves	-0.7
Visible imports fob	-187.2	Level of reserves	
Trade balance	26.8	end Dec.	156.5
Invisibles inflows	66.7	No. months of import cover	7.4
Invisibles outflows	-68.0	Official gold holdings, m oz	4.9
Net transfers	6.7	Foreign debt	129.7
Current account balance	32.1	– as % of GDP	32.8
– as % of GDP	8.1	– as % of total exports	45.2
Capital balance	-17.1	Debt service ratio	6.7
Overall balance	5.9		

Health and education

Health spending, % of GDP	6.5	Education spending, % of GDP	4.1
Doctors per 1,000 pop.	0.4	Enrolment, %: primary	103
Hospital beds per 1,000 pop.	2.1	secondary	129
Improved-water source access,		tertiary	49
% of pop.	97.8		

Society

No. of households, m	22.5	Cost of living, Dec. 2016	
Av. no. per household	3.0	New York = 100	77
Marriages per 1,000 pop.	...	Cars per 1,000 pop.	125
Divorces per 1,000 pop.	...	Colour TV households, % with:	
Religion, % of pop.		cable	9.9
Buddhist	93.2	satellite	4.9
Muslim	5.5	Telephone lines per 100 pop.	7.9
Christian	0.9	Mobile telephone subscribers	
Non-religious	0.3	per 100 pop.	152.7
Hindu	0.1	Broadband subs per 100 pop.	9.2
Jewish	<0.1	Internet users, % of pop.	39.3

a 2013

TURKEY

Area, sq km	785,000	Capital	Ankara
Arable as % of total land	26.9	Currency	Turkish Lira (YTL)

People

Population, m	78.7	Life expectancy: men	73.0 yrs
Pop. per sq km	100.3	women	79.3 yrs
Average annual growth		Adult literacy	95.7
in pop. 2015–20, %	0.9	Fertility rate (per woman)	2.1
Pop. aged 0–24, %	42.3	Urban population, 2020, %	75.7
Pop. aged 70 and over, %	4.9		per 1,000 pop.
No. of men per 100 women	96.7	Crude birth rate	15.7
Human Development Index	76.7	Crude death rate	5.8

The economy

GDP	$859bn	GDP per head	$10,915
GDP	YTL2,338bn	GDP per head in purchasing	
Av. ann. growth in real		power parity (USA=100)	43.2
GDP 2010–15	4.4%	Economic freedom index	65.2

Origins of GDP		**Components of GDP**	
	% of total		% of total
Agriculture	9	Private consumption	69
Industry, of which:	27	Public consumption	16
manufacturing	18	Investment	18
Services	65	Exports	28
		Imports	-31

Structure of employment

	% of total		% of labour force
Agriculture	20.4	Unemployed 2015	10.2
Industry	27.2	Av. ann. rate 2005–15	9.7
Services	52.4		

Energy

	m TOE		
Total output	15.6	Net energy imports as %	
Total consumption	131.3	of energy use	74
Consumption per head			
kg oil equivalent	1,568		

Inflation and finance

			av. ann. increase 2011–16
Consumer price			
inflation 2016	9.0%	Narrow money (M1)	18.9%
Av. ann. inflation 2011–16	8.4%	Broad money	15.3%
Treasury bill rate, Dec. 2016	14.00%		

Exchange rates

	end 2016		December 2016
YTL per $	3.52	Effective rates	2010 = 100
YTL per sdr	4.74	– nominal	...
YTL per €	3.70	– real	...

Trade

Principal exports		Principal imports	
	$bn fob		*$bn cif*
Agricultural products	26.3	Fuels	37.8
Transport equipment	18.6	Chemicals	29.0
Textiles & clothing	15.6	Mechanical equipment	24.4
Iron & steel	13.6	Transport equipment	21.8
Total incl. others	**143.8**	Total incl. others	**207.2**

Main export destinations		Main origins of imports	
	% of total		*% of total*
Germany	9.3	China	12.0
Iraq	5.9	Germany	10.3
United Kingdom	7.3	Russia	9.8
Italy	4.8	United States	5.4
EU28	44.5	EU28	38.0

Balance of payments, reserves and debt, $bn

Visible exports fob	152.0	Change in reserves	-16.9
Visible imports fob	-200.1	Level of reserves	
Trade balance	-48.1	end Dec.	110.5
Invisibles inflows	51.4	No. months of import cover	5.6
Invisibles outflows	-36.8	Official gold holdings, m oz	16.6
Net transfers	1.4	Foreign debt	397.7
Current account balance	-32.1	– as % of GDP	46.4
– as % of GDP	-3.7	– as % of total exports	195.0
Capital balance	10.1	Debt service ratio	26.9
Overall balance	-11.8		

Health and education

Health spending, % of GDP	5.4	Education spending, % of GDP	4.8
Doctors per 1,000 pop.	1.7	Enrolment, %: primary	107
Hospital beds per 1,000 pop.	2.5	secondary	100
Improved-water source access,		tertiary	86
% of pop.	100		

Society

No. of households, m	21.2	Cost of living, Dec. 2016	
Av. no. per household	3.7	New York = 100	72
Marriages per 1,000 pop.	7.8	Cars per 1,000 pop.	130
Divorces per 1,000 pop.	1.7	Colour TV households, % with:	
Religion, % of pop.		cable	7.0
Muslim	98.0	satellite	51.0
Non-religious	1.2	Telephone lines per 100 pop.	15.0
Christian	0.4	Mobile telephone subscribers	
Other	0.3	per 100 pop.	96.0
Hindu	<0.1	Broadband subs per 100 pop.	12.4
Jewish	<0.1	Internet users, % of pop.	53.7

UKRAINE

Area, sq km	603,500	Capital	Kiev
Arable as % of total land	56.2	Currency	Hryvnya (UAH)

People

Population, m	44.8	Life expectancy: men	66.2 yrs
Pop. per sq km	74.2	women	76.1 yrs
Average annual growth		Adult literacy	99.8
in pop. 2015–20, %	-0.5	Fertility rate (per woman)	1.5
Pop. aged 0–24, %	25.8	Urban population, 2020, %	70.8
Pop. aged 70 and over, %	11.3		per 1,000 pop.
No. of men per 100 women	86.3	Crude birth rate	10.7
Human Development Index	74.3	Crude death rate	15.7

The economy

GDP	$91bn	GDP per head	$2,030
GDP	UAH1,989bn	GDP per head in purchasing	
Av. ann. growth in real		power parity (USA=100)	13.6
GDP 2010–15	-2.3%	Economic freedom index	48.1

Origins of GDP		**Components of GDP**	
	% of total		% of total
Agriculture	14	Private consumption	67
Industry, of which:	26	Public consumption	20
manufacturing	14	Investment	15
Services	60	Exports	53
		Imports	-55

Structure of employment

	% of total		% of labour force
Agriculture	15.3	Unemployed 2015	9.1
Industry	24.7	Av. ann. rate 2005–15	7.7
Services	60.1		

Energy

	m TOE		
Total output	68.0	Net energy imports as %	
Total consumption	105.5	of energy use	27
Consumption per head			
kg oil equivalent	2,334		

Inflation and finance

			av. ann. increase 2011–16
Consumer price			
inflation 2016	15.1%	Narrow money (M1)	11.2%
Av. ann. inflation 2011–16	13.4%	Broad money	10.0%
Money market rate, Dec. 2016	13.63%		

Exchange rates

	end 2016		December 2016
UAH per $	27.19	Effective rates	2010 = 100
UAH per sdr	36.55	– nominal	44.97
UAH per €	28.61	– real	76.01

Trade

Principal exports		**Principal imports**	
	$bn fob		*$bn cif*
Food & beverages	14.6	Fuels	11.7
Non-precious metals	9.5	Machinery & equipment	8.0
Machinery & equipment	4.6	Chemicals	5.0
Fuels	3.1	Food & beverages	3.5
Total incl. others	**37.9**	Total incl. others	**36.3**

Main export destinations		**Main origins of imports**	
	% of total		*% of total*
Russia	12.8	Russia	19.3
Turkey	7.3	Germany	10.0
China	6.3	China	9.7
Egypt	5.5	Belarus	6.3
EU28	34.1	EU28	40.9

Balance of payments, reserves and debt, $bn

Visible exports fob	35.4	Change in reserves	5.8
Visible imports fob	-38.9	Level of reserves	
Trade balance	-3.5	end Dec.	13.3
Invisibles inflows	16.7	No. months of import cover	2.9
Invisibles outflows	-16.1	Official gold holdings, m oz	0.9
Net transfers	2.6	Foreign debt	122.8
Current account balance	-0.2	– as % of GDP	135.5
– as % of GDP	-0.2	– as % of total exports	211.3
Capital balance	1.2	Debt service ratio	56.9
Overall balance	0.8		

Health and education

Health spending, % of GDP	7.1	Education spending, % of GDP	5.9
Doctors per 1,000 pop.	3.5	Enrolment, %: primary	104
Hospital beds per 1,000 pop.	9.0	secondary	99
Improved-water source access,		tertiary	82
% of pop.	96.2		

Society

No. of households, m	17.7	Cost of living, Dec. 2016	
Av. no. per household	2.5	New York = 100	47
Marriages per 1,000 pop.	6.9	Cars per 1,000 pop.	163
Divorces per 1,000 pop.	3.0	Colour TV households, % with:	
Religion, % of pop.		cable	23.2
Christian	83.8	satellite	15.5
Non-religious	14.7	Telephone lines per 100 pop.	21.6
Muslim	1.2	Mobile telephone subscribers	
Jewish	0.1	per 100 pop.	144.0
Other	0.1	Broadband subs per 100 pop.	11.8
Hindu	<0.1	Internet users, % of pop.	48.9

UNITED ARAB EMIRATES

Area, sq km	83,600	Capital	Abu Dhabi
Arable as % of total land	0.4	Currency	Dirham (AED)

People

Population, m	9.2	Life expectancy: men	76.9 yrs
Pop. per sq km	110.0	women	79.1 yrs
Average annual growth		Adult literacy	93.0
in pop. 2015–20, %	1.4	Fertility rate (per woman)	2.4
Pop. aged 0–24, %	26.6	Urban population, 2020, %	86.8
Pop. aged 70 and over, %	0.5		per 1,000 pop.
No. of men per 100 women	274.0	Crude birth rate	10.0
Human Development Index	84.0	Crude death rate	1.8

The economy

GDP	$370bn	GDP per head	$40,250
GDP	AED1,360bn	GDP per head in purchasing	
Av. ann. growth in real		power parity (USA=100)	124.6
GDP 2010–15	4.7%	Economic freedom index	76.9

Origins of GDP		**Components of GDP**	
	% of total		% of total
Agriculture	1	Private consumption	45
Industry, of which:	48	Public consumption	13
manufacturing	...	Investment	28
Services	52	Exports	97
		Imports	-83

Structure of employment

	% of total		% of labour force
Agriculture	...	Unemployed 2015	3.8
Industry	...	Av. ann. rate 2005–15	3.8
Services	...		

Energy

	m TOE		
Total output	229.5	Net energy imports as %	
Total consumption	106.5	of energy use	-184
Consumption per head			
kg oil equivalent	7,756		

Inflation and finance

		av. ann. increase 2011–16	
Consumer price			
inflation 2016	3.6%	Narrow money (M1)	11.5%
Av. ann. inflation 2011–16	4.0%	Broad money	8.5%
Treasury bill rate, Dec. 2016	...		

Exchange rates

	end 2016		December 2016
			2010 = 100
AED per $	3.67	Effective rates	
AED per sdr	4.94	– nominal	129.72
AED per €	3.86	– real	...

Trade

Principal exports		Principal imports	
	$bn fob		$bn cif
Re-exports	134.8	Precious stones & metals	45.2
Crude oil	31.6	Machinery & electrical equip.	39.3
Gas	7.7	Vehicles & other transport	
		equipment	28.8
		Base metals & related products	13.2
Total incl. others	**300.4**	Total incl. others	**263.4**

Main export destinations		Main origins of imports	
	% of total		% of total
Oman	13.3	China	7.9
Japan	10.8	United States	6.7
India	9.4	India	6.2
Iran	7.4	Germany	4.1

Balance of payments, reserves and debt, $bn

Visible exports fob	300.4	Change in reserves	15.5
Visible imports fob	-223.9	Level of reserves	
Trade balance	76.6	end Dec.	93.9
Invisibles inflows	60.7	No. months of import cover	3.7
Invisibles outflows	-80.9	Official gold holdings, m oz	0.2
Net transfers	-39.6	Foreign debt	203.3
Current account balance	16.7	– as % of GDP	54.9
– as % of GDP	4.5	– as % of total exports	53.6
Capital balance	-3.2	Debt service ratio	5.3
Overall balance	15.3		

Health and education

Health spending, % of GDP	3.6	Education spending, % of GDP	...
Doctors per 1,000 pop.	2.5	Enrolment, %: primary	116
Hospital beds per 1,000 pop.	1.1	secondary	...
Improved-water source access,		tertiary	...
% of pop.	99.6		

Society

No. of households, m	1.7	Cost of living, Dec. 2016	
Av. no. per household	5.4	New York = 100	72
Marriages per 1,000 pop.	...	Cars per 1,000 pop.	195
Divorces per 1,000 pop.	...	Colour TV households, % with:	
Religion, % of pop.		cable	1.0
Muslim	76.9	satellite	98.4
Christian	12.6	Telephone lines per 100 pop.	23.6
Hindu	6.6	Mobile telephone subscribers	
Other	2.8	per 100 pop.	187.3
Non-religious	1.1	Broadband subs per 100 pop.	12.9
Jewish	<0.1	Internet users, % of pop.	91.2

UNITED KINGDOM

Area, sq km	244,000	Capital	London
Arable as % of total land	25.8	Currency	Pound (£)

People

Population, m	64.7	Life expectancy: men	79.4 yrs
Pop. per sq km	265.2	women	83.1 yrs
Average annual growth		Adult literacy	...
in pop. 2015–20, %	0.6	Fertility rate (per woman)	1.9
Pop. aged 0–24, %	30.1	Urban population, 2020, %	83.8
Pop. aged 70 and over, %	12.1		per 1,000 pop.
No. of men per 100 women	97.2	Crude birth rate	12.4
Human Development Index	90.9	Crude death rate	9.1

The economy

GDP	$2,863bn	GDP per head	$44,255
GDP	£1,873bn	GDP per head in purchasing	
Av. ann. growth in real		power parity (USA=100)	74.5
GDP 2010–15	2.0%	Economic freedom index	76.4

Origins of GDP		**Components of GDP**	
	% of total		% of total
Agriculture	1	Private consumption	65
Industry, of which:	19	Public consumption	19
manufacturing	10	Investment	17
Services	80	Exports	28
		Imports	-29

Structure of employment

	% of total		% of labour force
Agriculture	1.1	Unemployed 2015	5.3
Industry	18.5	Av. ann. rate 2005–15	6.5
Services	79.7		

Energy

	m TOE		
Total output	99.9	Net energy imports as %	
Total consumption	200.8	of energy use	40
Consumption per head			
kg oil equivalent	2,777		

Inflation and finance

			av. ann. increase 2011–16
Consumer price			
inflation 2016	0.7%	Narrow money (M1)	...
Av. ann. inflation 2011–16	3.7%	Broad money	5.1%
Treasury bill rate, Dec. 2016	0.05%		

Exchange rates

	end 2016		December 2016
£ per $	0.81	Effective rates	2010 = 100
£ per sdr	1.09	– nominal	97.97
£ per €	0.85	– real	105.96

Trade

Principal exports

	$bn fob
Machinery & transport equip.	163.7
Chemicals & related products	79.8
Mineral fuels & lubricants	33.2
Food, drink & tobacco	28.0
Total incl. others	**439.4**

Principal imports

	$bn cif
Machinery & transport equip.	237.4
Chemicals & related products	76.9
Food, drink & tobacco	59.5
Mineral fuels & lubricants	50.8
Total incl. others	**622.3**

Main export destinations

	% of total
United States	15.2
Germany	10.6
Switzerland	7.3
China	6.2
EU28	44.4

Main origins of imports

	% of total
Germany	14.9
China	9.8
United States	9.3
Netherlands	7.6
EU28	53.6

Balance of payments, reserves and aid, $bn

Visible exports fob	439.3	Overall balance	31.3
Visible imports fob	-622.2	Change in reserves	21.9
Trade balance	-182.9	Level of reserves	
Invisibles inflows	555.5	end Dec.	129.6
Invisibles outflows	-457.6	No. months of import cover	1.4
Net transfers	-37.7	Official gold holdings, m oz	10.0
Current account balance	-122.6	Aid given	18.6
– as % of GDP	-4.3	– as % of GDP	0.7
Capital balance	132.7		

Health and education

Health spending, % of GDP	9.1	Education spending, % of GDP	5.8
Doctors per 1,000 pop.	2.8	Enrolment, %: primary	108
Hospital beds per 1,000 pop.	2.9	secondary	128
Improved-water source access,		tertiary	57
% of pop.	100		

Society

No. of households, m	27.2	Cost of living, Dec. 2016	
Av. no. per household	2.4	New York = 100	89
Marriages per 1,000 pop.	4.5	Cars per 1,000 pop.	514
Divorces per 1,000 pop.	2.0	Colour TV households, % with:	
Religion, % of pop.		cable	14.4
Christian	71.1	satellite	41.7
Non-religious	21.3	Telephone lines per 100 pop.	52.0
Muslim	4.4	Mobile telephone subscribers	
Other	1.4	per 100 pop.	124.1
Hindu	1.3	Broadband subs per 100 pop.	38.6
Jewish	0.5	Internet users, % of pop.	92.0

UNITED STATES

Area, sq km	9,832,000	Capital	Washington DC
Arable as % of total land	16.9	Currency	US dollar ($)

People

Population, m	321.8	Life expectancy: men	77.3 yrs
Pop. per sq km	32.7	women	81.9 yrs
Average annual growth		Adult literacy	...
in pop. 2015–20, %	0.7	Fertility rate (per woman)	1.9
Pop. aged 0–24, %	32.6	Urban population, 2020, %	82.5
Pop. aged 70 and over, %	9.8		per 1,000 pop.
No. of men per 100 women	98.3	Crude birth rate	12.6
Human Development Index	92.0	Crude death rate	8.4

The economy

GDP	$18,037bn	GDP per head	$56,049
Av. ann. growth in real		GDP per head in purchasing	
GDP 2010–15	2.1%	power parity (USA=100)	100.0
		Economic freedom index	75.1

Origins of GDP		**Components of GDP**	
	% of total		% of total
Agriculture	1	Private consumption	68
Industry, of which:	20	Public consumption	14
manufacturing	12	Investment	20
Services	80	Exports	13
		Imports	-15

Structure of employment

	% of total		% of labour force
Agriculture	1.6	Unemployed 2015	5.3
Industry	18.5	Av. ann. rate 2005–15	6.8
Services	79.9		

Energy

	m TOE		
Total output	2,050.5	Net energy imports as %	
Total consumption	2,451.1	of energy use	9
Consumption per head			
kg oil equivalent	6,949		

Inflation and finance

			av. ann. increase 2011–16
Consumer price			
inflation 2016	1.2%	Narrow money (M1)	8.9%
Av. ann. inflation 2011–16	3.4%	Broad money	4.3%
Treasury bill rate, Dec. 2016	0.52%		

Exchange rates

	end 2016		December 2016
$ per sdr	1.34	Effective rates	2010 = 100
$ per €	1.05	– nominal	125.44
		– real	123.11

Trade

Principal exports

	$bn fob
Capital goods, excl. vehicles	539.4
Industrial supplies	426.0
Consumer goods, excl. vehicles	197.7
Vehicles & products	151.9
Total incl. others	**1,502.6**

Principal imports

	$bn fob
Industrial supplies	485.8
Capital goods, excl. vehicles	602.0
Consumer goods, excl. vehicles	594.3
Vehicles & products	349.2
Total incl. others	**2,248.2**

Main export destinations

	% of total
Canada	18.6
Mexico	15.7
China	7.7
Japan	4.2
EU28	18.2

Main origins of imports

	% of total
China	21.4
Canada	13.1
Mexico	13.1
Japan	5.8
EU28	18.9

Balance of payments, reserves and aid, $bn

Visible exports fob	1,510.3	Overall balance	-6.3
Visible imports fob	-2,272.9	Change in reserves	-50.7
Trade balance	-762.6	Level of reserves	
Invisibles inflows	1,533.8	end Dec.	383.7
Invisibles outflows	-1,089.2	No. months of import cover	1.4
Net transfers	-145.0	Official gold holdings, m oz	261.5
Current account balance	-463.0	Aid given	31.0
– as % of GDP	-2.6	– as % of GDP	0.2
Capital balance	188.9		

Health and education

Health spending, % of GDP	17.1	Education spending, % of GDP	4.9
Doctors per 1,000 pop.	2.5	Enrolment, %: primary	100
Hospital beds per 1,000 pop.	2.9	secondary	98
Improved-water source access,		tertiary	86
% of pop.	99.2		

Society

No. of households, m	124.5	Cost of living, Dec. 2016	
Av. no. per household	2.6	New York = 100	100
Marriages per 1,000 pop.	6.8	Cars per 1,000 pop.	375
Divorces per 1,000 pop.	2.8	Colour TV households, % with:	
Religion, % of pop.		cable	56.6
Christian	78.3	satellite	29.5
Non-religious	16.4	Telephone lines per 100 pop.	38.4
Other	2.0	Mobile telephone subscribers	
Jewish	1.8	per 100 pop.	117.6
Muslim	0.9	Broadband subs per 100 pop.	31.0
Hindu	0.6	Internet users, % of pop.	74.5

VENEZUELA

Area, sq km	912,050	Capital	Caracas
Arable as % of total land	2.9	Currency	Bolivar (Bs)

People

Population, m	31.1	Life expectancy: men	70.9 yrs
Pop. per sq km	34.1	women	79.0 yrs
Average annual growth		Adult literacy	95.4
in pop. 2015–20, %	1.3	Fertility rate (per woman)	2.3
Pop. aged 0–24, %	45.8	Urban population, 2020, %	89.3
Pop. aged 70 and over, %	3.9		per 1,000 pop.
No. of men per 100 women	99.1	Crude birth rate	18.5
Human Development Index	76.7	Crude death rate	5.7

The economy

GDP	$260bn	GDP per head	$8,363
GDP	Bs6,025bn	GDP per head in purchasing	
Av. ann. growth in real		power parity (USA=100)	29.5
GDP 2010–15	0.1%	Economic freedom index	27.0

Origins of GDP[a]		Components of GDP[a]	
	% of total		% of total
Agriculture	6	Private consumption	75
Industry, of which:	42	Public consumption	15
manufacturing	14	Investment	25
Services	53	Exports	17
		Imports	-31

Structure of employment

	% of total		% of labour force
Agriculture	7.4	Unemployed 2015	6.8
Industry	21.3	Av. ann. rate 2005–15	8.0
Services	71.1		

Energy

	m TOE		
Total output	169.5	Net energy imports as %	
Total consumption	82.7	of energy use	...
Consumption per head			
kg oil equivalent	...		

Inflation and finance

			av. ann. increase 2011–16
Consumer price			
inflation 2016	475.8%	Narrow money (M1)	89.0%
Av. ann. inflation 2011–16	46.9%	Broad money	61.3%
Money market rate, Dec. 2016	0.35%		

Exchange rates

	end 2016		December 2016
		Effective rates	2010 = 100
Bs per $	9.98	Effective rates	2010 = 100
Bs per sdr	13.41	– nominal	32.36
Bs per €	10.50	– real	...

Trade

Principal exports[b]		Principal imports[b]	
	$bn fob		*$bn cif*
Oil	85.6	Intermediate goods	25.9
Non-oil	3.2	Capital goods	11.1
		Consumer goods	8.9
Total	**88.8**	Total incl. others	**49.4**

Main export destinations		Main origins of imports	
	% of total		*% of total*
United States	35.4	United States	23.4
India	16.6	China	19.5
China	12.9	Brazil	12.4
Netherlands Antilles	8.2	Colombia	7.5

Balance of payments, reserves and debt, $bn

Visible exports fob	37.2	Change in reserves	-5.8
Visible imports fob	-36.5	Level of reserves	
Trade balance	0.8	end Dec.	15.6
Invisibles inflows	2.4	No. months of import cover	3.1
Invisibles outflows	-23.4	Official gold holdings, m oz	8.8
Net transfers	-0.2	Foreign debt	123.7
Current account balance	-20.4	– as % of GDP	26.0
– as % of GDP	-7.8	– as % of total exports	310.8
Capital balance	18.5	Debt service ratio	60.3
Overall balance	-4.5		

Health and education

Health spending, % of GDP	5.3	Education spending, % of GDP	...
Doctors per 1,000 pop.	...	Enrolment, %: primary	100
Hospital beds per 1,000 pop.	0.9	secondary	90
Improved-water source access,		tertiary	...
% of pop.	93.1		

Society

No. of households, m	7.9	Cost of living, Dec. 2016	
Av. no. per household	3.9	New York = 100	50
Marriages per 1,000 pop.	3.0	Cars per 1,000 pop.	114
Divorces per 1,000 pop.	...	Colour TV households, % with:	
Religion, % of pop.		cable	29.3
Christian	89.3	satellite	5.7
Non-religious	10.0	Telephone lines per 100 pop.	24.9
Muslim	0.3	Mobile telephone subscribers	
Other	0.3	per 100 pop.	93.0
Hindu	<0.1	Broadband subs per 100 pop.	8.2
Jewish	<0.1	Internet users, % of pop.	61.9

a 2014   b 2013

VIETNAM

Area, sq km	330,967	Capital	Hanoi
Arable as % of total land	20.7	Currency	Dong (D)

People

Population, m	93.4	Life expectancy: men	71.7 yrs
Pop. per sq km	282.2	women	80.8 yrs
Average annual growth		Adult literacy	94.5
in pop. 2015–20, %	1.0	Fertility rate (per woman)	1.8
Pop. aged 0–24, %	40.0	Urban population, 2020, %	36.8
Pop. aged 70 and over, %	4.7		per 1,000 pop.
No. of men per 100 women	97.9	Crude birth rate	16.2
Human Development Index	68.3	Crude death rate	5.9

The economy

GDP	$191bn	GDP per head	$2,048
GDP	D4,192trn	GDP per head in purchasing	
Av. ann. growth in real		power parity (USA=100)	10.6
GDP 2010–15	5.9%	Economic freedom index	52.4

Origins of GDP		**Components of GDP**	
	% of total		% of total
Agriculture	19	Private consumption	65
Industry, of which:	37	Public consumption	6
manufacturing	15	Investment	28
Services	44	Exports	90
		Imports	-89

Structure of employment

	% of total		% of labour force
Agriculture	43.6	Unemployed 2015	2.1
Industry	23.1	Av. ann. rate 2005–15	2.2
Services	33.3		

Energy

	m TOE		
Total output	43.5	Net energy imports as %	
Total consumption	57.2	of energy use	...
Consumption per head			
kg oil equivalent	...		

Inflation and finance

		av. ann. increase 2011–16	
Consumer price			
inflation 2016	2.0%	Narrow money (M1)	17.1%
Av. ann. inflation 2011–16	6.4%	Broad money	18.9%
Deposit rate, Oct. 2016	4.80%		

Exchange rates

	end 2016		December 2016
D per $	22,159.00	Effective rates	2010 = 100
D per sdr	29,789.01	– nominal	...
D per €	23,316.81	– real	...

Trade

Principal exports		Principal imports	
	$bn fob		*$bn cif*
Telephones & mobile phones	30.2	Machinery & equipment	27.6
Textiles & garments	22.8	Electronics, computers & parts	23.2
Computers & electronic products	15.6	Telephones & mobile phones	11.0
Footwear	12.0	Textiles	10.2
Total incl. others	**162.0**	Total incl. others	**165.8**

Main export destinations		Main origins of imports	
	% of total		*% of total*
United States	20.9	China	28.1
China	10.4	South Korea	15.7
Japan	8.8	Japan	8.1
South Korea	5.6	Taiwan	6.0

Balance of payments, reserves and debt, $bn

Visible exports fob	162.1	Change in reserves	-5.9
Visible imports fob	-154.7	Level of reserves	
Trade balance	7.4	end Dec.	28.3
Invisibles inflows	11.6	No. months of import cover	1.9
Invisibles outflows	-25.8	Official gold holdings, m oz	0.0
Net transfers	7.7	Foreign debt	77.8
Current account balance	0.9	– as % of GDP	40.7
– as % of GDP	0.5	– as % of total exports	41.6
Capital balance	1.6	Debt service ratio	3.5
Overall balance	-6.0		

Health and education

Health spending, % of GDP	7.1	Education spending, % of GDP	5.7
Doctors per 1,000 pop.	1.2	Enrolment, %: primary	109
Hospital beds per 1,000 pop.	2.0	secondary	...
Improved-water source access,		tertiary	29
% of pop.	97.6		

Society

No. of households, m	27.1	Cost of living, Dec. 2016	
Av. no. per household	3.4	New York = 100	73
Marriages per 1,000 pop.	...	Cars per 1,000 pop.	21
Divorces per 1,000 pop.	...	Colour TV households, % with:	
Religion, % of pop.		cable	17.8
Other	45.6	satellite	19.5
Non-religious	29.6	Telephone lines per 100 pop.	6.3
Buddhist	16.4	Mobile telephone subscribers	
Christian	8.2	per 100 pop.	130.6
Muslim	0.2	Broadband subs per 100 pop.	8.1
Jewish	<0.1	Internet users, % of pop.	52.7

ZIMBABWE

Area, sq km	390,757	Capital	Harare
Arable as % of total land	10.3	Currency	Zimbabwe dollar (Z$)[a]

People

Population, m	15.6	Life expectancy: men	60.8 yrs
Pop. per sq km	37.4	women	64.0 yrs
Average annual growth		Adult literacy	86.9
in pop. 2015–20, %	2.3	Fertility rate (per woman)	3.5
Pop. aged 0–24, %	62.5	Urban population, 2020, %	32.2
Pop. aged 70 and over, %	2.0		per 1,000 pop.
No. of men per 100 women	97.1	Crude birth rate	32.4
Human Development Index	51.6	Crude death rate	7.8

The economy

GDP	$14bn	GDP per head	$908
Av. ann. growth in real		GDP per head in purchasing	
GDP 2010–15	6.3%	power parity (USA=100)	3.2
		Economic freedom index	44.0

Origins of GDP		**Components of GDP**	
	% of total		% of total
Agriculture	13	Private consumption	86
Industry, of which:	28	Public consumption	23
manufacturing	11	Investment	14
Services	59	Exports	26
		Imports	-50

Structure of employment

	% of total		% of labour force
Agriculture	67.2	Unemployed 2015	5.1
Industry	7.4	Av. ann. rate 2005–15	5.4
Services	25.4		

Energy

	m TOE		
Total output	3.2	Net energy imports as %	
Total consumption	4.0	of energy use	...
Consumption per head			
kg oil equivalent	...		

Inflation and finance

		av. ann. increase 2011–16	
Consumer price			
inflation 2016	-1.6%	Narrow money (M1)	...
Av. ann. inflation 2011–16	2.8%	Broad money	...
Treasury bill rate, Dec. 2016	...		

Exchange rates

	end 2016		December 2016
Z$ per $	...	Effective rates	2010 = 100
Z$ per SDR	...	– nominal	...
Z$ per €	...	– real	...

Trade

Principal exports[b]		Principal imports[b]	
	$bn fob		$bn cif
Gold	0.8	Machinery & transport equip.	0.5
Platinum	0.8	Fuels & lubricants	0.4
Tobacco	0.5	Manufactures	0.3
Ferro-alloys	0.4	Chemicals	0.2
Total incl. others	**3.4**	Total incl. others	**4.7**

Main export destinations		Main origins of imports	
	% of total		% of total
South Africa	70.8	South Africa	46.1
Mozambique	15.1	Zambia	24.5
United Arab Emirates	5.4	China	3.9
Zambia	3.4	Botswana	3.7

Balance of payments, reserves and debt, $bn

Visible exports fob	3.6	Change in reserves	0.1
Visible imports fob	-6.0	Level of reserves	
Trade balance	-2.4	end Dec.	0.4
Invisibles inflows	0.6	No. months of import cover	0.7
Invisibles outflows	-1.9	Official gold holdings, m oz	0.0
Net transfers	2.1	Foreign debt	8.7
Current account balance	-1.5	– as % of GDP	60.6
– as % of GDP	-10.7	– as % of total exports	154.6
Capital balance	1.3	Debt service ratio	10.9
Overall balance	-0.2		

Health and education

Health spending, % of GDP	6.4	Education spending, % of GDP	8.4
Doctors per 1,000 pop.	0.1	Enrolment, %: primary	100
Hospital beds per 1,000 pop.	1.7	secondary	48
Improved-water source access,		tertiary	8
% of pop.	76.9		

Society

No. of households, m	3.1	Cost of living, Dec. 2016	
Av. no. per household	5.0	New York = 100	...
Marriages per 1,000 pop.	...	Cars per 1,000 pop.	54
Divorces per 1,000 pop.	...	Colour TV households, % with:	
Religion, % of pop.		cable	...
Christian	87.0	satellite	...
Non-religious	7.9	Telephone lines per 100 pop.	2.2
Other	4.2	Mobile telephone subscribers	
Muslim	0.9	per 100 pop.	84.8
Hindu	<0.1	Broadband subs per 100 pop.	1.1
Jewish	<0.1	Internet users, % of pop.	16.4

a   Zimbabwe adopted a multi-currency system in 2009. Its dollar was decommissioned in mid-2015.

b   2014

EURO AREA[a]

Area, sq km	2,678,181	Capital	–
Arable as % of total land	24.4	Currency	Euro (€)

People

Population, m	335.2	Life expectancy: men	79.8 yrs
Pop. per sq km	125.2	women	84.8 yrs
Average annual growth		Adult literacy	...
in pop. 2015–20, %	0.1	Fertility rate (per woman)	1.6
Pop. aged 0–24, %	25.7	Urban population, 2020, %	76.9
Pop. aged 70 and over, %	14.4		per 1,000 pop.
No. of men per 100 women	95.6	Crude birth rate	9.5
Human Development Index	89.7	Crude death rate	10.1

The economy

GDP	$11,606bn	GDP per head	$34,624
GDP	€10,459bn	GDP per head in purchasing	
Av. ann. growth in real		power parity (USA=100)	75.2
GDP 2010–15	0.7%	Economic freedom index	67.1

Origins of GDP		**Components of GDP**	
	% of total		% of total
Agriculture	2	Private consumption	55
Industry, of which:	25	Public consumption	21
manufacturing	17	Investment	20
Services	72	Exports	46
		Imports	-42

Structure of employment

	% of total		% of labour force
Agriculture	3.2	Unemployed 2015	10.8
Industry	23.6	Av. ann. rate 2005–15	9.8
Services	72.5		

Energy

	m TOE		
Total output	...	Net energy imports as %	
Total consumption	1,077.4	of energy use	...
Consumption per head			
kg oil equivalent	3,267		

Inflation and finance

		av. ann. increase 2011–16	
Consumer price			
inflation 2016	0.2%	Narrow money (M1)	8.1%
Av. ann. inflation 2011–16	3.3%	Broad money	3.6%
Interbank rate, Dec. 2016	-0.35%		

Exchange rates

	end 2016		December 2016
€ per $	0.95	Effective rates	2010 = 100
€ per SDR	1.28	– nominal	97.25
		– real	90.63

Trade[b]

Principal exports		Principal imports	
	$bn fob		*$bn cif*
Machinery & transport equip.	678.3	Machinery & transport equip.	483.8
Other manufactured goods	363.2	Other manufactured goods	407.0
Chemicals & related products	284.1	Mineral fuels & lubricants	296.1
Food, drink & tobacco	102.0	Chemicals & related products	167.2
Mineral fuels & lubricants	77.1	Food, drink & tobacco	97.9
Total incl. others	**1,612.6**	Total incl. others	**1,558.5**

Main export destinations		Main origins of imports	
	% of total		*% of total*
United States	20.8	China	20.3
China	9.5	United States	14.4
Switzerland	8.4	Russia	7.9
Turkey	4.4	Switzerland	5.9

Balance of payments, reserves and aid, $bn

Visible exports fob	2,339.9	Overall balance	42.1
Visible imports fob	-1,951.9	Change in reserves	-44.2
Trade balance	388.0	Level of reserves	
Invisibles inflows	1,570.8	end Dec.	701.6
Invisibles outflows	-1,437.6	No. months of import cover	2.5
Net transfers	-148.7	Official gold holdings, m oz	346.9
Current account balance	372.4	Aid given	
– as % of GDP	3.2	– as % of GDP	
Capital balance	-303.4		

Health and education

Health spending, % of GDP	10.4	Education spending, % of GDP	5.3
Doctors per 1,000 pop.	3.9	Enrolment, %: primary	...
Hospital beds per 1,000 pop.	5.6	secondary	...
Improved-water source access,		tertiary	...
% of pop.	99.9		

Society

No. of households, m, m	152.2	Colour TV households, % with:	
Av. no. per household	2.2	cable	41.0
Marriages per 1,000 pop.	3.5	satellite	25.4
Divorces per 1,000 pop.	1.8	Telephone lines per 100 pop.	31.0
Cost of living, Dec. 2016		Mobile telephone subscribers	
New York = 100	...	per 100 pop.	123.8
Cars per 1,000 pop.	516	Broadband subs per 100 pop.	37.2
		Internet users, % of pop.	78.3

a Data generally refer to the 18 EU members that had adopted the euro as at December 31
2014: Austria, Belgium, Cyprus, Estonia, Finland, France, Germany, Greece, Ireland, Italy,
Latvia, Luxembourg, Malta, Netherlands, Portugal, Slovakia, Slovenia and Spain.
b EU28, excluding intra-trade.

WORLD

Area, sq km	129,733,173	Capital	...
Arable as % of total land	10.9	Currency	...

People

Population, m	7,349.5	Life expectancy: men	69.5 yrs
Pop. per sq km	49.4	women	73.9 yrs
Average annual growth		Adult literacy	86.2
in pop. 2015–20	1.1	Fertility rate (per woman)	2.5
Pop. aged 0–24, %	42.3	Urban population, 2020, %	56.2
Pop. aged 70 and over, %	5.3		per 1,000 pop.
No. of men per 100 women	101.8	Crude birth rate	18.6
Human Development Index	71.7	Crude death rate	7.8

The economy

GDP	$74.2trn	GDP per head	$10,095
Av. ann. growth in real		GDP per head in purchasing	
GDP 2010–15	2.6%	power parity (USA=100)	29.3
		Economic freedom index	58.4

Origins of GDP		**Components of GDP**	
	% of total		% of total
Agriculture	4	Private consumption	58
Industry, of which:	28	Public consumption	17
manufacturing	15	Investment	24
Services	68	Exports	30
		Imports	-29

Structure of employment

	% of total		% of labour force
Agriculture	19.8	Unemployed 2015	5.7
Industry	28.8	Av. ann. rate 2005–15	5.9
Services	51.4		

Energy

	m TOE		
Total output	12,546.5	Net energy imports as %	
Total consumption	13,643.0	of energy use	-2.5
Consumption per head			
kg oil equivalent	1,929		

Inflation and finance

Consumer price			av. ann. increase 2011–16
inflation 2016	2.8%	Narrow money (M1)	
Av. ann. inflation 2011–16	2.8%	Broad money	
LIBOR $ rate, 3-month, Dec. 2016	0.98%		

Trade

World exports

	$bn fob		$bn fob
Manufactures	11,404.3	Ores & minerals	729.3
Fuels	2,105.2	Agricultural raw materials	248.6
Food	1,508.4		
		Total incl. others	**16,576.1**

Main export destinations		**Main origins of imports**	
	% of total		% of total
United States	13.1	China	13.9
China	8.7	United States	8.7
Germany	6.4	Germany	7.9
United Kingdom	3.9	Japan	4.2
Japan	3.6	France	3.2

Balance of payments, reserves and aid, $bn

Visible exports fob	16,082	Overall balance	...
Visible imports fob	-15,648	Change in reserves	-839
Trade balance	434	Level of reserves	
Invisibles inflows	8,413	end Dec.	12,383
Invisibles outflows	-8,296	No. months of import cover	6.2
Net transfers	-231	Official gold holdings, m oz	1,053
Current account balance	320	Aid given	
– as % of GDP	0.4	– as % of GDP	
Capital balance	...		

Health and education

Health spending, % of GDP	10	Education spending, % of GDP	4.7
Doctors per 1,000 pop.	1.5	Enrolment, %: primary	105
Hospital beds per 1,000 pop.	...	secondary	75
Improved-water source access,		tertiary	35
% of pop.	91.0		

Society

No. of households, m, m	2,012.2	Cost of living, Dec. 2016	
Av. no. per household	3.7	New York = 100	...
Marriages per 1,000 pop.	...	Cars per 1,000 pop.	132
Divorces per 1,000 pop.	...	Colour TV households, % with:	
Religion, % of pop.		cable	...
Christian	31.5	satellite	...
Muslim	23.2	Telephone lines per 100 pop.	12.6
Non-religious	16.3	Mobile telephone subscribers	
Hindu	15.0	per 100 pop.	106.6
Other	13.8	Broadband subs per 100 pop.	18.0
Jewish	0.2	Internet users, % of pop.	48.0

a OECD countries.

WORLD RANKINGS QUIZ

Test your knowledge with our new world rankings quiz. Answers can be found on the pages indicated.

Geography and demographics

1 Which country is the largest (by land area)?
   a Brazil **b** China **c** United States **d** Australia *page 12*

2 France's marine territory is 20 times its land area, true or false?
   a True **b** False *page 12*

3 Over half the world's mountains higher than 8,000m are in Nepal.
   a True **b** False *page 13*

4 Which river is longest?
   a Yangtze **b** Amazon **c** Mississippi *page 13*

5 Which desert is the largest?
   a Syrian **b** Great Basin **c** Patagonian *page 13*

6 Which is the largest of the Great Lakes?
   a Michigan **b** Superior **c** Huron *page 13*

7 Which of these has a population under 50m?
   a Colombia **b** South Korea **c** Tanzania **d** Turkey *page 14*

8 Afghanistan has a faster-growing population than Nigeria.
   a True **b** False *page 15*

9 Out of these, which has the most total births?
   a Angola **b** Germany **c** Japan **d** United Kingdom *page 16*

10 Ukraine has a lower fertility rate than Germany.
   a True **b** False *page 17*

11 Which of these has the highest proportion of people over the age of 70?
   a Austria **b** Italy **c** Japan **d** Spain *page 18*

12 Which city in Latin America has the biggest population?
   a Buenos Aires **b** Lima **c** Mexico City **d** São Paulo *page 19*

13 Out of these, which has the fastest rate of urban growth?
   a Nigeria **b** Russia **c** Uganda **d** Ukraine *page 20*

14 This country is the world's biggest source of migrants.
   a Mexico **b** India **c** Afghanistan **d** Bangladesh *page 22*

Economics and business

1   How many of the top ten fastest-growing economies in
1995–2005 remained so over the next decade?
a One **b** Three **c** Five **d** Eight   *pages 30–1*

2   Which country experienced the biggest decline in services
output over 2007–15?
a Bahamas **b** Greece **c** Italy **d** Japan   *page 32*

3   Which country scores lowest on the United Nations
Development Programme's Human Development Index?
a Yemen **b** Central African Rep. **c** South Sudan
d Afghanistan   *page 28*

4   On the Human Development Index, Iceland ranks ninth, but
adjusted for inequality, its ranking rises to:
a First **b** Sixth **c** Second **d** Fourth   *page 29*

5   Which non-Asian country receives the highest level of
remittances from workers in foreign countries?
a Mexico **b** Egypt **c** Germany **d** France   *page 36*

6   Which currency was most undervalued against the dollar in
2016?
a Hong Kong **b** China **c** India   *page 37*

7   Out of these, which has the highest foreign debt?
a Indonesia **b** Malaysia **c** South Korea **d** Taiwan   *page 40*

8   Which of these has the highest proportional household
debt?
a Finland **b** Ireland **c** Sweden **d** United Kingdom   *page 41*

9   Which country received the most foreign aid per person?
a Jordan **b** Lebanon **c** Syria **d** West Bank & Gaza *page 42*

10 Ethiopia had the highest growth in industrial output
between 2007–15.
a True **b** False   *page 44*

11 Which country depends most on agriculture?
a Mali **b** Liberia **c** Chad **d** Kenya   *page 46*

12 Which country produces the most coffee?
a Brazil **b** Colombia **c** Vietnam **d** Indonesia   *page 49*

13 Germany accounts for more than a fifth of zinc consumption in the EU28.
    a True **b** False

14 Which country produces most energy?
    a Canada **b** Indonesia **c** Australia **d** India

15 Japan is a bigger net energy importer than Iraq.
    a True **b** False

16 Which country has the highest labour-force participation rate?
    a Qatar **b** Rwanda **c** Greece **d** Italy

17 A higher proportion of women are working in Latvia than in Lithuania.
    a True **b** False

18 The average working week is longest in:
    a Turkey **b** Peru **c** Egypt **d** Hong Kong

19 A greater proportion of workers in Mali earn less than $2 per day than in Zimbabwe.
    a True **b** False

20 Over half of the world's 20 most expensive cities for office rents are in Asia.
    a True **b** False   *page 59*

21 Which country has the highest foreign direct investment inflows?
    a Germany **b** United Kingdom **c** Ireland
    d Netherlands   *page 59*

22 Which European country tied with Venezuela for the highest brain-drain score?
    a Romania **b** Moldova **c** Macedonia **d** Serbia   *page 60*

23 Which country spends the highest percentage of GDP on research and development?
    a United States **b** Israel **c** South Korea **d** Japan   *page 61*

24 On an index of innovation, which country scores highest?
    a Sweden **b** Hong Kong **c** United States
    d Switzerland   *page 61*

25 Amazon's market capitalisation is bigger than Microsoft's.
    a True **b** False   *page 62*

Politics and society

1 Where is primary school enrolment lowest?
  a Senegal **b** Mali **c** Syria **d** Sudan   *page 68*

2 Which country has the lowest adult literacy rate?
  a Chad **b** Afghanistan **c** Nigeria **d** Benin   *page 69*

3 Which country has the lowest marriage rate?
  a Iceland **b** Kuwait **c** Netherlands **d** Qatar   *page 70*

4 Which country has the highest divorce rate?
  a Cuba **b** Denmark **c** Russia **d** United States   *page 71*

5 In years, what is the mean age of marriage in India?
  a 16.7 **b** 17.8 **c** 18.2 **d** 19.5   *page 71*

6 Where is the biggest average household size?
  a Iraq **b** Libya **c** Pakistan **d** Oman   *page 72*

7 The cost of living is higher in Norway than in France.
  a True **b** False   *page 73*

8 Which country is the most generous?
  a United States **b** Myanmar **c** Sweden
  d Sri Lanka   *page 73*

9 Car use has grown most in the past 20 years in:
  a Argentina **b** Belarus **c** Canada **d** Kuwait   *page 76*

10 Germany has a bigger merchant fleet than the United
   States.
   a True **b** False   *page 80*

11 Which country had the most terrorist incidents in 2015?
   a Syria **b** Libya **c** India **d** Egypt   *page 83*

12 Which country emits the most carbon dioxide per person?
   a Poland **b** Qatar **c** Russia **d** United States   *page 85*

13 Which of these countries has the most forested land?
   a Bolivia **b** Colombia **c** Mexico **d** Peru   *page 87*

14 Which country has the most dams?
   a China **b** India **c** Spain **d** United States   *page 88*

15 The UK has a better environmental ranking than Denmark.
   a True **b** False   *page 89*

Health and welfare

1 Which of these countries has the highest life expectancy?
a Andorra **b** Finland **c** Hong Kong **d** Israel *page 90*

2 People in the United States live longer than people in the US Virgin Islands.
a True **b** False *page 90*

3 In Swaziland life expectancy is lower for women than men.
a True **b** False *page 91*

4 Which of these countries has the highest death rate?
a Belarus **b** Hungary **c** Romania **d** Russia *page 92*

5 Which country has the highest infant mortality rate?
a Angola **b** Burundi **c** Chad **d** Mali *page 93*

6 Diabetes prevalence is highest in:
a Qatar **b** Kuwait **c** Mauritius **d** Malaysia *page 94*

7 Which country has the higher incidence of cardiovascular disease?
a Belarus **b** Georgia **c** Russia **d** Ukraine *page 94*

8 Which country has the highest rate of deaths caused by respiratory disease?
a Bangladesh **b** China **c** India **d** Pakistan *page 94*

9 HIV/AIDS is most prevalent in which country?
a Botswana **b** Lesotho **c** South Africa
d Swaziland *page 95*

10 Zimbabwe has a higher death rate from AIDS than South Africa.
a True **b** False *page 95*

11 Health spending is lower in South Sudan than in Congo-Kinshasa.
a True **b** False *page 96*

12 Where has obesity grown most?
a United States **b** South Africa **c** Oman **d** Egypt *page 97*

13 Which country has the greatest food deficit?
a Haiti **b** North Korea **c** Zimbabwe **d** Ethiopia *page 97*

Culture and entertainment

1 Germany has more landline telephones per person than
   France.
   a True **b** False   *page 98*

2 Which country publishes the most new books per person?
   a Spain **b** France **c** Denmark **d** Italy   *page 100*

3 Which of these has the most total visits to the cinema?
   a Brazil **b** Japan **c** Russia **d** South Korea   *page 101*

4 The French make more visits to the cinema than the British.
   a True **b** False   *page 101*

5 Which country has the least-free press?
   a China **b** Eritrea **c** North Korea **d** Saudi Arabia   *page 102*

6 Which country has produced most Nobel prize winners?
   a Canada **b** Russia **c** Sweden **d** France   *page 103*

7 Tennis's Davis Cup has been won most by:
   a Germany **b** Argentina **c** France **d** Sweden   *page 104*

8 Which country has been the more efficient gold medal
   winner at summer Olympic games?
   a United States **b** China **c** Soviet Union
   d East Germany   *page 105*

9 Which country consumes the most beer per person?
   a Austria **b** Czech Republic **c** Germany **d** Poland   *page 106*

10 Americans are bigger tourist spenders than the Chinese.
   a True **b** False   *page 107*

11 Which of these has more smokers per person?
   a Belarus **b** China **c** Lebanon **d** Russia   *page 106*

12 Which of these saw the most tourist arrivals?
   a Germany **b** Russia **c** Turkey **d** United Kingdom   *page 107*

13 Australia saw the most gambling losses per person.
   a True **b** False   *page 106*

14 The United States has a higher circulation of newspapers
   than Japan.
   a True **b** False   *page 102*

Glossary

Balance of payments The record of a country's transactions with the rest of the world. The **current account** of the balance of payments consists of: visible trade (goods); "invisible" trade (services and income); private transfer payments (eg, remittances from those working abroad); official transfers (eg, payments to international organisations, famine relief). Visible imports and exports are normally compiled on rather different definitions to those used in the trade statistics (shown in principal imports and exports) and therefore the statistics do not match. The **capital account** consists of long- and short-term transactions relating to a country's assets and liabilities (eg, loans and borrowings). The **current and capital accounts**, plus an errors and omissions item, make up the **overall balance**. **Changes in reserves** include gold at market prices and are shown without the practice often followed in balance of payments presentations of reversing the sign.

Big Mac index A light-hearted way of looking at exchange rates. If the dollar price of a burger at McDonald's in any country is higher than the price in the United States, converting at market exchange rates, then that country's currency could be thought to be over-valued against the dollar and vice versa.

Body-mass index A measure for assessing obesity – weight in kilograms divided by height in metres squared. An index of 30 or more is regarded as an indicator of obesity; 25 to 29.9 as over-weight. Guidelines vary for men and for women and may be adjusted for age.

CFA Communauté Financière Africaine. Its members, most of the francophone African nations, share a common currency, the CFA franc, pegged to the euro.

Cif/fob Measures of the value of merchandise trade. Imports include the cost of "carriage, insurance and freight" (cif) from the exporting country to the importing. The value of exports does not include these elements and is recorded "free on board" (fob). Balance of payments statistics are generally adjusted so that both exports and imports are shown fob; the cif elements are included in invisibles.

CIS is the Commonwealth of Independent States, including Georgia, Turkmenistan and Ukraine.

Crude birth rate The number of live births in a year per 1,000 population. The crude rate will automatically be relatively high if a large proportion of the population is of childbearing age.

Crude death rate The number of deaths in a year per 1,000 population. Also affected by the population's age structure.

Debt, foreign Financial obligations owed by a country to the rest of the world and repayable in foreign currency. The **debt service ratio** is debt service (principal repayments plus interest payments) expressed as a percentage of the country's earnings from exports of goods and services.

Debt, household All liabilities that require payment of interest or principal in the future.

Economic Freedom Index The ranking includes data on labour and business freedom as well as trade policy, taxation, monetary policy, the banking system, foreign-investment rules, property rights, government spending, regulation policy, the level of corruption and the extent of wage and price controls.

Effective exchange rate The nominal index measures a currency's depreciation (figures below 100) or appreciation (figures over 100) from a base date against a trade-weighted basket of the currencies of the country's main trading partners. The real effective exchange rate reflects adjustments for relative movements in prices or costs.

EU European Union. Members are: Austria, Belgium, Bulgaria, Croatia, Cyprus, Czech Republic, Denmark, Estonia, Finland, France, Germany, Greece, Hungary, Ireland, Italy, Latvia, Lithuania, Luxembourg, Malta, Netherlands, Poland,

Portugal, Romania, Slovakia, Slovenia, Spain, Sweden and the United Kingdom.

Euro area The 19 euro area members of the EU are Austria, Belgium, Cyprus, Estonia, Finland, France, Germany, Greece, Ireland, Italy, Latvia, Lithuania, Luxembourg, Malta, Netherlands, Portugal, Slovakia, Slovenia and Spain. Their common currency is the euro.

Fertility rate The average number of children born to a woman who completes her childbearing years.

G7 Group of seven countries: United States, Japan, Germany, United Kingdom, France, Italy and Canada.

GDP Gross domestic product. The sum of all output produced by economic activity within a country. GNP (gross national product) and GNI (gross national income) include net income from abroad, eg, rent, profits.

Import cover The number of months of imports covered by reserves, ie, reserves ÷ $\frac{1}{12}$ annual imports (visibles and invisibles).

Inflation The annual rate at which prices are increasing. The most common measure and the one shown here is the increase in the consumer price index.

Life expectancy The average length of time a baby born today can expect to live.

Literacy is defined by UNESCO as the ability to read and write a simple sentence, but definitions can vary from country to country.

Median age Divides the age distribution into two halves. Half of the population is above and half below the median age.

Money supply A measure of the "money" available to buy goods and services. Various definitions exist. The measures shown here are based on definitions used by the IMF and may differ from measures used nationally. Narrow money (M1) consists of cash in circulation and demand deposits (bank deposits that can be withdrawn on demand). "Quasi-money" (time, savings and foreign currency deposits) is added to this to create broad money.

OECD Organisation for Economic Co-operation and Development. The "rich countries" club was established in 1961 to promote economic growth and the expansion of world trade. It is based in Paris and now has 35 members from July 1st 2016, when Latvia joined.

Official reserves The stock of gold and foreign currency held by a country to finance any calls that may be made for the settlement of foreign debt.

Opec Set up in 1960 and based in Vienna, Opec is mainly concerned with oil pricing and production issues. The current members (2017) are: Algeria, Angola, Ecuador, Equatorial Guinea, Gabon, Iran, Iraq, Kuwait, Libya, Nigeria, Qatar, Saudi Arabia, United Arab Emirates and Venezuela.

PPP Purchasing power parity. PPP statistics adjust for cost of living differences by replacing normal exchange rates with rates designed to equalise the prices of a standard "basket"of goods and services. These are used to obtain PPP estimates of GDP per head. PPP estimates are shown on an index, taking the United States as 100.

Real terms Figures adjusted to exclude the effect of inflation.

SDR Special drawing right. The reserve currency, introduced by the IMF in 1970, was intended to replace gold and national currencies in settling international transactions. The IMF uses SDRs for book-keeping purposes and issues them to member countries. Their value is based on a basket of the US dollar (with a weight of 41.73%), the euro (30.93%), the Chinese renminbi (10.92%), the Japanese yen (8.33%), and the pound sterling (8.09%).

List of countries

	Population	GDP	GDP per head	Area	Median age
	m, 2015	$bn, 2015	$PPP, 2015	'000 sq km	yrs, 2015
Afghanistan	32.5	19.7	1,908	653	17.5
Albania	2.9	11.4	11,242	29	34.3
Algeria	39.7	164.8	14,614	2,382	27.6
Andorra	0.07	2.8	45,186	0.0	41.6
Angola	25.0	103.0	7,393	1,247	16.1
Argentina	43.4	631.6	20,346	2,780	30.8
Armenia	3.0	10.5	8,465	30	34.6
Australia	24.0	1,229.7	47,652	7,741	37.5
Austria	8.6	377.2	47,186	84	43.2
Azerbaijan	9.8	50.8	17,325	87	30.9
Bahamas	0.4	8.9	22,313	14	32.4
Bahrain	1.4	31.1	45,829	1	30.3
Bangladesh	161.0	206.7	3,603	148	25.6
Barbados	0.3	4.4	15,523	0.0	38.5
Belarus	9.5	56.3	18,311	208	39.6
Belgium	11.3	455.3	43,961	31	41.5
Benin	10.9	8.3	2,053	115	18.6
Bermuda	0.06	5.9	56,807	0.0	39.0
Bolivia	10.7	33.2	6,970	1,099	24.1
Bosnia & Herz.	3.8	16.3	10,702	51	41.5
Botswana	2.3	14.4	15,314	582	24.2
Brazil	207.8	1,801.5	15,477	8,516	31.3
Brunei	0.4	12.9	82,913	6	30.6
Bulgaria	7.1	50.2	19,433	111	43.5
Burkina Faso	18.1	11.1	1,698	274	17.0
Burundi	11.2	3.0	699	28	17.6
Cambodia	15.6	17.8	3,485	181	23.9
Cameroon	23.3	28.4	3,121	475	18.5
Canada	35.9	1,552.8	45,601	9,985	40.6
Central African Rep.	4.9	1.6	614	623	20.0
Chad	14.0	11.0	2,183	1,284	16.0
Channel Islands	0.2	9.2	57,500[ab]	0.0	42.6
Chile	17.9	242.5	23,823	756	34.4
China	1,376.0	11,226.2	14,314	9,563	37.0
Colombia	48.2	291.5	13,834	1,142	30.0
Congo-Brazzaville	4.6	8.6	6,568	342	18.7
Congo-Kinshasa	77.3	38.5	811	2,345	16.9
Costa Rica	4.8	55.5	15,906	51	31.4
Croatia	4.2	48.7	21,704	57	42.8
Cuba	11.4	87.1	22,357	110	41.2
Cyprus	1.2	19.6	23,728	9	35.9
Czech Republic	10.5	185.2	32,193	79	41.5
Denmark	5.7	301.3	46,890	43	41.6
Dominican Rep.	10.5	68.2	14,276	49	26.1
Ecuador	16.1	100.2	11,506	256	26.6
Egypt	91.5	332.1	11,712	1,001	24.7
El Salvador	6.1	25.9	8,657	21	26.7

	Population	GDP	GDP per head	Area '000 sq	Median age
	m, 2015	$bn, 2015	$PPP, 2015	km	yrs, 2015
Equatorial Guinea	0.8	13.8	43,488	28	20.5
Eritrea	5.3	4.7	1,647	118	18.6
Estonia	1.3	22.5	28,742	45	41.7
Ethiopia	99.4	64.7	1,632	1,104	18.6
Fiji	0.9	4.4	8,924	18	27.6
Finland	5.5	232.5	40,953	338	42.5
France	64.4	2,420.2	41,395[c]	549	41.2
French Guiana	0.3	5.0	16,667[ab]	84	24.5
French Polynesia	0.3	5.1	23,833	4	31.5
Gabon	1.7	14.4	20,354	268	21.4
Gambia, The	2.0	0.9	1,651	11	16.8
Georgia	4.0	14.0	8,930	70	37.5
Germany	80.7	3,365.3	47,833	357	46.2
Ghana	27.4	37.4	4,212	239	20.6
Greece	11.0	195.0	25,964	132	43.6
Guadeloupe	0.5	12.0	25,532[ab]	2	39.4
Guam	0.2	5.7	24,410	1	30.1
Guatemala	16.3	63.8	7,743	109	21.2
Guinea	12.6	6.7	1,191	246	18.5
Guinea-Bissau	1.8	1.0	1,501	36	19.4
Guyana	0.8	3.2	7,221	215	24.7
Haiti	10.7	8.7	1,760	28	23.0
Honduras	8.1	20.7	5,078	112	23.4
Hong Kong	7.3	309.4	56,983	1	43.2
Hungary	9.9	121.7	26,419	93	41.3
Iceland	0.3	16.8	50,700	103	36.0
India	1,311.1	2,088.2	6,104	3,287	26.6
Indonesia	257.6	861.1	11,063	1,911	28.4
Iran	79.1	374.3	17,035	1,745	29.5
Iraq	36.4	179.8	15,941	435	19.3
Ireland	4.7	283.4	64,844	70	36.9
Israel	8.1	299.4	35,217	22	30.3
Italy	59.8	1,825.8	36,559	301	45.9
Ivory Coast	22.7	32.8	3,551	322	18.4
Jamaica	2.8	14.2	8,816	11	29.1
Japan	126.6	4,382.4	40,432	378	46.5
Jordan	7.6	37.6	10,895	89	22.5
Kazakhstan	17.6	184.2	25,037	2,725	29.3
Kenya	46.1	63.6	3,085	580	18.9
Kosovo	1.9	6.4	3,390	11	24.0
Kuwait	3.9	114.1	75,015	18	31.0
Kyrgyzstan	5.9	6.7	3,467	200	25.1
Laos	6.8	12.6	5,551	237	21.9
Latvia	2.0	27.0	24,504	64	42.9
Lebanon	5.9	50.8	14,106	10	28.5
Lesotho	2.1	2.4	3,187	30	21.0
Liberia	4.5	2.0	835	111	18.6

	Population	GDP	GDP per head	Area	Median age
	m, 2015	$bn, 2015	$PPP, 2015	'000 sq km	yrs, 2015
Libya	6.3	29.8	9,083	1,760	27.5
Liechtenstein	0.04	6.4	80,000	0.2	42.0
Lithuania	2.9	41.4	28,636	65	43.1
Luxembourg	0.6	56.8	94,815	3	39.2
Macau	0.6	46.2	107,192	0	37.9
Macedonia	2.1	10.1	13,891	26	37.5
Madagascar	24.2	9.7	1,468	587	18.7
Malawi	17.2	6.4	1,186	118	17.2
Malaysia	30.3	296.3	26,978	331	28.5
Maldives	0.4	3.2	15,014	0.3	26.4
Mali	17.6	13.1	2,028	1,240	16.2
Malta	0.4	10.3	40,650	0.3	41.5
Martinique	0.4	12.0	31,579[ab]	1	46.1
Mauritania	4.1	4.8	3,893	1,031	19.8
Mauritius	1.3	11.5	18,976	2	35.2
Mexico	127.0	1,151.0	17,592	1,964	27.4
Moldova	4.1	6.5	4,379	34	35.6
Monaco	0.04	6.3	169,750	0	56.0
Mongolia	3.0	11.7	12,054	1,564	27.3
Montenegro	0.6	4.0	16,652	14	37.6
Morocco	34.4	100.6	7,967	447	28.0
Mozambique	28.0	14.8	1,191	799	17.1
Myanmar	53.9	59.5	5,249	677	27.9
Namibia	2.5	11.5	10,240	824	21.2
Nepal	28.5	21.3	2,463	147	23.1
Netherlands	16.9	750.7	49,732	42	42.7
New Caledonia	0.3	8.9	29,211	19	33.1
New Zealand	4.5	173.3	37,346	268	38.0
Nicaragua	6.1	12.7	5,185	130	25.2
Niger	19.9	7.2	955	1,267	14.8
Nigeria	182.2	493.8	6,004	924	17.9
North Korea	25.2	16.3	1,587	121	33.9
Norway	5.2	386.6	68,473	385	39.1
Oman	4.5	69.8	39,329	310	29.0
Pakistan	188.9	271.1	4,931	796	22.5
Panama	3.9	52.1	22,403	75	28.7
Papua New Guinea	7.6	21.2	3,549	463	21.2
Paraguay	6.6	27.3	9,253	407	24.9
Peru	31.4	192.4	12,290	1,285	27.5
Philippines	100.7	292.5	7,387	300	24.2
Poland	38.6	477.1	26,213	313	39.6
Portugal	10.3	199.2	28,223	92	44.0
Puerto Rico	3.7	102.9	35,578	9	36.3
Qatar	2.2	164.6	143,817	12	30.7
Réunion	0.9	22.0	24,444[ab]	3	34.3
Romania	19.5	177.5	21,332	238	42.1
Russia	143.5	1,365.9	26,200	17,098	38.7

	Population	GDP	GDP per head	Area '000 sq	Median age
	m, 2015	$bn, 2015	$PPP, 2015	km	yrs, 2015
Rwanda	11.6	8.3	1,831	26	19.2
Saudi Arabia	31.5	651.8	54,105	2,150	28.3
Senegal	15.1	13.7	2,435	197	18.0
Serbia	8.9	37.2	10,979	88	40.6
Sierra Leone	6.5	4.5	1,558	72	18.5
Singapore	5.6	296.8	85,128	1	40.0
Slovakia	5.4	87.3	30,094	49	39.1
Slovenia	2.1	42.8	30,371	20	43.1
Somalia	10.8	5.9	410	638	16.5
South Africa	54.5	314.7	13,354	1,219	25.7
South Korea	50.3	1,382.8	36,907	100	40.6
South Sudan	12.4	12.5	1,913	644	18.6
Spain	46.1	1,193.6	34,985	506	43.2
Sri Lanka	20.7	81.2	11,914	66	32.3
Sudan	40.2	81.4	4,195	1,879	19.4
Suriname	0.5	4.9	17,396	164	29.0
Swaziland	1.3	3.9	8,441	17	20.5
Sweden	9.8	495.7	48,561	447	41.0
Switzerland	8.3	670.7	58,216	41	42.3
Syria	18.5	28.4	3,016	185	20.8
Taiwan	23.4	525.2	47,094	36	37.5
Tajikistan	8.5	7.9	2,827	141	22.5
Tanzania	53.5	45.6	2,593	947	17.3
Thailand	68.0	399.2	16,380	513	38.0
Timor-Leste	1.2	2.9	4,589	15	18.5
Togo	7.3	4.2	1,499	57	18.7
Trinidad & Tobago	1.4	23.6	32,359	5	33.8
Tunisia	11.3	43.2	11,292	164	31.2
Turkey	78.7	859.0	24,239	785	29.8
Turkmenistan	5.4	36.0	16,438	488	26.4
Uganda	39.0	25.1	2,055	242	15.9
Ukraine	44.8	90.9	7,601	604	40.3
United Arab Emirates	9.2	370.3	69,858	84	33.3
United Kingdom	64.7	2,863.3	41,741	244	40.0
United States	321.8	18,036.7	56,049	9,832	38.0
Uruguay	3.4	53.1	21,441	176	34.9
Uzbekistan	29.9	65.4	6,299	447	26.3
Venezuela	31.1	260.1	16,525	912	27.4
Vietnam	93.4	191.3	5,925	331	30.4
Virgin Islands (US)	0.1	3.8	37,920[ab]	0.4	41.0
West Bank & Gaza	4.7	13.4	2,850	6	19.3
Yemen	26.8	37.7	2,824	528	19.3
Zambia	16.2	21.2	3,838	753	16.9
Zimbabwe	15.6	14.2	1,798	391	18.9
Euro area (19)	335.2	11,606.0	40,580	2,759	43.8
World	7,349.5	74,196.0	15,630	129,733	29.6

a Latest available year.   b Estimate.
c Including French Guiana, Guadeloupe, Martinique and Réunion.

Sources

Academy of Motion Pictures
AFM Research
Airports Council International, *Worldwide Airport Traffic Report*

Bank of East Asia
Bloomberg
BP, *Statistical Review of World Energy*

CAF, *The World Giving Index*
CBRE, *Global Prime Office Occupancy Costs*
Central banks
Central Intelligence Agency, *The World Factbook*
Company reports
Cornell University
Council of Tall Buildings and Urban Habitat

The Economist, www.economist.com
Economist Intelligence Unit, *Cost of Living Survey; Country Forecasts; Country Reports; Liveability Index*
Encyclopaedia Britannica
Euromonitor International
Eurostat, *Statistics in Focus*

FIFA
Finance ministries
Food and Agriculture Organisation

Global Democracy Ranking
Global Entrepreneurship Monitor
Global Terrorism Database, University of Maryland
Government statistics

H2 Gambling Capital
The Heritage Foundation, *Index of Economic Freedom*
Holman Fenwick Willan

IFPI
IMD, *World Competitiveness Yearbook*
IMF, *International Financial Statistics*; *World Economic Outlook*
INSEAD
Institute for Criminal Policy Research
International Civil Aviation Organisation
International Cocoa Organisation, *Quarterly Bulletin of Cocoa Statistics*
International Coffee Organisation
International Commission on Large Dams
International Cotton Advisory Committee, *March Bulletin*
International Cricket Council
International Diabetes Federation, *Diabetes Atlas*
International Grains Council
International Institute for Strategic Studies, *Military Balance*
International Labour Organisation
International Olympic Committee
International Organisation of Motor Vehicle Manufacturers
International Publishers Association
International Rubber Study Group, *Rubber Statistical Bulletin*
International Sugar Organisation, *Statistical Bulletin*
International Telecommunication Union, *ITU Indicators*
International Union of Railways
Inter-Parliamentary Union

Johnson Matthey

McDonald's

National Institute of Statistics and Economic Studies

National statistics offices
Nobel Foundation

OECD, *Development Assistance Committee Report; Economic Outlook; Government at a Glance; OECD.Stat; Revenue Statistics*

Pew Research Centre, *The Global Religious Landscape*
Population Reference Bureau
Progressive Media

Reporters Without Borders, *Press Freedom Index*

Sovereign Wealth Fund Institute
Stockholm International Peace Research Institute
Swiss Re

Taiwan Statistical Data Book
The Times, *Atlas of the World*
Thomson Reuters

UN, *Demographic Yearbook; National Accounts; State of World Population Report; World Fertility Report*
UNCTAD, *Review of Maritime Transport; World Investment Report*
UNCTAD/WTO International Trade Centre
UN Development Programme, *Human Development Report*
UNESCO Institute for Statistics

UN High Commissioner for Refugees
UN Office on Drugs and Crime
UN, Population Division
UNAIDS
US Department of Agriculture
US Energy Information Administration
US Federal Aviation Administration

Visionofhumanity.org

WHO, *Global Health Observatory; Global Immunisation Data; World Health Statistics*
World Anti-Doping Agency
World Bank, *Doing Business; Global Development Finance; Migration and Remittances Data; World Development Indicators; World Development Report*
World Bureau of Metal Statistics, *World Metal Statistics*
World Economic Forum, *Global Competitiveness Report*
World Federation of Exchanges
World Health Organisation
World Intellectual Property Organization
World Tourism Organisation, *Yearbook of Tourism Statistics*
World Trade Organisation, *Annual Report*

Yale University